National Bureau of Economic Research, Inc.

Incorporated under the Membership Corporation Laws of the State of New York, January 29, 1920

ITS ORGANIZATION AND PURPOSES

THE National Bureau of Economic Research was organized in 1920 in response to a growing demand for exact and impartial determinations of facts bearing on economic, social, and industrial problems.

It seeks not only to find facts and make them known, but to determine them in such manner and under such supervision as to make its findings carry conviction to Liberal and Conservative alike.

Entire control of the Bureau is vested in a Board of twenty directors, representing learned and scientific societies, financial, industrial, agricultural, commercial, labor, and technical organizations.

Rigid provisions in the Charter and By-Laws guard the Bureau from becoming a source of profit to its members, directors, or officers and from becoming an agency for propaganda. No report of the Research Staff may be published without the approval of the Directors and any Director who dissents from any finding approved by a majority of the Board may have such dissent published with the majority report.

The members of the Board of Directors are as follows:

DIRECTORS AT LARGE

MIGRATION AND BUSINESS CYCLES

By

HARRY JEROME

OF THE STAFF OF THE

NATIONAL BUREAU OF ECONOMIC RESEARCH

INCORPORATED

With a Foreword by

WESLEY C. MITCHELL

NEW YORK

NATIONAL BUREAU OF ECONOMIC
RESEARCH, Inc.

1926

NATIONAL BUREAU OF ECONOMIC RESEARCH, Inc.

Publications in the order of their issue.

INCOME IN THE UNITED STATES

Volume I. A summary of an Investigation of the Amount and Distribution of Income in the United States, 1909-1919, intended for readers who are primarily interested in the results. 152 pages, (Fifth printing) $1.58 postpaid.

Volume II. A report giving in full the methods and estimates on which the results shown in Volume I are based. 440 pages, (Second printing) $5.15 postpaid.

DISTRIBUTION OF INCOME BY STATES IN 1919

A study of the share of each state in the national income with a special analysis of the amount and relative importance of farmers' income. 32 pages, (Third printing) $1.30 postpaid.

BUSINESS CYCLES AND UNEMPLOYMENT

Results of an investigation made for the President's Conference on Unemployment. By the staff of the Bureau with 16 collaborators. Twenty-one topics covered. This report summarizes the known facts of unemployment and describes the various methods suggested to control the business cycle and alleviate cyclical unemployment. 405 pages, $4.10 postpaid.

EMPLOYMENT, HOURS, AND EARNINGS
IN PROSPERITY AND DEPRESSION

Results of an inquiry conducted by the National Bureau of Economic Research, with the help of the U. S. Bureau of Markets and Crop Estimates and the Bureau of Census, for the President's Conference on Unemployment. Gives full details of investigation summarized in *Business Cycles and Unemployment* to which it is a companion volume. 147 pages, (Out of print.)

THE GROWTH OF AMERICAN TRADE UNIONS, 1880-1923

Results of a comprehensive investigation of trade union membership year by year; its fluctuations with the business cycle; effects of World War conditions; women in trade unions. Contains also a detailed analysis of the total working population. 170 pages, $3 postpaid.

INCOME IN THE VARIOUS STATES
ITS SOURCES AND DISTRIBUTION, 1919, 1920 AND 1921

This volume gives the total and per capita income carefully adjusted for every state, with special tables showing the incomes of farmers, wage earners, persons of large means, and other matter relevant to the purchasing power and economic conditions of the different parts of the country. 306 pages, $5 postpaid.

BUSINESS ANNALS

A descriptive summary of business conditions in United States, England, France, Germany, Austria, Russia, Sweden, Netherlands, Italy, Argentina, Brazil, Canada, South Africa, Australia, India, Japan and China, for periods from 36 to 136 years with an introduction *Business Cycles as Revealed by Business Annals.* 384 pages, $4 postpaid.

Copies of available reports may be obtained upon application
accompanied by remittance to

NATIONAL BUREAU OF ECONOMIC RESEARCH, INC.
474 West 24th Street, New York

PUBLICATIONS OF THE NATIONAL BUREAU OF
ECONOMIC RESEARCH, INCORPORATED

No. 9.

MIGRATION AND BUSINESS CYCLES

PRINTED IN THE U. S. A.

————————

THE MESSENGER PRESS
ST. ALBANS, VT.

FOREWORD

Migration and Business Cycles presents the results of investigations made by the National Bureau of Economic Research at the request of a committee of the National Research Council. It forms part of two series of studies. One series, planned by the Committee on Scientific Problems of Human Migration, deals with the character, causes, and effects of mass-movements of men. The second series, planned by the National Bureau, deals with the character, causes, and effects of cyclical fluctuations in economic activities.

The Committee on Scientific Problems of Human Migration was appointed in October, 1922, by the National Research Council on recommendation of the Council's Division of Anthropology and Psychology. Its duties were

(1) carefully to consider, from the point of view of natural science, the complex migrational situation resulting from the World War and from the virtual elimination of space as a barrier to movements of man and to race intermixture;

(2) to prepare a research program which might reasonably be expected to yield ultimately such reliable information concerning physical, mental, and social characteristics, relations and values of ethnic groups (races and peoples) as is necessary for the understanding and wise regulation of mass-movements of mankind; and

(3) to initiate, organize, support, coordinate, or otherwise further, in accordance with the best judgment of the group, important investigations.[1]

The members of this Committee as originally organized were Dr. Raymond Dodge, then Professor of Psychology at Wesleyan University, Dr. Frank R. Lillie, Professor of Zoology at the University of Chicago, Dr. John C. Merriam, President of the Carnegie Institution of Washington, Miss Mary Van Kleeck, Director of Industrial Studies in the Russell Sage Foundation, Dr. Clark Wissler, Curator

[1] See the report of Dr. Robert M. Yerkes, Chairman of the Committee, *Journal of Personnel Research*, October, 1924, vol. iii, p. 189.

of the Department of Anthropology in the American Museum of Natural History, and Dr. Robert M. Yerkes, Chairman of the Research Information Service of the National Research Council, and also of the Committee.

In preparation for their work, the Committee called a conference of anthropologists, biologists, economists, psychologists and sociologists interested in various aspects of migration. After surveying the field and considering numerous suggestions, the Committee decided that it could render the best service by promoting work upon certain fundamental problems which must be solved as preliminaries to the scientific study of the characteristics, causes and effects of migration. Each problem was referred to a group of technically qualified investigators. The various groups worked in severalty, by whatever methods were best adapted to their tasks. Meanwhile the Committee gave the program as a whole such unity as was possible, by holding occasional conferences, in which all the cooperating investigators took part. The scope of the work undertaken is indicated by the following partial list of topics: the possibility of developing reliable measures of the psychological characteristics of different ethnic groups, the influence of race upon pathology, the behavior of physical traits in race intermixture, and the sources of information concerning the causes of migration available in Europe. To defray the expenses incident to these inquiries, the National Research Council obtained a grant from the Laura Spelman Rockefeller Memorial.

Among the problems which the Committee on Scientific Problems of Human Migration thought important to investigate was the "Shortage and surplus of labor in the United States in its relations to immigration and emigration." This problem was referred to the National Bureau of Economic Research.

Before it received this request to cooperate in the migration program, the National Bureau had begun a series of researches into the phenomena of business cycles. One report within this field, made at the request of a committee of President Harding's Conference on Unemployment, had already been published under the title, *Business Cycles and Unemployment*. A second report was on the point of appearing—*Employment, Hours and Earnings in Prosperity and Depression*, by Dr. Willford I. King, Dr. Leo Wolman's monograph on *The Growth of American Trade Unions, 1880-1923*, was then well under way, and has since been printed. Dr. Frederick

R. Macaulay had begun an elaborate investigation of bond yields
and interest rates since 1859, which we hope will appear soon. Dr.
Willard L. Thorp was making two collections of materials dealing
with cyclical fluctuations—a collection, recently published, of
business annals for 17 countries during periods ranging from 36 to
136 years, and a collection of economic statistics which is well advanced. Finally, the present writer had in hand a general treatise upon Business Cycles, the first volume of which will be submitted
to the directors of the National Bureau within a few months. Since
the "shortage and surplus of labor in its relations to immigration
and emigration" is chiefly a problem of short-period oscillations, it
was obviously relevant to the National Bureau's existing scheme of
work.

At our request, the University of Wisconsin granted leave of
absence to Dr. Harry Jerome, Assistant Professor of Economics, in
order that he might assume charge of the new undertaking, and later
extended the leave. To the University, and particularly to its
Department of Economics, our hearty thanks are due. Aided by
a small corps of assistants and the advice of other members of the
National Bureau's staff, Dr. Jerome analyzed the voluminous, yet
incomplete, records of migration to and from the United States, and
compared these records with various indices of business activity
here and abroad. The present volume presents in concise form his
conclusions concerning the short-period fluctuations in the demand
for and supply of labor in the United States, and the role played by
migration in these fluctuations. The National Bureau hopes that
this carefully documented study of a problem too often treated in a
controversial spirit will prove useful to all who are interested in migrations and to all who are interested in business cycles.

Before Dr. Jerome had finished the present monograph, the
Committee on Scientific Problems of Human Migration asked
the National Bureau to undertake another investigation. This
concerns the problem of "Migration and the Mechanization of Industry"—that is, the relation between the conditions on which
relatively unskilled labor can be hired and the adoption of auto-
matic machinery for the performance of work which may be done
by hand. In May, 1924, the recently organized Social Science
Research Council appointed a Committe on Human Migration,
which included besides three members of the older Committee (Dr.
Yerkes, Miss Van Kleeck, and Dr. Wissler), Dr. Edith Abbott,

chairman, Professor John R. Commons, Professor John A. Fairlie, Dr. Robert F. Foerster, Professor Edward A. Miller, Professor Charles E. Merriam, Professor Frederick A. Ogg, Professor Carl Wittke, and the writer. The plan of co-operation between the old Committee and the new one transferred the "machinization study" to the Social Science Research Council, under whose auspices it has been carried nearly to completion by Dr. Jerome.

Finally, the Social Science Research Council has enabled the National Bureau to supplement the present study of short-period fluctuations of migration in the United States by a long-period investigation of mass movements of mankind over the earth. Of course, the preparation of a broad sketch of the great world migrations of the past three or four generations requires the critical examination of many estimates of population movements for years and countries in which accurate records are lacking. It requires also the use of all the relevant statistics compiled in any part of the world. In short, it is a project which calls for close international co-operation among the leading authorities upon population statistics. Dr. Walter F. Willcox, of Cornell University, is organizing this co-operation with the National Bureau, and, when the materials are assembled, he will prepare a report.

Like the National Research Council, the Social Science Research Council asked and obtained financial support for its migration studies from the Laura Spelman Rockefeller Memorial.

Belonging as it does to two series of studies, *Migration and Business Cycles* is designed to cover a limited field. The major issues with which it deals are summed up in two questions:

(1)   To what extent are fluctuations in migration attributable to fluctuations in employment?

(2)   To what extent, in turn, are fluctuations in migration an ameliorating influence, and to what extent an aggravating factor, in employment and unemployment fluctuations?

Dr. Jerome has sought to get the most definite answers to these questions which he can wring from the available records. Other phases of the problem he treats incidentally, if at all. Among the factors affecting migration which he passes over lightly are political conditions, steerage rates, and the methods adopted by steamship companies to stimulate passenger traffic. A scientific analysis of the causes and consequences of human migration, comprehensive in scope and thorough in detail, can be developed only by co-operative efforts, such as the committees of the National Research Council and the Social Science Research Council are promoting. Many intensive investigations of specific issues, like the present report, must be made before we can attain the well-rounded knowledge needed as a basis for private opinion and public policy regarding migration.

In accordance with the established procedure of the National Bureau, Dr. Jerome's present monograph was submitted in manuscript to our Board of Directors. Criticisms made by members of the Board have resulted in various improvements upon the original draft. This process of criticism and betterment through which the National Bureau's reports pass before publication involves much labor upon the part of the Directors;—labor which is mostly self-effacing, for almost all the suggestions are incorporated in the text before publication. It is but just to state that this volume, like its predecessors, owes much more than appears to the acumen, the wide and varied experience, of the Directors.

WESLEY C. MITCHELL.

CONTENTS

CHAPTER VI

CHAPTER VII

CHAPTER VIII

LIST OF CHARTS

LIST OF TABLES

MIGRATION AND BUSINESS CYCLES

by

HARRY JEROME

assisted by

EDITH H. HANDLER

LAURA WEISSBUCH

CAROLINE WHITNEY

CHAPTER I

THE PROBLEM

The Nature of Modern Migration.

In significant respects, the great migratory movement to the United States in recent decades differs from earlier migrations. The migration of the semi-barbaric races which conquered the countries of southern and western Europe was a concerted, hostile movement of whole peoples, moving as military or political units. Likewise the early colonization of the Western Hemisphere by European peoples was largely by organized groups or under direct political authorization and for governmental purposes.

In contrast, the European emigration of recent history has been essentially a peaceful phenomenon of individual and family movement, although attaining an enormous scale which has given it a significance at least comparable to any of the earlier movements.

The motives for this movement of millions of people must be sought in the conditions which lead the individual to break established ties and risk a new start in a strange country. These motives, as well as the effects of the resulting migration, are as varied and complex as human life itself, and the minute details could be ascertained only by examination of the histories of the individual migrants. But general tendencies are more significant than an unwieldly mass of detail; and, because of the great numbers involved, significant major tendencies can best be discovered by the use of the statistical methods suitable for the quantitative analysis of mass phenomena. Accordingly, this monograph presents the results of a quantitative analysis of migratory movements.

While it is a part of a comprehensive coordinated program of investigation of the fundamental problems of migration, the present report is restricted primarily to the results of one phase of a survey of the economic causes and effects of migration, with particular regard to the supply of labor in the United States.

Migration and the Supply of Labor.

The significance of the problem of the relation of immigration to labor supply and the desirability of subjecting it to a close analysis

is suggested by incidents which took place in the years 1920 and
1921.   In hearings before the House Committee on Immigration
and Naturalization in April, 1920, it was testified that "there is a
labor shortage in practically every industry.   It amounts
to not less than that of 5,000,000 men.   In addition there is a dearth
of agricultural labor and of domestic servants to an extent difficult
of calculation."   And it was urged that under the circumstances,
"a policy looking to the exclusion of the immigrant would hamper
and curtail our natural development and lead to a world-wide
calamity."[1]

Within a few months after the above testimony was given, it was
obvious that industry was entering a depression period, and in
September, 1921, the President's Conference on Unemployment
met in Washington to consider measures for the relief of from "four
to five million unemployed resulting from the business slump of
1921."[2]

It seems a far cry from circumstances which could by
anyone be interpreted as indicating a shortage of at least five
million men to a condition where, in contrast, the numbers of unemployed are estimated in terms of millions.   It would appear
desirable that a more definite connotation should be given to the
terms "labor supply" and "labor shortage," and that particular
consideration should be given to the relation of the business cycle
to the validity of estimates of surplus or shortage in the supply of
labor.   is the purpose of this study.

The Long-Time and Short-Time Points of View.

In seeking to determine the relation of migration to the demands
of industry for man-power, a distinction may well be made between
what may be appropriately designated, respectively, as the long-
time and the short-time points of view.   From the long-time point
of view we are concerned with the relatively permanent adjustments
in industry which are hampered, furthered, or necessitated by
changes in the volume of immigration.   To treat this phase of the

[1]Statements included in a memorial adopted at the National Conference on Immigration, and submitted to the House Committee by Mr. Marshall.   *U. S. Immigration
and Naturalization Committee* (House) Hearings, 66 Con., 1-3 Sess., 1919-1921, p. 38.
This estimate of 5,000,000 shortage was apparently obtained by computing the net
immigration which would have taken place if the 1914 rate of immigration and emigration had continued, and making an additional allowance for the shorter hours in
industry in recent years.

[2]National Bureau of Economic Research, *Business Cycles and Unemployment*, Foreword by Herbert Hoover, p. v.

subject adequately it would be necessary to determine the extent to which migration has dominated the direction and the amount of industrial growth in the United States—that is, the extent to which the major changes in our industrial development and occupational distribution have been closely related to changes in the volume, type, or geographical distribution of immigration and emigration.

Even more significant would be an inquiry into the readjustments which may in the future be set in motion by modifications in the volume or type of migration. Will a decrease in the annual accession of laborers from abroad set in motion significant readjustments in industrial tendencies? Will the vacuum created by restricting immigration stimulate internal migration of the negro, intensify the country-to-city movement, or lead to a better utilization of the available man-power through improvements in methods of organization and administration or through more effective labor-saving devices? Or, if none of the above developments is adequate to enable industries to maintain the customary rate of progress, must we see a check to industrial advancement? All these are fascinating questions worthy of intensive and sustained research, and it is hoped that we may in subsequent reports give attention to these phases of the problem. The present study is made from what we have designated as the short-time point of view.

Migration and Business Cycles.

The queries we have just suggested are concerned chiefly with long-run tendencies. Equally significant is the relation of migration to those fluctuations in industrial activity which mark the various stages in the business cycle or accompany the round of the seasons.

In recent years the attention of students of economic affairs has been focused upon the phenomena of the business cycle, with its alternating periods of prosperity and depression, and the accompanying pendulum swing of employment from an apparent shortage of labor to severe unemployment or a relative surplus of labor. It is in this undulation of employment conditions that the most obvious and tangible instances of labor surplus and labor shortage arise. Demand for labor, like demand for any commodity, means demand for a given quantity at a given price. Supply means supply at a given price. Labor shortage and labor surplus, consequently, are relative terms, to be interpreted in terms of relation to demand at the prevailing wages. Obviously, however, if due allowance is made for changes in the level of prices, there is a relative labor shortage when employers are unable to hire laborers at wages which have been customary; and likewise a labor surplus when workmen, able and willing, are unable to find employment at what has been the prevailing wage.

This monograph is devoted primarily to consideration of these short-period aspects of the relation of migration to labor supply, in an effort to determine whether migration tends to intensify or to minimize the intensity of the business cycle and particularly whether that phase of the business cycle most directly and obviously inimical to human welfare—the unemployment phase—is rendered more or less severe in its effects because of migratory movements.

The Questions for Solution.

The objects of our inquiry may be conveniently summarized in the following questions to which answers are sought in the analysis set forth in the subsequent chapters:

1. To what extent do cyclical and seasonal fluctuations in migration correspond, in time and degree, with fluctuations in industrial activity, particularly as measured by employment or unemployment?

2. What noteworthy variations in cyclical and seasonal fluctuations appear when migrants are classified by sex, prior occupation, race, or country of origin?

3. What is the relative influence of the "push" or the "pull" upon fluctuations in migration; that is, are such fluctuations primarily determined by changes in the country of emigration or in the country of immigration?

4. What is the economic significance of the ascertained tendencies?

The Conflicting Interpretations.

A scrutiny of the scientific and popular literature of immigration reveals diverse interpretations of the effect of migration upon the fluctuations in employment which may, for the sake of brevity, be designated as the "safety-valve" and the "maladjustment" theories of migration.

Those who advance the *safety-valve theory* look optimistically upon the effect of immigration and urge that the coming and going of the alien immigrant and the alien emigrant are so timed that they lessen the inequalities in employment due to seasonal and cyclical variations in industrial activity. The immigrant, they say, comes and goes as he is wanted, aiding us when the need for men is greatest, departing to his native country when jobs are scarce.

The maladjustment theory. On the other hand, those who take a more pessimistic view urge that migration fails to synchronize well with the seasonal and cyclical fluctuations in industry and to that extent increases unemployment in dull seasons of the year and in periods of industrial depression. They suggest that when industry begins to slacken, immigration continues, and even if it decreases in volume, the change comes too slowly to aid materially in the improvement of employment conditions.* Furthermore, it is suggested, the very fact that a new supply of labor is available in times of industrial expansion is a vicious influence in that it enables the employer to enlarge the scope of his operations readily, and by this very expansion increases the intensity of the subsequent depression.[3]

As usual in such cases, there is doubtless some element of truth in both points of view—that which stresses the susceptibility of migration to employment conditions, and that which stresses the imperfections of such adjustments. The relative credence to be given to these conflicting interpretations can be determined only by close scrutiny of the ways in which the tide of migration ebbs and flows with seasonal and cyclical changes in industrial activity.

Summary of the Contents of Succeeding Chapters.

The first of the following chapters is devoted to a sketch of the major features of immigration into the United States, partly to indicate the reasons for the selection of the elements to which special attention is given and the reasons for the methods of analysis which are applied, and partly for the convenience of those readers who have not given close attention to the character of immigration into this country in recent decades. This chapter can be scanned quickly by the reader who is familiar with the major features of immigration to the United States.

To facilitate the study of the relation of migration to employment conditions, it is necessary to have before us a picture of the alternations in prosperity and depression during the period covered by our analysis. Accordingly, in the third chapter, we turn to a

[3]See the argument by Professor Gustav Cassel to the effect that immigration aggravates the severity of depressions, *The Theory of Social Economy*, Vol. II, pp. 545-547.
*Cf. Director's footnote "a", p. 120.

survey of the pertinent information concerning industrial conditions and particularly concerning employment. The hurried reader who is interested primarily in conclusions and little in method may find it advantageous to skip this chapter on employment indices (Chapter III) and proceed directly to the comparisons between industrial conditions and migratory movements.

With these preliminary pictures of the nature of the immigrant stream and of employment conditions before us, we proceed, in Chapters IV to VI, inclusive, first to a survey in broad outline of the cyclical movement in migration, then to a more detailed analysis of the movements of migration, particularly in the decades since 1890, there being for this period, especially during the years immediately preceding the Great War, a relative abundance of detailed monthly data concerning migration.

In Chapter VII attention is turned to differences in the cyclical movements of selected elements in migration, in order to ascertain the relative extent to which employment conditions affect the movement of immigrants as compared with nonimmigrants, of males as compared with females, or of workers as compared with those immigrants having no occupation.

The question naturally arises as to whether the economic conditions which influence migration to the United States are primarily those of the country of immigration or whether the alternations of prosperity and depression in the country of emigration may not exercise an equally strong influence on the time and volume of migration. Hence Chapter VIII is devoted to a consideration of peculiarities in the fluctuations of immigration from leading countries and to changes in economic conditions in those countries, as bearing on the relative power of the "push" or the "pull" in determining changes in the volume of migration.

While the cyclical aspects of migration are of most significance for the purposes of this study, it is also pertinent to inquire concerning the degree to which the seasonal distribution of migration harmonizes with the seasonal distribution of employment in those industries in which large numbers of immigrants are employed. Chapter IX is devoted to such a survey.

In the concluding chapter, we bring together the significant relations and conclusions developed in the earlier chapters.

CHAPTER II

SIGNIFICANT FEATURES OF MIGRATION

Purpose of Chapter.

For readers who have not given special attention to the immigration problem, it may be helpful to review briefly the characteristic phases of the flow of population to our shores, and particularly to stress those features which have a significant bearing on the particular inquiry to which we have set ourselves. In the first place, let us take note of the chief sources of information and the terminology to be used in the following pages.

SOURCES, TERMINOLOGY, AND COMPREHENSIVENESS OF MIGRATION STATISTICS[1]

Sources.

Except where otherwise specified, all tables and other statistics in this monograph refer to immigration into, or emigration from, the United States. Official annual statistics of immigration are first available with the year ending September 30, 1820; quarterly figures, with the year ending June 30, 1858; and monthly figures, with the year ending June 30, 1889. However, as noted below, the meaning and comprehensiveness of these statistics have varied from time to time.

From 1820 to 1874 immigration statistics were gathered by the Department of State; for the period 1867 to June, 1895, by the U. S. Bureau of Statistics; and from July, 1892, to date, by the U. S. Bureau of Immigration. In the four years in which the data of the Bureau of Statistics and of the Bureau of Immigration overlap, there is a considerable discrepancy in the numbers reported (see footnote to Table 1). The smaller figures, which are those now published as official, were compiled by the Bureau of Immigration. The reason for this discrepancy is not stated in the official publications of the departments concerned nor is it apparent upon examination of the data. It may be that the larger figures published by the

[1]See, also, the footnotes to Table 1 and to Tables I and II in the Appendix.

Bureau of Statistics include many who were counted by the Bureau of Immigration as temporary or nonimmigrant arrivals.[2]

Terminology.

At no time has there been a complete record of all persons entering or leaving the territory of the United States. Particularly on the land boundaries, an attempt at a complete count would be difficult of realization. Furthermore, even at the present time, certain classes of arrivals and departures are treated as "non-statistical" and do not enter into the published migration statistics. For example, "one year residents of Canada, Newfoundland or Mexico, who come for a stay of less than six months; and aliens who habitually cross and recross the land boundaries of the United States"[3] are treated as "non-statistical aliens" and not recorded.

Persons passing over our borders, aside from those who arrive or depart clandestinely, and those who, for reasons just cited, are treated as non-statistical, are classified as citizens or aliens. For recent years, the Bureau of Immigration has published statistics of the number of citizens departing to take up permanent residence abroad. Inasmuch as naturalized citizens are included, a minute appraisal of the movement of the foreign-born elements in our population would include the departing citizens. For example, after the Great War, thousands of naturalized Poles, and many of Polish descent born in this country, emigrated to share in the fortunes of the newly reorganized Poland. In this study, however, attention is concentrated chiefly upon the movement of aliens, and particularly, though not exclusively, upon the coming and going of those officially listed as immigrant or emigrant aliens, as contrasted with nonimmigrant and nonemigrant aliens.[4]

In the terminology used by the Bureau of Immigration, an immigrant alien is a non-resident of this country who enters with the declared intention of establishing a permanent residence, while a nonimmigrant alien is an alien resident of the United States returning from a temporary visit abroad or a non-resident entering for a stay of less than a year.

Likewise, an alien emigrant is an alien resident of the United States leaving for a relatively permanent sojourn abroad; and an alien nonemigrant is either an alien who originally entered as a

---

[2]This interpretation of the discrepancy was suggested by the Acting Commissioner-General of the U. S. Bureau of Immigration, in a letter to the writer, dated May 9, 1924.
[3]U. S. Bureau of Immigration, *General Order No. 13*, July 24, 1923, p. 16.
[4]See Chapter VII for comparison of immigrants and nonimmigrants.

nonimmigrant and is now leaving after having been in this country less than one year, or he is an alien resident of the United States leaving for a temporary sojourn abroad.

It should be noted that the definition of "immigrant" for purposes of the quota restriction acts of recent years differs somewhat in scope from the traditional meaning of the term as above defined.

Ordinarily in official and popular use, the terms immigrant, emigrant, immigration, and emigration refer to the relatively permanent immigrant or emigrant and exclude from consideration the nonimmigrant and nonemigrant groups; and, as a rule, that practice is followed in this monograph. However, it should be noted that for some purposes the citizen and nonimmigrant alien elements should not be ignored. Unless the arrivals and departures of these groups balance—and they do not—they should logically be included in a study of the contributions which migration makes to population. Also, in our present inquiry, the reaction to employment conditions of the aliens arriving or departing temporarily from our shores may be as significant as the fluctuations in the movements of immigrants and emigrants proper. In fact, it would seem reasonable to expect that the volume of migration of workers who come for only a temporary residence would be especially sensitive to changing conditions of employment.

In the following pages, the terms *immigrants* and *emigrants* refer ordinarily to those relatively permanent alien arrivals and departures officially designated as immigrants and emigrants; the terms *alien arrivals* and *alien departures* include, in addition, the nonimmigrant and nonemigrant group, respectively; and the terms *total arrivals* and *total departures* are inclusive of all recorded arrivals and departures of both citizens and aliens.

In some instances the term *permanent* has been used for immigrants and emigrants and *temporary* for the nonimmigrants and nonemigrants; but these terms should not be interpreted too literally, as the classification is based upon the declared intention, and intentions may be either misstated or subsequently changed. The arriving alien who declares an intention of establishing a permanent residence in this country may find conditions less agreeable than expected and emigrate within a few months. The fact that in the seventeen years from July 1, 1907, to June 30, 1924, the recorded total of nonimmigrants was only 2,485,789, while that of nonemigrants was 3,097,567, indicates either that thousands of incoming aliens declare an intention of permanent sojourn but change their minds and leave after a short stay, or that many alien residents upon leaving declare an intention of only a temporary sojourn abroad but do not return to this country as they had intended.

Variations in Comprehensiveness.

In addition to the above distinctions among citizens, immigrant aliens, and nonimmigrant aliens, it is necessary to note that the official statistics of immigration have not always been equally comprehensive and do not have exactly the same connotation throughout the period of a little more than a century for which they are available. The footnotes to the tables contain much of the detail concerning the varying comprehensiveness. For example, the data which are officially published for the annual totals of immigration[5] cover, prior to the fiscal year beginning July 1, 1867, all recorded arrivals of aliens, without discrimination as to length of intended residence; for the period ending June 30, 1903, they cover immigrants as differentiated from nonimmigrants; for the next three years, "aliens admitted" (though apparently this does not actually include nonimmigrants); and for subsequent years, only immigrants admitted. In brief, to make the data strictly comparable throughout the entire period, it would be necessary to make allowance for the inclusion or non-inclusion of, first, nonimmigrants, or those with announced intention of temporary residence only; and second, would-be immigrants debarred from entry.

Also, there are variances due to the circumstance that in the early period there was no attempt made to record residents of adjoining countries, Mexico and Canada, as they passed over our boundaries. In fact, the early records of the number of Europeans entering the United States via Canada are quite imperfect. For the period from July, 1885, to October, 1893, the statistics entirely omit such arrivals through Canada. Subsequent to October, 1893, the records include foreigners arriving at Canadian ports en route to this country, and more recently, they also include residents of Canada and Mexico who pass our boundary lines for a stay of six months or longer, although they are not counted as immigrants unless a stay of a year or more is intended.

The above-mentioned discrepancies in the official statistics of immigration, while significant for some purposes, are not important enough when we are primarily interested in cyclical fluctuations to

[5]United States Immigration Commission, *Statistical Review of Immigration*: 1820-1910, p. 4.

prevent us from treating the series as reasonably homogeneous throughout the entire period for which the official statistics are available.

Fiscal and Other Non-calendar Immigration Years.[6]

Through most of the period included in our immigration records, the year covered by the officially published annual statistics does not coincide with the calendar year. For the years 1820 to 1831, inclusive, the annual immigration statistics refer to the twelve months ending September 30th of the given year; for 1833 to 1842, inclusive, the immigration and calendar years coincide; for 1844 to 1850, the immigration year again terminates September 30th; for 1851 to 1856, the year ends December 31st; and beginning with 1858 and continuing until the present time, the official immigration year ends June 30th.

We shall use the term *fiscal years* for twelve-month periods which end on June 30th. To illustrate, the phrase "in the years 1863 to 1892 (fiscal)," means from July 1, 1867, to June 30, 1892, inclusive. Non-calendar years not ending on June 30th will be appropriately indicated.

PERTINENT FEATURES OF MIGRATION TO AND FROM THE UNITED STATES

Violence of the Major Fluctuations.

The significance of the facts revealed by the subsequent analysis of the quarterly and monthly statistics of migration will be clearer if we first make a preliminary survey of the larger movements in the flow of immigration. In Chart I, we have a curve representing the volume of immigration in each year in a period of slightly over a century, beginning with the year ending September 30, 1820.[7] The picture is one of successive waves, the crest of the major waves occurring, respectively, in 1854 (calendar year) and 1873, 1882, 1892, 1907, 1914, and 1921 (fiscal years). In each case the following decline corresponds approximately to a period of industrial depression in this country. We shall return in later chapters to a closer scrutiny of these relations.

While the general sweep of the curve is upward until checked by the Great War and the restrictive conditions of the post-war period,

[6]See Table 1.

[7]For the extent to which these data are not strictly comparable throughout the entire period, see the earlier section in this chapter entitled, "Variations in Comprehensiveness."

the fluctuations in volume are relatively so large that the trend, particularly for anything short of very long periods, is to a large extent obscured by the violence of the fluctuations. Moreover, on closer analysis, it is found that some major elements in migration have been declining while others were increasing in number. In all, the magnitude of the major fluctuations in immigration has led us in some instances, particularly where short periods are under consideration, to analyze the data without attempting to eliminate

CHART 1

FLUCTUATIONS IN THE NUMBER OF IMMIGRANTS, BY YEARS: 1820-1924[a]

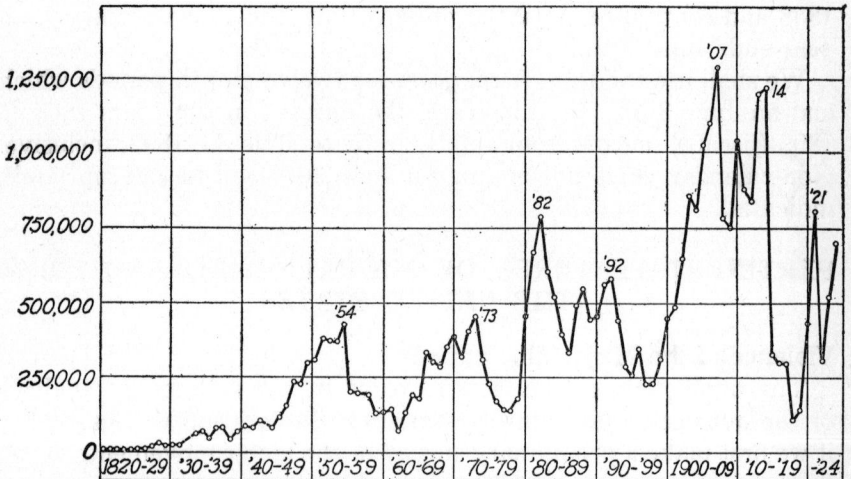

[a]Numerical data in Table 1.

whatever trend may be present; and for long-period studies, in order to bring out clearly the current alternations in prosperity and depression, trends have been computed by the flexible method of the moving average, which tends to eliminate the effect of the larger swings such as the general decline from the early eighties to the late nineties as well as the general upward trend of immigration.

The best data for comparing migration and industrial conditions apply to the years subsequent to 1890 and particularly to the period from 1907 to 1923. Obviously, however, the direction and degree of a significant trend throughout this period is largely a matter of conjecture.

TABLE 1.—OFFICIALLY RECORDED IMMIGRATION INTO THE UNITED STATES:
1820-1924ᵃ

(Thousands of Persons)

PERIOD	IMMIGRATION	PERIOD	IMMIGRATION	PERIOD	IMMIGRATION
YEAR ENDED SEPT. 30		YEAR ENDED DEC. 31		1886........	334.2
				1887........	490.1
1820.........	8.4ᵇ	1851........	379.5	1888........	546.9
1821.........	9.1	1852........	371.6	1889........	444.4
1822.........	6.9	1853........	368.6	1890........	455.3
1823.........	6.4	1854........	427.8	1891........	560.3
1824.........	7.9	1855........	200.9	1892........	579.7ᵉ
1825.........	10.2	1856........	195.9	1893........	439.7ᵉ
1826.........	10.8	1857........	c	1894........	285.6ᵉ
1827.........	18.9			1895........	258.5ᵉ
1828.........	27.4	YEAR ENDED JUNE 30		1896........	343.3
1829.........	22.5	1858........	191.9	1897........	230.8
1830.........	23.3	1859........	129.6	1898........	229.3
1831.........	22.6	1860........	133.1	1899........	311.7
1832.........	c	1861........	142.9	1900........	448.6
		1862........	72.2	1901........	487.9
YEAR ENDED DEC. 31		1863........	132.9	1902........	648.7
1833.........	58.6	1864........	191.1	1903........	857.0
1834.........	65.4	1865........	180.3	1904........	812.9
1835.........	45.4	1866........	332.6	1905........	1026.5
1836.........	76.2	1867........	303.1	1906........	1100.7
1837.........	79.3	1868........	282.2ᵈ	1907........	1285.3
1838.........	38.9	1869........	352.8	1908........	782.9
1839.........	68.1	1870........	387.2	1909........	751.8
1840.........	84.1	1871........	321.4	1910........	1041.6
1841.........	80.3	1872........	404.8	1911........	878.6
1842.........	104.6	1873........	459.8	1912........	838.2
1843.........	c	1874........	313.3	1913........	1197.9
		1875........	227.5	1914........	1218.5
YEAR ENDED SEPT. 30		1876........	170.0	1915........	326.7
1844.........	78.6	1877........	141.9	1916........	298.8
1845.........	114.4	1878........	138.5	1917........	295.4
1846.........	154.4	1879........	177.8	1918........	110.6
1847.........	235.0	1880........	457.3	1919........	141.1
1848.........	226.5	1881........	669.4	1920........	430.0
1849.........	297.0	1882........	798.0	1921........	805.2
1850.........	310.0	1883........	603.3	1922........	309.6
		1884........	518.6	1923........	522.9
		1885........	395.3	1924........	706.9

ᵃ Compiled from the U. S. Bureau of Immigration, *Annual Report of the Commissioner General of Immigration, Fiscal Year Ended June 30, 1924*, p. 122.

ᵇFor 1820 to 1867, these statistics pertain to "Aliens Arriving," including that class of arrivals later designated as nonimmigrants.

ᶜIn these periods the available statistics cover other than twelve-month periods. In the fifteen months from October 1, 1831, to December 31, 1832, 60, 482 alien arrivals are recorded; in the nine months from January 1 to September 30, 1843, 52,496; in the three months from October 1 to December 31, 1850, 59,976; and in the six months from January 1 to June 30, 1857, 112,123.

ᵈFor the fiscal years 1868 to 1903, inclusive, these statistics are designated in the official publications as including "Immigrants Arriving;" for the years 1904 to 1906, inclusive, "Aliens Admitted;" and from 1907 to date, "Immigrant Aliens Admitted." However, it would appear from other data given in the reports of the Commissioner General of Immigration that in all years after 1867, the statistics given in the above table do not include nonimmigrants.

ᵉThe numbers of immigrants as compiled by the U. S. Bureau of Statistics for these years are: 1892, 623,084; 1893, 502,917; 1894, 314,467; 1895, 279,948. *Monthly Summary of Commerce and Finance*, June, 1903, p. 4364.

Marked Seasonal Variation.

An examination of the quarterly and monthly data on immigration reveals a marked, and, on the whole, a regular seasonal variation. This is clearly evidenced by Chart 2. The upper section of

CHART 2

THE MARKED SEASONAL MOVEMENT IN IMMIGRATION: 1885-1924
Ratio Scale

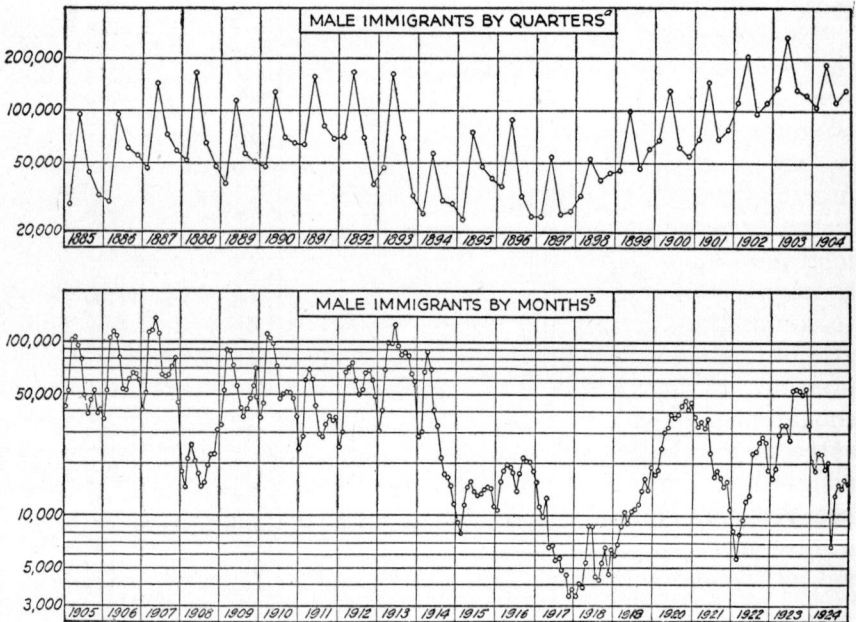

ªNumerical data in Appendix Table I.
ᵇNumerical data in Appendix Table II.

this chart presents the quarterly data for 1885 to 1904 (calendar years) showing invariably a relatively large immigration in the second quarter comprising April, May, and June. In the lower section of the chart, covering the period 1905 to 1924 by months, a similar marked seasonal variation appears prior to the Great War. During and immediately after the war, the seasonal is somewhat distorted and subordinated. After 1921, the influence of the per centum limit law, permitting twenty per cent of the admissible quota to enter in any one month, beginning in July, has caused the seasonal variation to differ markedly from that characteristic of the pre-war period.

Obviously it would be difficult to trace the response of migration to cyclical changes in industry without making allowance for the strong seasonal tendencies. Consequently, in most instances, the quarterly and monthly data on migration have been corrected for typical seasonal variation before they were used in comparisons with employment or other indices of business conditions.

Heavy Emigration.

Comprehensive data concerning emigration are available only for the period beginning on July 1, 1907. Prior to that date an approximation of the volume of emigration is afforded by statistics of outgoing steerage passengers furnished to the Government officials by the courtesy of the steamship companies. Both the approximations available prior to 1907 and the subsequent more exact statistics indicate clearly that an adequate analysis of the effect of migration upon labor supply must rest upon emigration as well as immigration statistics. Is the volume of emigration large relative to immigration? Does the net movement (immigration less emigration) show a decided response to industrial prosperity or depression? Is there ever a net outgo? The answers to these questions should help us in our quest. Consequently, in Chapter V and succeeding chapters attention has been given to fluctuations in emigration as well as in immigration. Statistics of the proportion between immigration and emigration of selected races are given in a subsequent section of this chapter; and the estimated or recorded net movement in the fiscal years 1900 to 1924 inclusive, is given in Table 10 on page 50. In the years 1908 to 1924, in which direct statistics of departures are available, the volume of alien departures was equal to 51 per cent of the volume of arrivals, but the ratio of departures to arrivals varies widely in the several years.

Preponderance of Males.

Immigration to the United States has been preponderantly male in every year from 1820 to 1923, except the fiscal year of 1922, when the ratio of males fell to 48.4 per cent of the total immigration. Chart 3 portrays the percentage distribution by sexes throughout the entire period for which data are available.[8]

[8]For the fiscal years 1820 to 1867, inclusive, this chart is based upon the distribution as estimated by the Immigration Commission in its *Statistical Review of Immigration,*

In most of the years since the Civil War, males have constituted from sixty to seventy per cent of the total immigration. Furthermore, while many foreign-born women are engaged in gainful occupations in this country, the percentage of foreign-born males so employed is much higher; hence the bulk of the recent immigrants

CHART 3

THE PREPONDERANCE OF MALES IN IMMIGRATION

The cross-hatched portion represents the per cent of total immigration wh'ch males constituted in each year: 1820-1924.

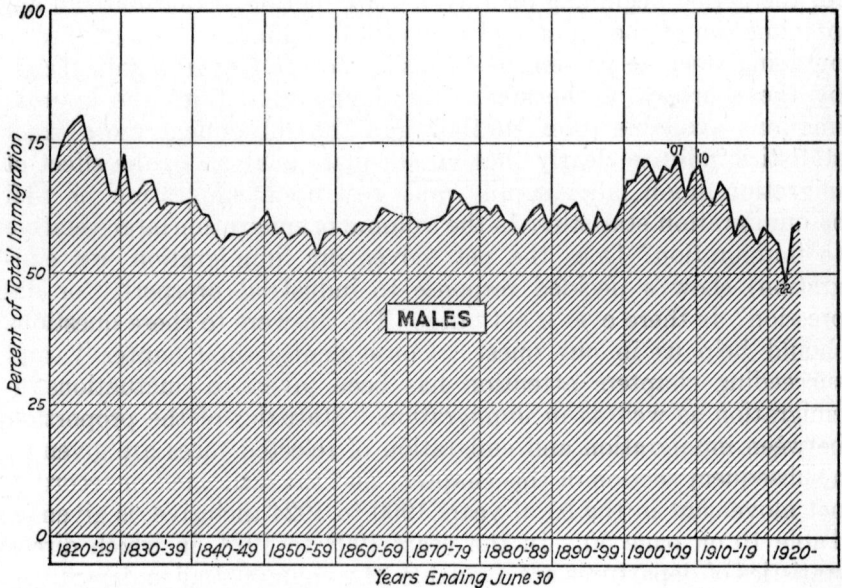

Years Ending June 30

.Numerical data in Table 2.

who enter industry are doubtless male immigrants, particularly in certain industries. In 1920, 89.3 per cent of foreign-born males, but only 18.4 per cent of foreign-born females, were gainfully employed. Few women engage in mining, in construction, or in railway maintenance. Of the 733,936 persons listed in the 1920 Census of Occupations as coal mine operatives, only 1,495 were females; of

1820-1910, p. 6; for the years 1869-1910, upon computations in the same publication based upon the recorded immigrant arrivals classified by sex; and for subsequent years, directly upon data published by the U. S. Bureau of Immigration.

the 470,199 steam railroad laborers, only 6,586; of the 623,203 "building, general, and not specified laborers," only 15,128; and of the 115,836 laborers in "road and street building and repairing," only 163.

TABLE 2.——PROPORTION OF MALES IN IMMIGRATION, FOR YEARS ENDING JUNE 30TH; 1820-1924[a]

YEAR ENDING JUNE 30	PER CENT OF TOTAL	YEAR ENDING JUNE 30	PER CENT OF TOTAL	YEAR ENDING JUNE 30	PER CENT OF TOTAL
1820	69.8	1855	58.8	1890	61.9
1821	74.2	1856	57.8	1891	63.2
1822	77.5	1857	53.9	1892	62.4
1823	79.0	1858	57.8	1893	63.8
1824	80.1	1859	58.2	1894	59.3
1825	74.2	1860	58.6	1895	57.6
1826	70.9	1861	57.1	1896	61.9
1827	71.7	1862	58.4	1897	58.5
1828	65.4	1863	60.1	1898	59.2
1829	65.2	1864	59.4	1899	62.6
1830	72.5	1865	59.9	1900	67.8
1831	64.4	1866	62.7	1901	67.9
1832	65.6	1867	62.0	1902	71.9
1833	67.5	1868	*	1903	71.5
1834	67.8	1869	60.9	1904	67.6
1835	62.0	1870	60.8	1905	70.6
1836	63.8	1871	59.3	1906	69.5
1837	63.4	1872	59.3	1907	72.4
1838	63.3	1873	60.0	1908	64.8
1839	64.0	1874	60.4	1909	69.2
1840	64.2	1875	61.5	1910	70.7
1841	61.5	1876	65.8	1911	64.9
1842	61.0	1877	64.9	1912	63.2
1843	57.4	1878	62.3	1913	67.5
1844	56.0	1879	62.9	1914	65.6
1845	57.7	1880	62.9	1915	57.2
1846	57.5	1881	61.4	1916	61.0
1847	57.9	1882	63.2	1917	59.1
1848	58.9	1883	60.3	1918	55.9
1849	60.0	1884	59.5	1919	59.0
1850	62.2	1885	57.3	1920	57.6
1851	57.7	1886	60.1	1921	55.8
1852	58.8	1887	62.6	1922	48.4
1853	56.7	1888	63.2	1923	58.8
1854	57.6	1889	59.2	1924	59.9

[a]For the years 1820 to 1867, these are approximate percentages computed by the United States Immigration Commission, and published in their *Statistical Review of Immigration 1820-1910*, pp. 5-6, which also gives the percentages for 1868 to 1910, inclusive, as computed from the official statistics of immigrants classified by sex. The percentages for subsequent years are computed from the statistics published by the U. S. Bureau of Immigration.
*Not reported.

It is apparent from the above stated facts that the fluctuations of male immigration are more significant than the movement of total immigration when the reaction of the flow of working immigrants to employment conditions is under consideration. For this reason, male immigration, rather than the immigration of both sexes, is the primary immigration series used in this study. It may be noted, in passing, that the percentage of male immigration is relatively high in prosperous years, such as the fiscal years of 1907 and 1910, and relatively low in the succeeding depression periods, suggesting, as would be expected, that the male element is the more sensitive to industrial conditions.

In emigration, males constitute even a larger proportion than in immigration. This proportion was highest in the depression year 1908 (See Table 3). Since the collection of emigration statistics

TABLE 3.—PROPORTION OF MALES IN EMIGRATION: 1908-1924*
Years ending June 30th

Year	Total emigrants	Males	Per cent
1908.............	395,073	342,883	86.8
1909.............	225,802	159,009	70.4
1910.............	202,436	154,842	76.5
1911.............	295,666	238,922	80.8
1912.............	333,262	275,970	82.8
1913.............	308,190	251,808	81.7
1914.............	303,338	242,208	79.8
1915.............	204,074	168,072	82.4
1916.............	129,765	106,625	82.2
1917.............	66,277	48,427	73.1
1918.............	94,585	71,352	75.4
1919.............	123,522	101,167	81.9
1920.............	288,315	237,748	82.5
1921.............	247,718	189,134	76.4
1922.............	198,712	143,223	72.1
1923.............	81,450	54,752	67.2
1924.............	76,789	57,313	74.6

*These data, compiled from the reports of the Commissioner General of Immigration, do not include departing citizens or non-emigrant aliens.

began in 1908, males have constituted at least seventy per cent of the total in every year but 1923 (fiscal). The restriction of immigration has tended to decrease the proportion of males in emigration as well as in immigration.

Country of Origin—the "Old" and "New" Immigration.

So much of the discussion of immigration in recent years has revolved around the relative merits of the so-called "old" and "new" elements in immigration that it seems desirable to indicate their relative contributions to the immigrant stream.   The "old" immigration came from northern and western Europe; the "new" comes from eastern and southern Europe and Turkey in Asia.

An examination of Table 4 and Chart 4 reveals that prior to 1896,

CHART 4

THE CHANGING CHARACTER OF IMMIGRATION.

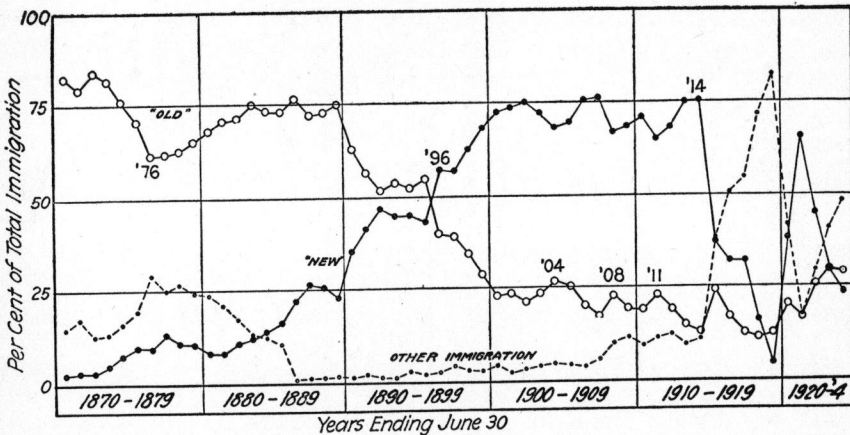

Years Ending June 30

.Numerical data in Table 4.

the majority of immigrants were of the "old" strain.   In the year ending June 30, 1896, the "new" immigration rose to 57 per cent of the total and since that date, until the Great War, held a clear preponderance over the immigration from northern and western Europe.   During the conduct of hostilities a large proportion of the immigrants came from Canada and Mexico, and in more recent years, the quota acts have been a restraining influence upon European immigration, particularly from the countries furnishing the "new" immigration.

Leading Immigrant Races or Peoples.[9]

Recognizing that a German immigrant does not always come from Germany or an Italian from Italy, and that it may be desirable

[9]The term "race" is used throughout this volume, not necessarily to designate a group defined according to strict ethnological principles, but to refer to one of the some

TABLE 4.—PERCENTAGE DISTRIBUTION OF IMMIGRANTS ACCORDING TO "OLD" AND "NEW" SOURCES, BY YEARS: 1870-1924[a]

100 per cent=the total number of immigrants for whom country of origin is known

YEAR ENDING JUNE 30	"OLD"[b]	"NEW"[c]	OTHER[d]	YEAR ENDING JUNE 30	"OLD"[b]	"NEW"[c]	OTHER[d]
1870	82.3	2.5	15.1	1900	23.1	72.4	4.4
1871	79.3	3.2	17.5	1901	23.7	73.6	2.6
1872	83.8	3.3	13.0	1902	21.4	75.0	3.6
1873	81.6	4.9	13.5	1903	23.8	72.1	4.1
1874	76.0	7.8	16.1	1904	26.8	68.4	4.9
1875	70.4	10.0	19.6	1905	25.6	69.9	4.5
1876	61.2	9.9	28.8	1906	20.2	75.7	4.0
1877	61.6	13.3	25.1	1907	17.7	76.2	6.0
1878	62.6	10.8	26.6	1908	22.8	66.9	10.4
1879	65.1	10.5	24.5	1909	19.6	68.5	11.9
1880	67.9	8.3	23.7	1910	19.4	70.9	9.6
1881	70.6	8.3	21.0	1911	23.0	65.2	11.8
1882	71.4	10.8	17.8	1912	19.2	68.1	12.7
1883	74.5	12.2	13.4	1913	15.3	74.9	9.9
1884	73.4	14.1	12.5	1914	13.5	75.2	11.3
1885	73.0	16.4	10.7	1915	24.2	37.4	38.3
1886	76.5	22.1	1.3	1916	17.1	32.2	50.7
1887	72.1	26.4	1.4	1917	13.0	32.2	54.8
1888	72.6	25.8	1.5	1918	11.7	16.4	71.9
1889	74.9	23.1	2.0	1919	12.8	4.7	82.5
1890	62.8	35.3	1.8	1920	20.3	38.3	41.5
1891	56.7	41.2	2.1	1921	17.2	65.3	17.5
1892	51.9	46.6	1.5	1922	25.7	44.9	29.4
1893	53.9	44.9	1.2	1923	29.9	29.4	40.7
1894	52.1	44.9	3.0	1924	28.8	23.2	48.0
1895	54.7	43.2	2.1				
1896	40.0	57.0	2.9				
1897	39.0	56.8	4.2				
1898	34.5	62.4	3.2				
1899	28.9	68.0	3.1				

[a]For 1870-1910, from the United States Immigration Commission, *Statistical Review of Immigration 1820-1910*; for 1911-1924, computed from statistics published by the U. S. Bureau of Immigration. Prior to 1906, immigrants were recorded by the country from which they departed; thereafter by the country of last permanent residence.

[b]The "old" sources include the countries of northern and western Europe, namely: Belgium, Denmark, France, Germany, the Netherlands, Norway, Sweden, Switzerland, and the United Kingdom.

[c]The "new" sources include the countries of eastern and southern Europe now known as Austria, Hungary, Czechoslovakia, Jugoslavia, Bulgaria, Finland, Greece, Italy, Poland, Portugal, Rumania, Russia, Spain, Turkey in Europe, and certain other small European countries designated as "other Europe;" also Turkey in Asia.

[d]"Other countries" includes all sources of immigration not included in "old" and "new" sources as above defined. In recent years most of this group came from Canada and Mexico. The fact noted in this chapter that immigrants from or through Canada were, in earlier periods, recorded incompletely or not at all, limits the comparability of the above percentage distributions.

forty groups for which statistics are given by the Bureau of Immigration under the caption "races or peoples." For a discussion of these "races or peoples," see the *Reports of the United States Immigration Commission*, Vol. 9, *Dictionary of Races or Peoples*.

to have statistics of the immigration of races like the Slovaks, Poles, and Hebrews[10] which either constitute only a part of the immigration from some one country or, on the other hand, an important fraction of the immigration from two or more countries, the U. S. Bureau of Immigration began in 1899 to collect statistics of immigration by race or people. Beginning with the fiscal year ending June 30, 1908,

CHART 5

GROSS AND NET IMMIGRATION OF SELECTED RACES:
JULY 1, 1907, TO JUNE 30, 1923.

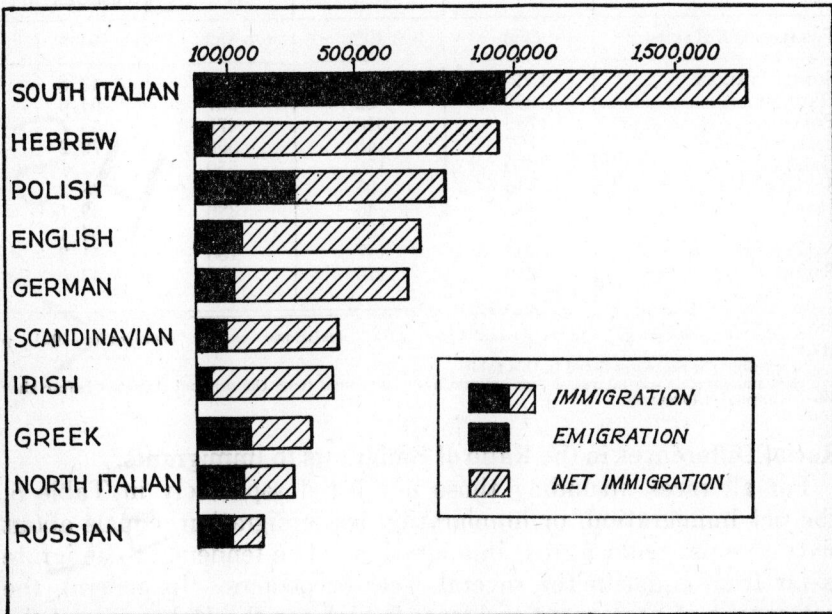

.Numerical data in Table 5.

similar statistics are available for emigration. The numerical facts concerning the immigration and emigration of the nine races which contributed the largest numbers of immigrants in the sixteen years from July 1, 1907, to June 30, 1923, are given in Table 5 and Chart 5. Though it is not the tenth in number of immigrants, the Russian race is also included to facilitate comparison with the numbers of

[10]Objection is sometimes made to the use of the word Hebrew as indicating a race. Here again we have followed the practice of the Bureau of Immigration in designating the Hebrews as a "race or people."

certain non-Russian races, such as the Poles and Hebrews, many of whom come from Russia. It will be noted that the three leading races in number of immigrants were the South Italians, Hebrews, and Poles, in the order named.

TABLE 5.—IMMIGRATION AND EMIGRATION OF LEADING RACES: 1908-1923[a]

(Thousands of persons)

RACE	IMMIGRATION	EMIGRATION	NET IMMIGRATION	
			NUMBER[c]	PER CENT OF IMMIGRATION
TOTAL—ALL RACES[b]	9,950	3,498	6,452	64.8
SOUTH ITALIAN.........	1,724	970	755	43.8
HEBREW...............	959	52	907	94.6
POLISH...............	789	318	471	59.7
ENGLISH..............	707	146	560	79.2
GERMAN..............	670	120	550	82.1
SCANDINAVIAN.........	449	98	351	78.2
IRISH...............	433	46	386	89.1
GREEK...............	366	169	198	54.1
NORTH ITALIAN........	302	147	155	51.3
RUSSIAN.............	210	110	100	47.6

[a]Compiled from data given in the *Annual Report of the Commissioner General of Immigration*, 1923, p 117-118.
[b]Including the races not listed in this table.
[c]Net immigration = immigration less emigration. Computed from the original statistics before they were reduced to thousands.

Racial Differences in the Ratio of Emigrants to Immigrants.

For all races, including those not listed separately in Table 5, the net immigration, or immigration less emigration, equals about sixty-five per cent of gross immigration. The tendency to emigrate is far from equal in the several races or peoples. In general, the percentage of permanent residents is high for the Hebrews and the races of northern and western Europe and low for the races of southern and eastern Europe except the Hebrews. Though the incoming South Italians far exceeded in number the immigrants of any other race, the net immigration for this race was only forty-four per cent of arriving immigrants in the fiscal years 1908 to 1923; while it was almost ninety-five per cent for the Hebrews, eighty-nine per cent for the Irish, and over eighty per cent for the Germans. In other words, the Germans, Irish, and Hebrews ordinarily come to stay; but large numbers of the South Italian immigrants, after a more or less short period of labor and saving, return to their native land, as has been their custom for decades in this and other countries to which they have emigrated. This practice has given rise to the statement that the Italian comes and goes as he is wanted. The accuracy of this statement we shall consider more at length in later pages.

We shall find it interesting, in subsequent analysis, to note whether this relatively temporary nature of the immigration of certain races is accompanied by an appreciably greater susceptibility to cyclical influences. We have seen that for every ten South Italians arriving in the United States approximately six of that race depart as emigrants. Is their departure closely correlated with the business cycle?

Occupations of Immigrants.

The great bulk of immigrants have been engaged in their native countries in relatively unskilled occupations, as agricultural or common laborers, and in this country enter, on the whole, occupations of the unskilled or semi-skilled grade. In many instances entrance in this country into the ranks of common labor is not necessarily due to incapacity for more skilled occupations, but in part to the inability or failure of the immigrant to capitalize his past experience. Thousands of former farmers and agricultural workers find their way into factory, mine, or construction camp; and many skilled handicraftsmen, handicapped by differences in language and different methods of production, find an inadequate market for their specialized skill and drift into the ranks of the unskilled or at most semi-skilled.

The above conclusions rest upon a comparison of the information obtained by the U. S. Bureau of Immigration concerning the occupations of immigrants prior to their entry and the occupations of emigrants while in this country, and also upon collateral evidence in the decennial Census of Occupations, the reports of the Immigration Commission in 1910, and various fragmentary studies. This evidence, though not complete, is reasonably conclusive as to the major tendencies.

As shown by the 1910 and 1920 Census of Occupations, between forty and fifty per cent of the foreign born workers enter mechanical and manufacturing pursuits; while less than fifteen per cent are found in the agricultural pursuits (Table 6). The tendency for the foreign born to engage in the unskilled labor of certain industries is evidenced by the data in Table 7. Of all employed in agriculture,

TABLE 6.—OCCUPATIONAL DISTRIBUTION OF FOREIGN-BORN WHITES:
1910 and 1920[a]

OCCUPATION	1910		1920	
	NUMBER	PER CENT	NUMBER	PER CENT
ALL OCCUPATIONS	7,811,502	100.0	7,746,460	100.0
AGRICULTURE, FORESTRY, AND ANIMAL HUSBANDRY....................	1,096,911	14.0	931,561	12.0
EXTRACTION OF MINERALS...........	463,036	5.9	377,138	4.9
MANUFACTURING AND MECHANICAL INDUSTRIES.....................	3,389,430	43.4	3,634,249	46.9
TRANSPORTATION..................	692,412	8.9	547,613	7.1
TRADE.........................	771,782	9.9	860,530	11.1
PUBLIC SERVICE..................	99,772	1.3	127,280	1.6
PROFESSIONAL SERVICE.............	202,699	2.6	231,719	3.0
DOMESTIC AND PERSONAL SERVICE.....	921,808	11.8	769,193	9.9
CLERICAL OCCUPATIONS.............	173,652	2.2	267,177	3.4

[a]Compiled from the U. S. Bureau of the Census, *Fourteenth Census of the United States*, Vol. IV, pp. 340-341. These occupation statistics include persons ten years of age or over.

TABLE 7.—THE PROPORTION OF FOREIGN-BORN WHITES IN THE TOTAL OF THE
GAINFULLY EMPLOYED AND AMONG "LABORERS," BY OCCUPATIONAL
GROUPS: 1910 and 1920[a]

Per Cent.

INDUSTRY	ALL LISTED IN THE OCCUPATION		THOSE LISTED AS LABORERS	
	1910	1920	1910	1920
ALL GAINFULLY EMPLOYED	20.5	18.6	27.4[b]	23.3[c]
AGRICULTURE, FORESTRY AND ANIMAL HUSBANDRY....................	8.7	8.5	9.8	9.8
EXTRACTION OF MINERALS...........	48.0	34.6	50.1	d
MANUFACTURING AND MECHANICAL INDUSTRIES.....................	31.9	28.4	38.5	31.2
TRANSPORTATION..................	26.3	17.9	50.1	31.5
TRADE..........................	21.4	20.3	34.5	25.2
PUBLIC SERVICE, NOT ELSEWHERE SPE-FIED.........................	21.7	16.5	40.1	29.3
PROFESSIONAL SERVICE.............	12.0	10.8	23.6[e]	e
DOMESTIC AND PERSONAL SERVICE.....	24.4	22.6	31.5	26.0

[a]Compiled from the *Thirteenth Census of the United States, Vol. IV, Occupation Statistics*, and the *Fourteenth Census of the United States, Vol. IV, Occupations*.
[b]Includes mining and quarrying and is consequently not exactly comparable with the 1920 total.
[c]Excludes mining and quarrying.
[d]The 1920 Census does not classify laborers separately in this industry.
[e]The 1910 Census listed some laborers in "occupations connected with professional service," but the 1920 Census gave no laborers under the designation "professional service."

for example, in 1910, only 8.7 per cent were foreign born, whereas 48.0 per cent of those in mining and 31.9 per cent of those in manufacturing and mechanical pursuits have a foreign nativity. Of those classified as laborers in 1910, however, the foreign born represent 50.1 per cent of those in mining, 38.5 per cent in manufacturing and mechanical pursuits, and 27.4 per cent of all classified as laborers.

It is obvious that for reasons of incapacity or difficulty in adjustment to American conditions, the immigrant is doing more than his per capita proportion of the common labor of industry. If the statistics gave us separate data for the newly arrived immigrant it seems unquestionable that an even greater proportion would be found in the ranks of the unskilled.

The percentage of laborers is particularly high among the immigrants of certain races. To illustrate, for the immigration years 1899 to 1910, three-fourths or more of the Greeks, the Slovaks, the South Italians, and the Poles were either general laborers or farm laborers. On the other hand, forty per cent or more of the Scotch, English, Welsh, and Hebrews are listed as skilled.

Occupational Changes.

The preponderance of unskilled among the immigrants and the tendency, particularly among the farmers and agricultural laborers, to abandon their old-country occupations upon arrival and thus to lose any opportunity fully to utilize their previous industrial experience, is clearly evidenced by the statistics of occupations of immigrants and emigrants in Table 8.

In the immigration years 1908 to 1923, 26 per cent of immigrants were classified as "laborers," while 70 per cent of emigrants are placed in this class. On the other hand, 25 per cent of immigrants and less than 2 per cent of emigrants are listed as farm laborers; and the skilled who compose 22 per cent of the immigrants were only 12 per cent of the emigrants. Even after allowing for a considerable degree of probable inaccuracy in the data, and also for the fact that probably a smaller proportion of foreign-born farmers and and farm laborers than of industrial workers emigrate, the conclusion seems unavoidable that many from the "farm laborer" and "skilled" occupations are in this country engaged in unskilled occupations in factories, mines, and construction operations. Mr. Louis Block[11]

[11] *Quarterly Publication of the American Statistical Association*, June, 1921, pp. 750-764, "Occupations of Immigrants Before and After Coming to the United States."

reached similar conclusions by comparing the occupational statistics of immigration in the decade 1900 to 1910 with the Census record of increases in the numbers in the several occupations.

Obviously, the unskilled elements in immigration and the cyclical variations in the employment of the unskilled worker in American industry are particularly worthy of attention in studying the relation of migration to the business cycle.

TABLE 8.—OCCUPATIONS OF IMMIGRANTS AND EMIGRANTS: JULY 1, 1907, TO JUNE 30, 1923[a]

OCCUPATION	NUMBERS			PER CENT OF NUMBER DECLARING AN OCCUPATION	
	IMMIGRANTS	EMIGRANTS	NET[b]	IMMIGRANTS	EMIGRANTS
TOTAL............	9,949,740	3,498,185	+6,451,555	....	....
ALL OCCUPATIONS	6,904,963	2,909,956	+3,995,007	100.0	100.0
LABORERS.........	1,821,038	2,031,444	— 210,406[c]	26.4	69.8
FARM LABORERS....	1,733,556	46,163	+1,687,393[c]	25.1	1.6
SKILLED OCCUPATIONS.........	1,517,121	356,515	+1,160,606	22.0	12.3
PROFESSIONAL OCCUPATIONS......	177,127	43,249	+ 133,878	2.6	1.5
OTHER OCCUPATIONS	1,656,121	432,585	+1,223,536	24.0	14.9
WITHOUT OCCUPATION (INCLUDING WOMEN AND CHILDREN)	3,044,777	588,229	+2,456,548	....	....

[a]Compiled from the annual reports of the United States Commissioner General of Immigration for the years 1908 to 1923, inclusive.
[b]Net = immigrants less emigrants.
[c]The apparent excess of emigrant over immigrant laborers is probably caused by a large number of immigrants declaring their occupation as "agricultural laborer" on arrival and as "laborer" at departure.

Though the foreign born are found in other industries in considerable numbers, the industries which are particularly worthy of our attention are factory employment, coal mining, railroad maintenance, and construction work. Employment in these industries is clearly subject to cyclical variations and the immigrant is an important element in each, both in absolute numbers and in proportion to the native born.

The Volume of Immigration Relative to Population.

The significance of a given volume of immigration becomes more obvious when it is compared with population. In Table 9 we have a comparison between the population of the United States at the

decennial census periods and the volume of immigration during the
ten years centering at July 1st of the census year. It will be noted
that immigration was relatively greatest in the decade from July
1, 1846, to June 30, 1855, in which period the average annual immigration was about equal to one and one-quarter per cent of the
total population. In no subsequent decade has the average annual
ratio of immigration to population fallen below one-half of one per
cent or much exceeded one per cent.

TABLE 9.—AVERAGE ANNUAL IMMIGRATION COMPARED WITH POPULATION,
BY DECADES*

DATE OF CENSUS	POPULATION (THOUSANDS)	AVERAGE ANNUAL IMMIGRATION	
		NUMBER (THOUSANDS)ᵃ	RATIO TO POPULA-TION (PER CENT)
JUNE 1-1830................	12,866	34	.26
JUNE 1-1840................	17,069	77	.45
JUNE 1-1850................	23,192	296	1.28
JUNE 1-1860................	31,443	158	.50
JUNE 1-1870................	38,558	338	.88
JUNE 1-1880................	50,156	406	.81
JUNE 1-1890................	62,948	439	.70
JUNE 1-1900................	75,995	540	.71
APRIL 15-1910.............	91,972	942	1.02
JAN. 1-1920................	105,711	389ᵇ	.37

ᵃThe population data are from the 1920 Census, Vol. II, p. 29; the average annual immigration is
computed from data in the 1924 *Annual Report of the Commissioner General of Immigration*, p. 122, and from
mimeographed bulletins of the U. S. Bureau of Immigration for the last six months of 1924, and, except in
the last case, is the average over ten years centered at July 1st of the census year.
ᵇAverage for ten years centered at January 1, 1920.

If we turn to a year-by-year comparison, we find, as would be
expected, a greater variation in the ratio of immigration to population. In Table 10 is given a comparison between the total number
of alien arrivals in fiscal years ending June 30th, and the estimated
population on January 1st of the corresponding years,[12] and also a
comparison between population and the net alien movement—that
is, arrivals less departures.

It should be noted that the data in Table 9 include only those
aliens officially recorded as immigrants, but that in Table 10 and
Table 11 nonimmigrants and nonemigrants are also included; hence
in the immediately following paragraphs the term "immigration"
refers to all arriving aliens.

[12]This estimate of population was prepared by Dr. W. I. King, of the National Bureau
of Economic Research, and is based upon interpolations between the decennial censuses
with the aid of immigration data and the available statistics of births and deaths.

In the quarter century from 1900 to 1924, there have been substantial fluctuations in the relative volume of migration, even if the war period is excluded. The maximum was reached in 1907, just before the depression of 1907-1908, with an annual immigration equivalent to 1.7 per cent of the population.

The barriers created by war conditions checked immigration to such an extent that it dropped to a small fraction of its former volume, reaching low ebb in the year ending June 1918, with two

TABLE 10.—RATIO OF GROSS AND NET ALIEN ARRIVALS TO POPULATION
1900-1924[a]

| YEAR ENDING JUNE 30 | POPULATION[b] (THOUSANDS) | ALIEN ARRIVALS | | | |
| | | THOUSANDS | | RATIO TO POPULATION (PER CENT) | |
		GROSS[a]	NET[a]	GROSS[a]	NET[a]
1900	75,891	474	308	0.63	0.41
1901	76,714	518	327	0.68	0.43
1902	77,933	679	475	0.87	0.61
1903	79,385	885	635	1.11	0.80
1904	80,852	841	449	1.04	0.56
1905	82,326	1,067	662	1.30	0.80
1906	84,078	1,166	825	1.39	0.98
1907	86,153	1,438	1,021	1.67	1.19
1908	88,001	925	210	1.05	0.24
1909	89,357	944	544	1.06	0.61
1910	91,530	1,198	818	1.31	0.89
1911	93,165	1,030	512	1.11	0.55
1912	94,458	1,017	402	1.08	0.43
1913	96,144	1,427	815	1.48	0.85
1914	98,213	1,403	769	1.43	0.78
1915	99,710	434	50	0.44	0.05
1916	101,055	367	126	0.36	0.12
1917	102,590	363	216	0.35	0.21
1918	103,852	212	19	0.20	0.02
1919	104,524	237	21	0.23	0.02
1920	105,711	622	194	0.59	0.18
1921	107,412	978	552	0.91	0.51
1922	109,135	433	87	0.40	0.08
1923	110,688	673	473	0.61	0.43
1924	112,684	879	663	0.78	0.59

[a]Gross = Alien immigrants and nonimmigrants; net = gross arrivals less alien emigrants and nonemigrants.
  As emigration statistics were not compiled prior to July 1, 1907, the number of departing aliens in the earlier years is estimated from the statistics of departing steerage passengers, by assuming that the ratio between departing aliens and departing steerage passengers which obtained for the period from July 1, 1907, to June 30, 1914, is applicable to the period from July 1, 1899, to June 30, 1907.
  [b]These population estimates are for January 1st, and were prepared by Dr. W. I. King, of the staff of the National Bureau of Economic Research.

alien arrivals to each one thousand population. By 1920, the incoming flow was gaining momentum and in the fiscal year of 1921 reached almost a pre-war level at 0.9 per cent. The depression of 1921 brought a marked reduction in the ratio during the fiscal year 1922, but in the two subsequent years, despite the restrictions of the three per centum quota law, the annual volume increased to over one-half of one per cent of the population.

Net arrivals exceeded one per cent of the population only in 1907, was relatively low in the depression years (fiscal) of 1904, 1908, 1911-1912, and particularly 1922, and, in some of the war years almost reached the vanishing point. In the year ending June 30, 1924, they had rallied, despite restrictive legislation, to over one-half of one per cent of the estimated population on January 1, 1924.

It may well be questioned whether a comparison between total immigration and total population is the most significant for our purposes. As we are concerned with the contribution of immigration to the supply of labor, a more significant ratio is obtained by comparing the number of alien arrivals (excluding those recorded as having "no occupation") with the estimated total number of gainfully employed in the United States. It might be even more pertinent to compare arrivals with the number of gainfully employed in those sections of the country in which the aliens settle in large numbers, but for the present at least we shall rest content with the comparison based upon data for the entire country.

Arriving aliens are classified according to the occupations followed in their home countries. Those, including women and children, who have no gainful occupations are placed in a "no occupation" group, the remainder, exclusive of the "no occupation" group, may, with substantial accuracy, be designated as "working immigrants." Though many immigrants ultimately become independent farmers or set up in business for themselves, the great bulk of them, particularly in the period immediately after their arrival, become wage earners in factories, mines, building construction, or on farms. Consequently, an appropriate standard with which to compare the number of "working immigrants" is the number of wage earners in industry. In Table 11 such a comparison has been made between the gross and net arrivals of alien workers and the estimated number of wage earners attached to the leading industries. The workers considered "attached" to a given industry are those who look to that industry as their chief occupation, although they may be temporarily out of employment. During the years 1909 to 1913, the ratio of the annual arrivals of alien workers to the number of wage earners attached to the leading industries ranged from 3.45 per cent in 1909 to 4.96 per cent in 1913. During the war the ratio dropped to less than one per cent, but recovered in 1920 to almost two per cent. It is obvious that the incoming tide of alien workers is ordinarily an appreciable fraction of the total number of wage

TABLE 11.—RATIOS OF GROSS AND NET ARRIVALS OF ALIEN WORKERS TO THE NUMBER OF WAGE EARNERS ATTACHED TO THE LEADING INDUSTRIES, BY FISCAL YEARS: 1909-1921

YEAR ENDING JUNE 30	WAGE EARNERS[a] (THOUSANDS)	ALIEN WORKERS ARRIVING[b]		NET ARRIVALS OF ALIEN WORKERS[c]	
		THOUSANDS	RATIO TO WAGE EARNERS (PER CENT)	THOUSANDS	RATIO TO WAGE EARNERS (PER CENT)
1909	19,736	680.5	3.45	345.9	1.75
1910	20,250	897.7	4.43	593.3	2.93
1911	20,742	743.2	3.58	319.3	1.54
1912	21,134	738.6	3.49	240.2	1.14
1913	21,601	1071.1	4.96	575.0	2.66
1914	22,158	1029.9	4.65	524.4	2.37
1915	22,464	282.1	1.26	[d]29.7	[d]0.13
1916	22,764	239.7	1.05	52.1	0.23
1917	22,998	237.7	1.03	134.3	0.58
1918	22,315	147.4	0.66	[d]3.0	[d]0.01
1919	22,098	156.2	0.71	[d]15.5	[d]0.07
1920	22,798	403.8	1.77	66.0	0.29
1921	23,330	629.9	2.70	314.8	1.35

[a]Includes wage earners attached to factories, transportation and communication, mines and quarries, construction and building, agriculture and "unclassified industries." Computed from estimates for calendar years prepared by Dr. W. I. King.
[b]All arriving aliens (both immigrant and nonimmigrant) less those listed as having no occupation.
[c]All alien workers arriving less all departing aliens (both emigrant and nonemigrant) except those listed as having no occupation.
[d]Excess of departures over arrivals.

earners. However, it is also true that an immigration of three per cent may be a helpful influence in one phase of the cycle and an unwelcome and aggravating factor in another. The volume of immigration must be considered in relation to the contemporaneous conditions of employment before its real importance can be appraised. Also, allowance must be made for the offsetting factor of emigration. To these problems we shall turn our attention in subsequent chapters.

CHAPTER SUMMARY

Upon the facts presented in this chapter, we have based the following major conclusions concerning the immigration elements to be selected for study and the method to be used in their analysis.

1.   Primary, though not exclusive, attention should be given to those alien arrivals and departures ordinarily designated, respectively, as alien immigrants and alien emigrants.

2.   For our purpose, the volume of male immigration is more significant than the volume of total immigration.

3.   Owing to the violence of the major fluctuations in immigration, the estimation of trends in the subsequent chapters is, in most cases, by the flexible method of moving averages, with adjustments in some instances to iron out minor irregularities.

4.   Immigration movements are characterized by strong seasonal fluctuations for which adjustment must be made to facilitate the study of cyclical fluctuations.

5.   The increasing fraction of total immigration contributed by the peoples of southern and eastern Europe in the years before the Great War suggests the desirability of special attention to the cyclical fluctuations in the leading elements of this group.

6.   Immigrants of the various races or peoples exhibit marked differences in the extent to which they establish a permanent residence in this country, indicating the desirability of comparing cyclical fluctuations in emigration by race or people.

7.   A large proportion of immigrants engage in relatively unskilled occupations in factories, mines, and construction operations; hence special attention should be given to fluctuations in employment in these industries and particularly to variations in the market for common labor.

8.   Lastly, the relative volume of migration compared with population is indicated by the fact that while, in this century, the annual number of net alien arrivals has exceeded one per cent of the total population only in 1907, in some of the years just before the Great War, the number of net arrivals of alien workers was equivalent to more than two per cent of the total number of wage earners attached to the leading industries in the United States.

CHAPTER III

EMPLOYMENT OPPORTUNITIES FOR IMMIGRANTS

The Significance of a Measure of Employment Opportunity.

With the passing of the era of abundant and fertile free land, industrial employment rather than agricultural opportunity has been the lodestone attracting the foreign worker to our shores. Particularly within the last three or four decades the typical immigrant has been a prospective wage earner seeking employment in factory, mine, or construction camp.

Data concerning fluctuations in the employment of wage earners are, accordingly, particularly pertinent to our study. The cycle of employment is the aspect of the business cycle which is of direct meaning to the immigrant. It is the most tangible measure of the conditions affecting his economic welfare; and hence it affords the obvious and logical basis for appraising the influence upon migration of fluctuations in economic opportunities and the celerity with which immigration and emigration currents respond to such changes.

The Ideal Measure.

The ideal index of employment, for our purpose, would cover all of those occupations in which immigrants engage in large numbers and would indicate, not merely the variations in the number of workers employed, but also the extent of part-time and over-time employment.

Not only that, but to give a complete picture of the relative economic opportunity afforded the immigrant, our ideal index would be adjusted to variations in real wage rates, that is, in money rates reduced to terms of comparable purchasing power by allowance for changes in the prices of those articles which comprise the budget of the immigrant worker. In short, such an index would make allowance for both the volume of employment and the real rate of compensation and thus measure changes in the real earnings in the immigrant industries.

An index of employment portraying the condition of employment for the unskilled laborer would be particularly valuable, for it is the concensus of opinion of commentators on employment conditions that this class bears the chief brunt of cyclical and seasonal variations in employment, and furthermore, it is the immigrant who makes up a large part of the unskilled labor group.

For much of our analysis, monthly, or at least quarterly, rather than annual data are essential. Annual data serve well to give indications of general tendencies, but the picture which may be drawn with them is necessarily only in broad outline and permits symptomatic details to be obscured. For example, with only annual data, it becomes impossible to determine, with any reasonable degree of precision, whether the immigrant tide slackens in premonition of an impending industrial slump, or, on the contrary, begins to ebb only after employment has been on the decline for several months.

Lastly, if we could have an equally comprehensive index of fluctuations of economic opportunities in the country from which immigrants come, we should feel excellently equipped for the task before us.

The data actually available do not make possible the construction of such an ideal index as that just outlined, but, nevertheless, afford, in our judgment, a basis for reasonably accurate conclusions, particularly when reinforced by other indices of industrial activity.

Types of Employment Statistics.

The principal sources of information concerning employment conditions in the United States are of four types: (1) *indirect evidences of employment conditions* as found in statistics of production and such even less direct indices of employment opportunities as are afforded by prices, clearings, and other indicators of business activity; (2) records of the *average number of wage earners employed* during the month, or the number employed on a given day, as shown by payroll data; (3) statistics of the *percentage of trade union members unemployed*; and (4) *employment office statistics*, giving the ratio of applicants to jobs. All four of these types have been utilized in the subsequent analysis, although the primary index of factory employment by months, for the period beginning with 1889, has been constructed from statistics of the average number employed, supplemented for a portion of the period by trade union statistics of unemployment.

ANNUAL STATISTICS OF INDUSTRIAL CONDITIONS

To obtain a picture of the major features of changes in employment conditions, let us first turn our attention to the fluctuations in various series of annual data which serve as more or less satisfactory indicators of conditions in the several industries in which immigrants find employment.

For this purpose we have used the following series: for factory employment, an index of estimated average number employed, 1890 to 1922; for coal mining, the number of tons of anthracite and bituminous coal, respectively, produced each year from 1870 to 1922; for construction, the annual increase in the operated mileage of railroads from 1891 to 1916 and an index of the estimated annual total value of construction from 1902 to 1920; for railway maintenance, the average number of trackmen employed from 1889 to 1914; and for general industrial and business conditions, several series, including the value of imports of merchandise 1870 to 1923, pig iron production 1870 to 1923, the clearings index computed by the Federal Reserve Bank of New York for 1876 to 1923, wholesale prices 1870 to 1922, and Professor E. E. Day's index of manufacture 1899 to 1923.

For convenience in comparison, these series have been charted in two groups, on pages 59 and 62, one group consisting of those series which refer to calendar years (Tables 12-A and 12-B and Chart 6); and the other group, those series which refer to fiscal years ending June 30th (Tables 13-A and 13-B and Chart 7).

The Calendar Year Group.

The annual production of pig iron, bituminous coal, and anthracite coal, respectively, an index of the physical volume of manufacturing, an index of the estimated total value of construction, the number of railway trackmen employed, and an index of wholesale prices comprise the calendar year group. Pig iron is discussed more fully at subsequent points in this chapter. A few words concerning the reason for choice of some of the other series are pertinent.

Railway Employment.

Large numbers of immigrants are employed in the maintenance of railway track and roadbeds, and, consequently, we have included in our evidences of employment conditions a curve showing the fluctuations in the numbers of railway trackmen, other than section foremen, on June 30th of each year from 1889 to 1914.

Coal Mining.

The United States Geological Survey has published statistics of the movement of men employed and of days worked in anthracite and bituminous mining, respectively, for the years 1890 to 1921, and statistics of the production of coal are available from 1870 to date. Based upon a careful study of the returns filed with them, the Survey reaches the conclusion that the figures of the average number employed represent "not the average number of men actually working at any one time, nor the aggregate number of men who have worked at any time during the year, nor the absolute average number on the payrolls, but rather the number of men commonly dependent on the mine for employment." Hence, by multiplying the average number of men employed in each year by the average number of days worked, we obtain a figure which affords a better index of employment conditions in the mines than the average number of employed. To illustrate, the reported average number of men employed in bituminous mines is even greater in the depression year of 1908 than in 1907, but the number of days worked was but 193 as compared with 223 in 1907.

The resulting estimate of employment was compared with the statistics of bituminous coal production, which are available for a longer period, and the two series were found to agree so closely that the longer, or production series, has been used for an indicator of probable conditions of employment in the bituminous coal industry. In like manner, the production of anthracite coal is used as an approximate index of employment in that phase of mining.

Construction.

Especially valuable for our purposes would be a comprehensive index of the number of men, particularly of common laborers, employed upon new construction—buildings, sewers, railways, and streets and highways—but unfortunately no such index is available. Fragmentary evidence is furnished by statistics of building permits, miles of railroad constructed, and building contracts awarded, but none of these series is both comprehensive enough and available over a sufficiently long period to afford an adequate index of employment conditions over the period in which we wish to study the relations of migration and employment. Statistics of the miles of

railroad constructed, partly on a calendar year and partly on a
fiscal year basis, are available throughout the period covered by
Charts 6 and 7 (1870-1923); but the best of the construction indices,
the volume of building covered by contracts awarded, is available
only beginning in 1910 and has changed somewhat in scope during
this period. However, an estimate of the annual total value of
construction is given in Chart 6 as a rough index of employment
conditions in the construction industry.

The Fiscal Year Group.

To aid in the identification of boom and depression periods when
data applying to fiscal years ending June 30th are considered, we
have used annual statistics of the number of miles of railroad constructed, imports of merchandise, the estimated average daily production of pig iron, the estimated average number employed in
factories, and an index of business conditions compiled by Mr.
Carl Snyder, of the Federal Reserve Bank of New York.

The curve for factory employment represents an estimate based
primarily upon data more fully described later in this chapter in
connection with monthly estimates of employment. This curve
presumably underestimates somewhat the size of the fluctuations in
factory employment, in that it gives no consideration to part-time
employment and, also, particularly in the earlier years, is based
primarily upon data for Massachusetts, in which State industrial
conditions were probably relatively stable.

The mileage of railroad constructed is significant because it
reflects general industrial conditions and because immigrant laborers
in large numbers have been employed as laborers in such construction.

Method of Interpreting the Accompanying Charts (6 and 7).

The several series discussed in the above paragraphs are plotted
in Charts 6 and 7, which are so-called "ratio charts," or charts with
the vertical scale so proportioned that equal percentage declines
between any two years are represented by equal vertical declines on
the curves involved. If one curve declines ten per cent in 1900,
and another series ten per cent in 1900 and also in 1904, in each of
these three cases the vertical drop on the chart would be the same.
In like manner, equal percentage increases are represented by equal
vertical rises in the respective curves. Hence, despite the fact that
the series are expressed in widely different units, it is possible, by

inspection of these charts, to approximate with the eye the relative change in different years or in the several curves for any one year.

Depression Years.

When examining the fluctuations in migration, we shall have frequent occasion to refer to the depression years in industry. These years of depression may be quite satisfactorily identified for preliminary comparisons by examination of Charts 6 and 7, on

CHART 6

INDICES OF ECONOMIC CONDITIONS, BY CALENDAR YEARS: 1870-1923.

Ratio scale

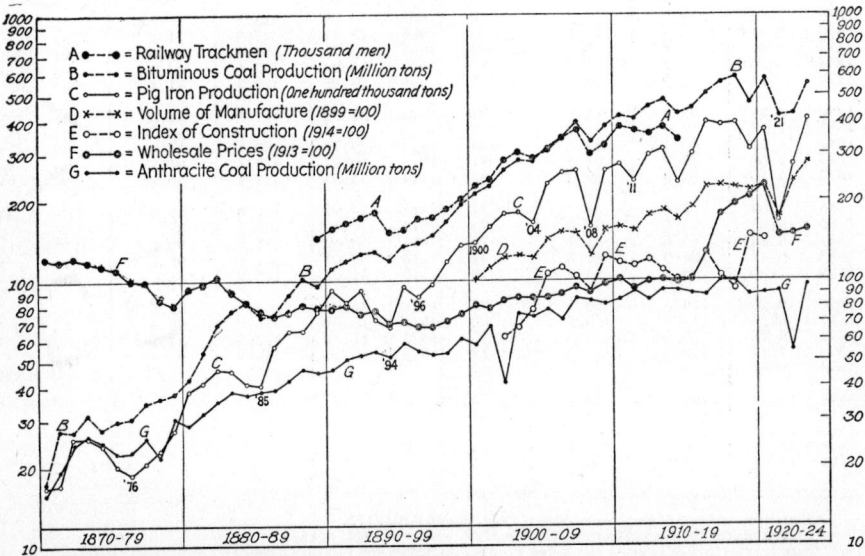

A ●--● = Railway Trackmen *(Thousand men)*
B ●--● = Bituminous Coal Production *(Million tons)*
C ○——○ = Pig Iron Production *(One hundred thousand tons)*
D ✕--✕ = Volume of Manufacture *(1899=100)*
E ○--○ = Index of Construction *(1914=100)*
F ●—● = Wholesale Prices *(1913=100)*
G ●—● = Anthracite Coal Production *(Million tons)*

.Numerical data in Tables 12-A and 12-B.

pages 59 and 62, which show the relative fluctuations in the annual statistics. With the exception of the clearings index of business, the data plotted in these charts have not been corrected for the growth element, hence a mild depression tendency may be evidenced merely by a slackening in the rate of increase rather than by a decided downward slope of the curve. The fluctuations in the production of pig iron, when they are reasonably well supported by the other series, have been taken as the primary determinants of which years should be designated as depression years.

Calendar Years.

From Chart 6, page 59, in which calendar year totals are plotted, we note that in the period since 1870 the slack years appear to be

TABLE 12-A—INDICES OF ECONOMIC CONDITIONS, BY CALENDAR YEARS, 1870-1923

YEAR	PRODUCTION (MILLION TONS)			WHOLE-SALE PRICES[c] 1913 = 100	YEAR	PRODUCTION (MILLION TONS)			WHOLE-SALE PRICES[c] 1913 = 100
	PIG IRON[a]	BITUMIN-OUS COAL[b]	ANTHRA-CITE COAL[b]			PIG IRON[a]	BITUMIN-OUS COAL[b]	ANTHRA-CITE COAL[b]	
1870	1.67	17.4	15.7	122	1900	13.79	212.3	57.4	81
1871	1.71	27.5	19.3	118	1901	15.88	225.8	67.5	79
1872	2.55	27.2	24.2	123	1902	17.82	260.2	41.4	84
1873	2.56	31.4	26.2	118	1903	18.01	282.7	74.6	86
1874	2.40	27.8	24.8	114	1904	16.50	278.7	73.2	86
1875	2.02	29.9	22.5	110	1905	22.99	315.1	77.7	86
1876	1.87	30.5	22.8	100	1906	25.31	342.9	71.3	89
1877	2.07	34.8	25.7	99	1907	25.78	394.8	85.6	94
1878	2.30	36.2	21.7	85	1908	15.94	332.6	83.3	90
1879	2.74	37.9	30.2	81	1909	25.80	379.7	81.1	97
1880	3.84	42.8	28.6	94	1910	27.30	417.1	84.5	101
1881	4.14	54.0	31.9	97	1911	23.65	405.9	90.5	93
1882	4.62	68.4	35.1	103	1912	29.73	450.1	84.4	99
1883	4.60	77.3	38.5	91	1913	30.97	478.4	91.5	100
1884	4.10	83.0	37.2	83	1914	23.33	422.7	90.8	98
1885	4.04	72.8	38.3	77	1915	29.92	442.6	89.0	101
1886	5.68	74.6	39.0	74	1916	39.43	502.5	87.6	127
1887	6.42	88.6	42.1	76	1917	38.62	551.8	99.6	177
1888	6.49	102.0	46.6	81	1918	39.05	579.4	98.8	194
1889	7.60	95.7	45.5	79	1919	31.02	465.9	88.1	206
1890	9.20	111.3	46.5	78	1920	36.93	568.7	89.6	226
1891	8.28	117.9	50.7	80	1921	16.69	415.9	90.5	147
1892	9.16	126.9	52.5	75	1922	27.22	422.3[a]	54.7[a]	149
1893	7.12	128.4	54.0	77	1923	40.36	545.4[a]	95.4[a]	154
1894	6.66	118.8	51.9	69					
1895	9.45	135.1	58.0	70					
1896	8.62	137.6	54.3	67					
1897	9.65	147.6	52.6	67					
1898	11.77	166.6	53.4	70					
1899	13.62	193.3	60.4	75					

[a]Statistical Abstract of the United States, 1923, pp. 264-265, 272.
[b]United States Geological Survey, Coal in 1919, 1920 and 1921, p. 482.
[c]Based, prior to 1891, upon the index number compiled by Joseph L. Snider, "Wholesale Prices in the United States, 1866-91", in the Review of Economic Statistics, April, 1924, pp. 93-118, especially p. 112, converted to 1913 base; for 1891 to 1923, upon the index number of the United States Bureau of Labor Statistics, Bulletin 335, p. 9, and Survey of Current Business, Feb., 1923, p. 135.

as follows: first, a slump in the late seventies, the exact year differing in the several series; then 1885, 1888 (slight), 1893 and 1894, 1896 or 1897, 1902 in anthracite coal, due to strikes, 1904, 1908 (severe), 1911 (relatively mild), 1914 and to a lesser extent 1915 and 1919, 1921 (severe), and 1922. Further indication of the depression characteristic of these years is found in Chart 8 on a subsequent page, in which are plotted pig iron production and a composite index of economic conditions, with their trends eliminated.

TABLE 12-B.—INDICES OF ECONOMIC CONDITIONS, BY CALENDAR YEARS: 1889-1923

YEAR	VOLUME OF MANUFAC- TURE 1899 = 100[a]	VALUE OF CONSTRUC- TION[b] 1914 = 100	RAILWAY TRACK- MEN (THOUS- ANDS)[c]	YEAR	VOLUME OF MANUFAC- TURE 1899 = 100	VALUE OF CONSTRUC- TION 1914 = 100	RAILWAY TRACK- MEN (THOUS- ANDS)
1889	...	....	145	1910	159	116.6	379
1890	...	....	157	1911	153	112.8	363
1891	...	....	164	1912	177	119.2	357
1892	...	....	172	1913	184	109.4	377
1893	...	....	180	1914	169	100.0	337
1894	...	....	151				
1895	...	....	155	1915	189	101.5	...
1896	...	....	170	1916	225	127.6	...
1897	...	....	172	1917	227	103.7	...
1898	...	....	184	1918	223	92.2	...
1899	...	....	202	1919	218	147.0	...
1900	101	....	227	1920	227	143.3	...
1901	112	....	239	1921	174	.....	...
1902	122	61.8	281	1922	238	.....	...
1903	124	66.7	301	1923	277	.....	...
1904	122	77.3	289				
1905	143	106.3	311				
1906	152	112.0	344				
1907	151	103.2	367				
1908	126	90.5	299				
1909	155	123.6	321				

[a]Professor E. E. Day's index of the physical volume of production in manufacture, unadjusted for secular trend, *Review of Economic Statistics*, July, 1924, p. 200.

[b]An estimate compiled by Dr. W. I. King, and based, prior to 1909, chiefly upon building permits in selected cities for which continuous records are available; subsequent to 1908 this index also includes estimates based on construction by the Federal Government and by railways.

[c]Compiled from Interstate Commerce Commission, *Statistics of Railways in the United States*. Includes "trackmen other than section foremen"; as of June 30th of each year.

Fiscal Years.

In many instances migration data are available by fiscal years ending June 30th rather than by calendar years. Consequently, it is desirable to note what fiscal years are marked by depression conditions. In Chart 7 are given five series which are available on the fiscal year basis. The shift to the fiscal year basis does not make much change in the years which stand out as depression years. For the data compiled on the fiscal year basis we find that the relatively low years include the late seventies, 1885, 1894, 1897

(1898 for imports), 1901 (slight), 1904, 1908 (and 1909, also, for clearings), 1914 and 1915, 1919, and 1921 and 1922.

CHART 7

INDICES OF ECONOMIC CONDITIONS, BY FISCAL YEARS: 1870-1923.

Ratio Scale

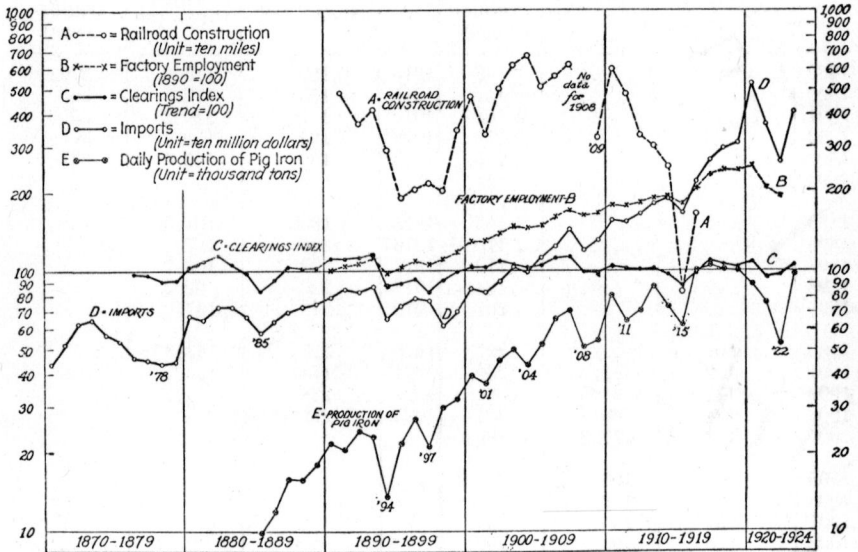

•Numerical data in Tables 13-A and 13-B.

Pig Iron Production and a Composite Index of Business Cycles.

Pig iron is basic to many manufacturing industries and to much construction work, and, in the form of machinery or other products of iron and steel, is supplementary to practically all industrial activities, hence fluctuations in the production of pig iron ordinarily bear a close relation to the volume of industrial activity. This relationship has been frequently noted in previous statistical studies of economic conditions. For example, Professor E. E. Day, in his construction of an index of manufacturing, compares annual statistics of pig iron production with his index and finds a striking similarity in the fluctuations of the two series.[1] Because of this

[1]*Review of Economic Statistics*, 1920, p. 367, "The correspondence of pig-iron production with manufacture, when both are adjusted for secular trend, is extraordinary. The correlation coefficient is .97." (Based upon the period 1899-1919).

close association between pig iron and industrial activity, we have
made frequent use of pig iron production in comparisons with
migratory fluctuations in this and other countries, partly because
direct employment figures are not available and partly because it is

TABLE 13-A.—INDICES OF ECONOMIC CONDITIONS, BY FISCAL YEARS
ENDING JUNE 30TH: 1870-1923

YEAR	MERCHAN- DISE IMPORTS[a] (MILLION DOLLARS)	CLEARINGS INDEX OF BUSINESS (TREND = 100)[b]	DAILY PIG IRON PRODUC- TION[c] (THOUS- AND TONS)	YEAR	MERCHAN- DISE IMPORTS[a] (MILLION DOLLARS)	CLEARINGS INDEX OF BUSINESS (TREND = 100)[b]	DAILY PIG IRON PRODUC- TION (THOUS- AND TONS)
1870	436.0	....	....	1900	849.9	102.9	39.9
1871	520.2	....	....	1901	823.2	102.8	37.1
1872	626.6	....	....	1902	903.3	108.4	45.4
1873	642.1	....	....	1903	1025.7	106.2	50.0
1874	567.4	....	....	1904	991.1	102.7	43.6
1875	533.0	....	....	1905	1117.5	104.9	52.6
1876	460.7	96.9	....	1906	1226.6	111.9	65.5
1877	451.3	96.1	....	1907	1434.4	112.2	70.6
1878	437.1	91.4	....	1908	1194.3	99.0	51.4
1879	445.8	90.4	....	1909	1311.9	98.0	54.3
1880	668.0	102.8	....	1910	1556.9	103.9	80.3
1881	642.7	107.9	....	1911	1527.2	100.6	64.6
1882	724.6	114.4	....	1912	1653.3	100.4	70.4
1883	723.2	105.6	....	1913	1813.0	100.8	87.3
1884	667.7	98.0	....	1914	1893.9	96.6	73.3
1885	577.5	83.8	9.9	1915	1674.2	88.0	62.3
1886	635.4	92.1	11.9	1916	2197.9	97.9	101.1
1887	692.3	103.3	15.6	1917	2659.4	108.2	106.0
1888	724.0	101.7	15.8	1918	2945.7	105.6	101.6
1889	745.1	103.4	18.1	1919	3095.7	103.5	100.1
1890	789.3	110.1	21.8	1920	5238.4	107.7	89.4
1891	844.9	111.2	20.7	1921	3654.5	94.3	75.8
1892	827.4	111.7	24.4	1922	2608.1	96.3	52.6
1893	866.4	115.0	23.2	1923	4068.6	105.1	97.8
1894	655.0	86.9	13.6				
1895	732.0	89.3	21.7				
1896	779.7	92.3	27.2				
1897	764.7	82.7	21.3				
1898	616.0	91.7	30.0				
1899	697.1	98.4	32.5				

[a]U. S. Bureau of Foreign and Domestic Commerce, *Monthly Summary of Commerce and Finance.*
[b]An average of monthly figures of an index of business conditions based upon clearings outside New
York, corrected for trend, compiled by Mr. Carl Snyder, Federal Reserve Bank, New York, *Journal of the
American Statistical Association*, September, 1924, p. 335.
[c]Annual averages computed from monthly data published in the *Iron Age*, and based prior to October,
1902, upon the number of furnaces in blast and thereafter upon monthly statistics of pig iron produced.

not improbable that pig iron, related as it is to other industries as well as manufacturing, may be an index of employment opportunities for immigrants at least as significant as the ordinary index of numbers employed in factories, which at best does not make adequate allowance for part-time employment.

TABLE 13-B.—INDICES OF ECONOMIC CONDITIONS, BY FISCAL YEARS
ENDING JUNE 30TH: 1890-1922

YEAR	NUMBER EMPLOYED IN FACTORIES[a] (1890 = 100)	MILES OF RAILROAD[b] CONSTRUCTED	YEAR	NUMBER EMPLOYED IN FACTORIES (1890 = 100)	MILES OF RAILROAD CONSTRUCTED
1890	100.0	. . . .	1910	177.7	5,908
1891	103.5	4,844	1911	176.9	4,740
1892	107.0	3,656	1912	181.2	3,301
1893	112.4	4,143	1913	189.5	3,003
1894	97.3	2,899	1914	190.3	2,511
1895	102.7	1,895	1915	180.4	831
1896	108.6	2,053	1916	208.3	1,653
1897	105.9	2,163	1917	233.9	. . . .
1898	110.5	2,026	1918	243.3	. . . .
1899	117.5	3,466	1919	242.2	. . . .
1900	128.2	4,628	1920	253.0	. . . .
1901	129.3	3,324	1921	208.1	. . . .
1902	138.2	4,965	1922	192.7	. . . .
1903	146.8	6,169			
1904	145.7	6,690			
1905	148.4	5,084			
1906	160.2	5,565			
1907	170.2	6,188			
1908	162.6	. . . .			
1909	165.9	3,238			

[a]An estimate for the United States, based upon Census of Manufactures statistics for census years and on interpolations in intervening years with the aid of State employment and unemployment statistics.
[b]*Statistical Abstract of the United States.* In 1908 and the subsequent years, these data exclude switching and terminal companies hence are not strictly comparable with those for the years prior to 1908.

To indicate the extent to which the fluctuations in pig iron production are similar to those of other indices of economic conditions, there is given in Chart 8 a comparison between pig iron production and a composite index of business conditions, both expressed as deviations from computed trends. This composite index is one computed by Professor W. F. Ogburn and Dorothy S. Thomas, using nine economic series, namely: wholesale prices (1870-1913), commercial failures (1870-1920), bituminous coal production

(1870-1920), pig iron production (1870-1920), railroad freight ton mileage (1882-1920), bank clearings outside New York (1881-1915), employment in Massachusetts (1889-1920), railroad mileage constructed (1870-1888), and imports (1870-1888).[2]

CHART 8

CYCLES IN ECONOMIC CONDITIONS IN THE UNITED STATES: 1870-1919[a]

Unit= one standard deviation

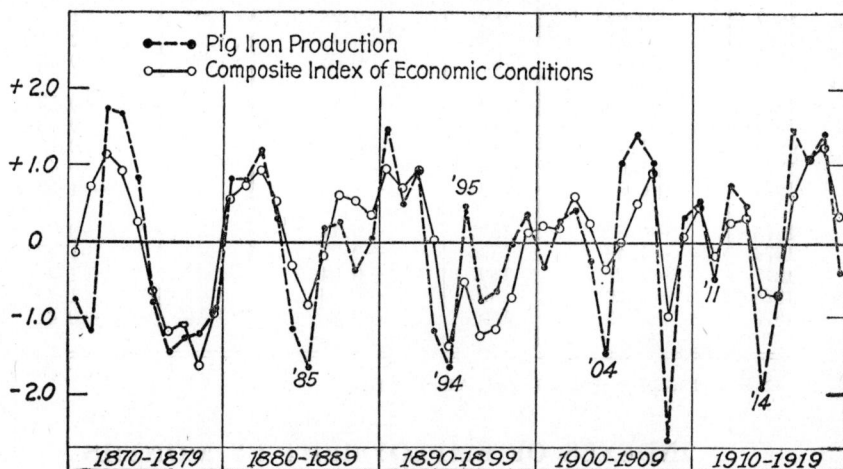

[a]The numerical data for pig iron are in Table 14. For source of the "Composite Index," see accompanying text.

It will be noted that all major cycles and most of the minor fluctuations are common to the two curves, that there is no lag of sufficient extent to be obvious in these annual data, and that only in a few years are changes in the two series opposite in direction. It appears that, on the whole, no marked differences in results will arise whether pig iron production or such a composite index as that plotted in Chart 8 is used in analyzing annual cycles in economic conditions.

[2]"The Influence of the Business Cycle on Certain Social Conditions," *Journal of the American Statistical Association*, September, 1922, p. 327.

TABLE 14.—CYCLES OF PIG IRON PRODUCTION, BY CALENDAR YEARS: 1860-1919ᵃ

Percentage deviations from a seven-year moving average, expressed in multiples of their standard deviation (12.68 per cent)

YEAR	PIG IRON PRODUCTION	YEAR	PIG IRON PRODUCTION	YEAR	PIG IRON PRODUCTION
1860	+0.97	1880	+0.82	1900	—0.32
1861	—1.23	1881	+0.80	1901	+0.28
1862	—0.99	1882	+1.20	1902	+0.41
1863	—0.20	1883	+0.29	1903	—0.25
1864	+0.65	1884	—1.15	1904	—1.48
1865	—1.62	1885	—1.67	1905	+1.03
1866	+0.09	1886	+0.17	1906	+1.40
1867	—0.02	1887	+0.25	1907	+1.03
1868	+0.13	1888	—0.38	1908	—2.61
1869	+0.28	1889	+0.06	1909	+0.32
1870	—0.78	1890	+1.47	1910	+0.53
1871	—1.17	1891	+0.50	1911	—0.50
1872	+1.74	1892	+0.91	1912	+0.72
1873	+1.68	1893	—1.16	1913	+0.48
1874	+0.84	1894	—1.65	1914	—1.92
1875	—0.80	1895	+0.47	1915	—0.74
1876	—1.43	1896	—0.77	1916	+1.48
1877	—1.27	1897	—0.64	1917	+1.06
1878	—1.20	1898	—0.03	1918	+1.42
1879	—0.88	1899	+0.36	1919	—0.41

ᵃComputed from data given in Table 12-A for 1870-1919.

INDEXES OF EMPLOYMENT BY MONTHS

We have previously noted the desirability of a monthly index of employment conditions. For the quarter century preceding the Great War it has been possible to build up by the synthesis of somewhat fragmentary series, an index of factory employment. This index has been supplemented by an index of monthly changes in pig iron production. Charts of the cyclical movements in these two series are given in Chapter V. The methods of compilation are set forth in the subsequent pages of this chapter.

The Census of Manufactures.

The United States Census of Manufactures furnishes a virtually complete census of the number of wage earners employed in factories, by months, for the years 1899, 1904, 1914, 1919, and 1921. In taking the census of manufactures in 1899 workers in the hand

and neighborhood industries were included, but in the subsequent censuses only factory workers were counted, hence in order to make the 1899 figures comparable with those for the later years, it was necessary to adjust them to exclude, as far as practicable, the number of workers in hand and neighborhood industries.

Other Available Monthly Statistics.

Although varying in their comprehensiveness and throughout a portion of the period lacking in strict continuity, monthly statistics of the average number of wage earners in Massachusetts factories are available for the period 1889 to 1922.[3] For the years 1889 to 1906, inclusive, a census of manufactures was taken annually, and included the number of wage earners employed by the reporting concerns, by months, over a period of two years. The fraction of the total represented by the reporting factories varied from year to year, but, due to the fact that each annual report covers two years, it is possible to splice the reports together to produce a consecutive index.

Beginning with 1907 the annual Massachusetts Census of Manufactures is intended to be a substantially complete enumeration rather than a mere sample, and each census covers only twelve months instead of twenty-four as previously. An examination of the data indicates that for the first years following this change in method the census did not approach a complete enumeration with equal consistency; and adjustments, more completely indicated below, have been made to make the series approximately homogeneous.

Somewhat similar statistics of wage earners employed are available for New Jersey. Two special inquiries afford some evidence of employment conditions in the State from June, 1893, to May, 1895, and an annual survey of factory wage workers, by months, covers the period from 1895 to 1919, inclusive.[4] The fraction represented by the firms reporting has not been invariable and the samples do not overlap in the way that the Massachusetts statistics did prior to 1907, so that splicing estimates have been necessary in utilizing the New Jersey statistics.

Quarterly statistics of the percentage of trade union members unemployed in Massachusetts are available beginning with 1908,

[3]The results of the 1923 Census of Manufactures were not available in time for use in this study.

[4]See Table 16 on a later page in this chapter.

and have been used in supplemental studies, but have not been incorporated in the major index of employment conditions.

Similar statistics, however, for trade union unemployment in New York State, by months, have been utilized in widening the scope of our employment index during the years 1904-1914.

An index of factory employment in New York State is available beginning in June, 1914, and in the following year the United States Bureau of Labor Statistics began an index of factory employment. In the post-war period still more complete data are available. The Federal Reserve Board has consolidated various series into an index of industrial employment for the years 1919 to 1923, and has also published an "index of the labor market" showing the fluctuations in the ratio of applicants to jobs in the operations of the public employment offices during the period January, 1919, to December, 1923.[5]

Previous Studies in Employment Fluctuations.

Several economists have utilized the series described above, together with supplementary information, in the construction of more or less comprehensive estimates of the course of employment and unemployment. Mr. Hornell Hart made an estimate of the volume of unemployment by months during the period 1902 to 1917, inclusive;[6] Mr. Ralph D. Hurlin, of the Staff of the Russell Sage Foundation utilized the Massachusetts data in constructing a picture of "Three Decades of Employment Fluctuations";[7] and Professor William A. Berridge, in a series of valuable studies presented in the *Review of Economic Statistics* and elsewhere,[8] has analyzed the cyclical fluctuations in employment from 1903 to date.

As employment is the primary measure of immigrant opportunity used in this study, and as it is desirable to carry our comparisons through as long a period as possible, it has seemed advisable to prepare an index especially for our purposes rather than to rely

[5]*Federal Reserve Bulletin*, Dec., 1923 (index of industrial employment); and Feb., 1924 ("labor market" index).

[6]Hornell Hart, *Fluctuations in Unemployment in Cities of the United States, 1902-1917*, Studies from the Helen S. Trounstine Foundation, Vol. 1, No. 2, pp. 47-59.

[7]Ralph D. Hurlin, "Massachusetts Employment in Factories," *Annalist*, Oct. 24, 1921, pp. 387-388.

[8]Cf. articles in the *Journal of the American Statistical Association*, March, 1922, pp. 42-55, and June, 1922, pp. 227-240; the *Review of Economic Statistics*, January, 1922, pp. 1-56; the *Federal Reserve Bulletin*, December 1923, pp. 1272-1279, and February, 1924, pp. 83-87; also his volume entitled *Cycles of Unemployment in the United States, 1903-1922*.

solely upon any of the available series or analytic studies.   However, these valuable pioneer studies have been utilized in some of the subsequent comparisons, and have afforded many suggestions for the preparation of our special employment index.

Index of Factory Employment, by Months, 1889-1923.

The index of employment opportunity which is most extensively used in the subsequent chapters is an *Index of Factory Employment*, representing an estimate obtained by the synthesis of some of the employment and unemployment series mentioned in above paragraphs.   This index covers the period from January 1, 1889, to December, 1923, by months.   For 1889 to 1894 the estimate is based upon Massachusetts data; for 1895 to 1903, on statistics for Massachusetts and New Jersey; for 1904 to 1919, New York is added; and for the years subsequent to 1919, the New Jersey series ceases to be available and the index rests upon data for New York and Massachusetts alone.   For the period subsequent to 1914 other employment series are available and are used to corroborate the evidence presented by the *Index of Factory Employment*.   The methods used in welding the available fragmentary data into a continuous comparable index may be briefly summarized as follows:

1. The Census of Manufactures' statistics of wage earners employed in factories in the years 1899, 1904, 1909, 1914, 1919, and 1921, were adjusted for known variations in their comprehensiveness, in order to make them as comparable as possible throughout the entire period.
2. Estimates, by months, of the number employed in factories in each of the three States—Massachusetts, New Jersey, and New York—were made by using the Census data for the given State as basing points and interpolating between Census years by means of indexes constructed from the available employment and unemployment (inverted) data for the given State.
3. The separate State estimates of numbers employed were then added together to get a consolidated estimate for the groups, and from this estimate an index, with the average for 1914 = 100, was computed, due allowance being made for the changes in 1895, 1904, and 1920 in the number of States included

The monthly figures for this *Index of Factory Employment*, in terms of percentages of the 1914 average, are given in Table IV in the Appendix, for the convenience of investigators who may wish

to make use of them. More details of its construction are given
in the following paragraphs.

The Estimate for Massachusetts.[9]

An examination of Chart 9 will aid in following the process used
in constructing the estimate of factory employment in Massachusetts. The fragments of curves in the lower part of the chart

CHART 9

ILLUSTRATION OF METHOD OF ESTIMATING FACTORY EMPLOYMENT
IN MASSACHUSETTS[a]

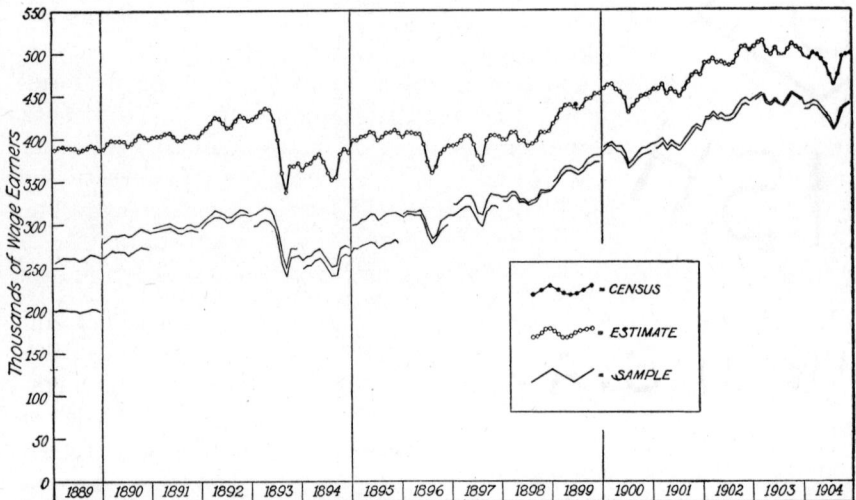

[a]See explanation in accompanying text.

represent the unadjusted data for numbers employed in identical
establishments. Each fragment is twenty-four months long and,
for the second twelve months, runs substantially parallel to the
succeeding fragment. The upper curve on the chart represents the
revised estimate of factory employment in Massachusetts obtained
by (1) splicing the fragments together at the December points which
are common to two fragments, and (2) raising the resulting index
to make it consistent with the complete enumeration of the Census
years.

The black circle for 1899 represents the Census average for that

[9]See Table 15.

year adjusted for the exclusion of hand and neighborhood industries. Adjusted figures by months were not obtainable. For 1904, and all subsequent Census years, the Census monthly data represented by

TABLE 15.—ESTIMATES OF FACTORY EMPLOYMENT IN MASSACHUSETTS, BY MONTHS, 1889-1922[a]

Thousands of persons

YEAR	JAN.	FEB.	MAR.	APR.	MAY	JUNE	JULY	AUG.	SEPT.	OCT.	NOV.	DEC.
1889	388	391	391	390	390	390	386	388	390	393	391	388
1890	389	395	399	398	398	398	392	395	400	405	402	400
1891	402	403	404	406	407	403	399	399	403	404	403	402
1892	408	413	418	425	424	418	413	414	421	426	425	421
1893	423	426	432	435	434	421	399	360	337	368	368	371
1894	364	370	371	378	381	373	360	352	355	382	388	384
1895	398	398	402	403	407	406	398	402	406	407	410	406
1896	402	406	406	405	405	393	373	360	367	382	387	391
1897	391	393	398	403	403	393	380	374	397	404	404	402
1898	399	399	406	406	397	397	391	394	397	407	407	408
1899	417	424	433	438	439	436	433	436	445	446	451	451
1900	458	462	463	456	454	446	430	437	444	449	450	452
1901	456	457	462	451	457	453	449	456	465	473	476	474
1902	488	489	493	488	489	486	485	487	496	506	507	503
1903	507	511	514	501	498	505	497	496	504	510	506	503
1904	493	493	499	497	492	485	473	463	474	495	497	499
1905	511	518	524	525	524	520	517	523	532	531	534	536
1906	549	552	556	555	554	550	546	549	555	563	570	570
1907	579	589	595	590	586	584	575	580	584	586	574	545
1908	533	527	523	514	510	513	510	518	544	563	563	561
1909	566	573	580	577	576	576	573	581	595	602	604	613
1910	624	628	628	622	616	601	587	594	597	606	614	614
1911	612	614	619	612	600	592	587	593	605	615	620	620
1912	612	608	621	617	620	620	612	614	626	638	645	646
1913	640	642	641	630	617	611	595	607	617	622	625	622
1914	627	629	634	628	619	612	596	589	589	591	587	580
1915	584	592	600	598	595	597	596	608	619	639	651	659
1916	677	687	698	697	692	689	686	688	689	702	719	725
1917	727	734	738	721	710	706	696	693	704	716	731	737
1918	723	728	741	735	734	734	730	724	717	701	720	708
1919	696	677	681	679	689	705	716	727	736	742	752	766
1920	757	749	756	748	739	720	697	684	669	657	611	558
1921	533[a]	559	574	578	584	585	578	584	596	598	598	596
1922	593	604	603	585	584	588	589	603	629	649	662	662

[a]Computed, by methods described in the accompanying text, from statistics of manufactures, by months, published annually in *Public Document No. 36* by the Massachusetts Bureau of Statistics of Labor for the years 1886 to 1907, by the Bureau of Statistics for 1908 to 1918, and by the Department of Labor and Industries subsequent to 1919. For the years 1904, 1909, 1914, 1919, and 1921 the above estimates are the U. S. Census of Manufactures' statistics for Massachusetts.

A portion of the original data from which the above estimates were computed are republished in *Bulletin 310* of the U. S. Bureau of Labor Statistics.

the solid b'ack dots are used. For each intercensal period any discrepancy which appears between the index and the Census is prorated over the intervening months so that the final curve shows no sudden changes at the junctures with the Census years.

After 1907, as previously noted, the annual censuses do not overlap, and it becomes necessary to estimate the December-to-January change.

December-to-January Interpolations.

Beginning in 1907, as we have noted, the Massachusetts Census of Industries was designed to be virtually a complete census. However, on plotting the data, it became apparent that in some years, particularly in those immediately after the abandonment of the former method of making each census cover twenty-four months, in order to make the series reasonably continuous, it would be necessary to substitute for the December-to-January change which is indicated by the raw data, an estimated percentage change. This was done for the December-to-January change of 1906-07, 1907-08, 1908-09, 1909-10, 1913-14, 1914-15, and 1918-19. For the other years since 1907, it was judged, upon the basis of a comparison of the raw data, that no adjustments were necessary.

The principle upon which these interpolations were made is that the best clew to the joint effect of the seasonal and cyclical influences is found in the typical relation in the past of the December-to-January change to the changes in contiguous months. Two estimates were made for each year in question. For one, the median ratio in the years 1889-1906 between the November-to-December and the December-to-January movements was found and this ratio assumed to hold in the years for which the actual December-to-January movement was not known. A similar estimate was made for the relation of the December-to-January change to the January-to-February change. The two estimates were then averaged for the final estimate.

For 1923 the estimate is based upon the index of employment in Massachusetts, recently inaugurated by the Massachusetts Bureau of Statistics. The final result of the Massachusetts computation is an estimate of the average number of wage earners employed in factories with a product of $500 or more, from 1889 to 1923 by months.

The Estimate for New Jersey.[10]

A similar estimate was constructed for New Jersey. Inasmuch as the New Jersey data are based, particularly in the early years,

TABLE 16.—ESTIMATES OF FACTORY EMPLOYMENT IN NEW JERSEY,
BY MONTHS: 1893-1919[a]

Thousands of persons

YEAR	JAN.	FEB.	MAR.	APR.	MAY	JUNE	JULY	AUG.	SEPT.	OCT.	NOV.	DEC.
1893	...	...	...	...	...	196	178	160	155	155	152	148
1894	143	143	147	152	153	151	150	152	156	160	165	162
1895	163	164	171	175	172	169	167	171	175	179	178	178
1896	176	177	177	177	173	169	162	161	169	172	170	173
1897	173	179	181	184	183	180	173	175	188	190	185	184
1898	183	186	191	192	192	191	184	186	193	196	195	195
1899	199	203	208	212	215	218	210	215	222	224	222	221
1900	225	226	230	232	232	228	219	220	224	227	225	225
1901	227	231	235	237	238	236	231	233	239	245	245	244
1902	251	254	258	263	262	257	252	257	265	271	270	269
1903	267	268	274	273	273	270	262	262	266	269	265	262
1904	259	262	267	269	268	264	258	264	272	273	269	267
1905	274	277	284	289	287	286	280	282	290	294	296	294
1906	300	304	310	315	315	315	307	311	317	322	322	321
1907	328	329	335	334	340	337	327	329	334	336	323	303
1908	296	295	296	297	293	292	286	294	302	311	312	310
1909	313	313	318	322	322	322	318	324	335	342	343	343
1910	343	347	354	355	354	352	340	347	352	358	360	357
1911	350	352	356	358	354	352	344	350	354	358	359	355
1912	359	363	367	367	372	370	365	372	379	381	386	385
1913	384	385	378	375	371	369	376	385	390	392	393	386
1914	376	378	381	384	383	379	371	367	372	373	362	356
1915	356	363	372	379	386	393	400	408	418	431	440	446
1916	446	453	465	470	473	477	478	478	486	492	499	501
1917	496	500	504	499	498	497	495	498	506	513	519	519
1918	518	524	533	539	546	551	560	558	560	549	538	530
1919	505	485	482	490	496	503	511	517	519	528	530	538

[a]For 1895 to 1919, the above estimates were computed, by methods described in the accompanying text, from the U. S. Census of Manufactures' statistics of numbers employed in New Jersey factories for the years 1904, 1909, 1914, and 1919, supplemented by statistics of employment in reporting factories published annually by the New Jersey Bureau of Statistics of Labor and Industries for the years prior to 1914, and by the Bureau of Industrial Statistics of New Jersey for 1914 to 1919. The estimates prior to 1895 are based chiefly on fragmentary data contained in two special "panic inquiries" covering the periods from June, 1893, to May, 1894, and June, 1894, to May, 1895, respectively, and were not used in computing the index of manufacturing given in Table IV, in the appendix.

upon a sample representing each year a varying proportion of the total, it was necessary to make an estimate of the December-to-January movement. For the years 1889-1909 the known or estimated change in Massachusetts was used. For the years 1909-

[10]See Table 16.

1914 the changes as shown by the raw data were accepted; for 1914-1919, the New Jersey data are given the same movement as exhibited by the industrially-akin State of New York.

The Estimate for New York.[11]

In making the estimates of the average number employed in New York factories, which cover the period 1904 to 1922, inclusive, the interpolations between Census data were made for the years 1905-

TABLE 17.—ESTIMATES OF FACTORY EMPLOYMENT IN NEW YORK STATE, BY MONTHS: 1904-1922[a]

Thousands of persons

YEAR	JAN.	FEB.	MAR.	APR.	MAY	JUNE	JULY	AUG.	SEPT.	OCT.	NOV.	DEC.
1904	817	839	857	862	849	836	829	853	892	905	888	856
1905	858	872	871	899	904	902	911	920	897	917	922	930
1906	923	909	916	915	924	951	967	967	956	951	962	936
1907	963	952	963	958	946	966	990	983	942	804	801	740
1908	710	690	694	669	687	719	848	909	837	874	893	912
1909	945	971	992	989	984	981	977	999	1041	1063	1060	1045
1910	1068	1068	1039	1037	1040	1047	1073	1073	1068	1053	1049	1022
1911	1037	1059	1058	1060	1038	1060	1081	1082	1082	1082	1052	1007
1912	1046	1085	1077	1079	1050	1032	1038	1101	1107	1101	1064	1032
1913	1083	1096	1071	1069	1062	1070	1074	1076	1088	1081	1059	1023
1914	1056[a]	1078	1095	1084	1067	1053	1034	1037	1067	1073	1035	1015
1915	1014	1034	1033	1042	1061	1071	1059	1048	1099	1109	1150	1170
1916	1169	1199	1198	1238	1216	1215	1204	1213	1254	1253	1284	1304
1917	1291	1290	1310	1288	1276	1265	1253	1231	1251	1271	1280	1289
1918	1277	1297	1307	1295	1294	1293	1313	1280	1278	1225	1255	1244
1919	1179	1182	1188	1195	1187	1192	1228	1261	1273	1260	1282	1311
1920	1318	1305	1333	1319	1295	1283	1279	1245	1231	1207	1130	1042
1921	966[a]	998	1018	1014	992	985	985	999	1028	1040	1027	1003
1922	982	1014	1025	1014	1025	1035	1035	1067	1088	1119	1140	1161

[a]The above estimates were computed, by methods described in the accompanying text, from the U.S. Census of Manufactures' statistics of numbers employed in New York factories for the years 1904, 1909 1914, 1919, and 1921, with interpolations for the intervening years computed from data on unemployment among trade union members for the years 1905 to 1913, and from data on employment in representative factories from 1915 to 1922, published by the New York State Department of Labor.

1908 and 1910-1913, inclusive, upon the basis of the trade union statistics of unemployment; and for the subsequent years upon the index of factory employment published by the New York State Department of Labor.

In utilizing the trade union figures, an index of unemployment in the factory trades, weighted by the numbers in each trade, was

[11]See Table 17.

computed. For the years 1909-1914, this index exhibited fluctuations considerably more violent than exhibited by the same series in 1904-1908 or by the census data in 1909 and 1914. Consequently, in order to get a consecutive series on a reasonably homogeneous basis, the fluctuations of the trade union unemployment data were scaled down in the ratio which they bore in 1914 to the fluctuations shown by the Census.

Monthly Production of Pig Iron.

For evidence supplementary to that afforded by our index of factory employment by months, we have used monthly statistics of pig iron production. The original figures were adjusted for seasonal variation by a method designed to make allowance for the tendency of the typical seasonal variation to change over a long period of years. The method used is developed by Dr. W. I. King in an article published in the *Journal of the American Statistical Association*.[12] His data, seasonally corrected, were used for the years 1905 to 1914, and together with figures obtained by similar methods for the years 1884 to 1904, were corrected for a computed trend based upon a seven-year moving average smoothed to eliminate minor irregularities. Small fluctuations were then ironed out by taking a three-month moving average of the indices obtained by correction for trend and seasonal variation. The results appear in Chart 14 in Chapter V.

The Numerical Volume of Employment and Unemployment.

Information concerning the actual number of workers represented by fluctuations in employment or unemployment is scant. We have made use, however, of two studies of this nature. The first, covering unemployment in non-agricultural occupations during the years 1902 to 1917, by months, was made by Professor Hornell Hart.[13] The method used, as described by Professor Hart, was to ascertain for each year and month the total number of persons normally occupied in non-agricultural pursuits, and to subtract from these normal supply figures the estimated "connected demand" for labor. This "connected demand" for labor was determined "by a synthesis of widely scattered information on employment fluctuations," chiefly from various Federal and State statistical publica-

[12]"An Improved Method for Measuring the Seasonal Factor," September, 1924.
[13]Hornell Hart, *Fluctuations in Unemployment in Cities of the United States, 1902 to 1917*, Studies from the Helen S. Trounstine Foundation, Volume 1, Number 2.

tions.   Owing to the fragmentary nature of the data available, there is necessarily a considerable margin of error in these estimates, and hence the comparisons made with their aid must be interpreted as giving roughly approximate rather than closely accurate results.

A second estimate of the actual numbers represented by fluctuations in employment is found in the study made by Dr. W. I. King for the 1921 depression period and described more fully in Volume V of the publications of the National Bureau of Economic Research, *Employment Hours and Earnings in Prosperity and Depression, 1920-1922.*   Based upon returns from a large number of employers in various lines of industry, estimates were made of the changes in numbers employed from the first quarter of 1920 to the first quarter of 1922, inclusive.   From these estimates, which are given by industries, we have selected, in Chapter VI, those industries which are most significant from the point of view of employment opportunities for immigrants and made comparisons with the number of immigrants and emigrants during the period covered by the estimates.

CHAPTER SUMMARY

The direct and indirect indices of employment conditions to be utilized in the following chapters include (1) for the entire period over which immigration statistics are available, the annual statistics of imports of merchandise; (2) for the decades between the Civil War and 1890, annual statistics of pig iron production and quarterly statistics of imports of merchandise; (3) for the period beginning in 1890, estimates of factory employment and of pig iron production, by months, and (4) particularly in the post-war years, various short-period indices of employment conditions, the description of some of which is deferred to the chapters in which they are used.

In this chapter we have noted the nature of the major series of statistics of economic conditions to be used, made some comparisons between these indices and other evidences of economic activity, and indicated the methods used in putting these employment data into convenient form for statistical comparisons.   The subsequent chapters are devoted chiefly to the analysis of fluctuations in immigration with the aid of the employment indexes to which attention has been directed in this chapter.

CHAPTER IV

IMMIGRATION AND BUSINESS CYCLES PRIOR TO 1890

Economic Motives for Migration.

Even with no direct knowledge of the statistics of immigration, one would be led to expect that variations in economic conditions in the United States would exercise a large influence upon the number of incoming aliens. It will be granted that the hope of economic betterment is not the sole motive for emigration. Religious or political persecution, racial discrimination, or the mere love of adventure may be the impelling force. But, in the main, the emigrant is a seller of labor, seeking the best price for his services, and hence not apt to be attracted by a stagnant market. Furthermore, for many prospective immigrants the financing of the trip becomes easier when times are prosperous in the United States, for at such times friends and relatives who have previously emigrated are in a better position to remit funds for the trip. Approximately one third of the total number of immigrants have their passage paid by relatives.[1] Even those who pay their own way are apt to find it easier to obtain the necessary funds in periods of prosperity in the United States, for, as we shall note more in detail in a subsequent chapter, periods of prosperity in the United States are ordinarily accompanied by prosperity in the country of emigration, when savings are more readily accumulated and property more easily disposed of.[2]

Lastly, the increasing facility of communication tends, we should expect, to decrease the lag between industrial slumps and the consequent decreases in immigration.

Opinions of Authorities on Immigration Problems.

The arguments just cited for expecting a close relationship between fluctuations in industry and immigration are uniformly supported by the conclusions of various authorities who have given consideration to this problem.

[1] 32.1 per cent in the seven fiscal years, 1908-1914, inclusive.
[2] See discussion of this point in Chapter VIII.

For example, in the reports of the U. S. Industrial Commission, the conclusion is reached, after a comparison of the course of wholesale prices and immigration, "that there is a striking coincidence, since the year 1868, between business conditions and the volume of immigration" so that "it may be said that immigration since the Civil War is a reflection of industrial conditions."[3]

However, that the adjustment of migration to employment conditions is not perfect is suggested by J. W. Jenks and W. Jett Lauck in their analysis of the immigrant as a dynamic factor in industry. "The statement," they say, "that the influx and the outgo of foreign-born workmen automatically adjusts itself to activity or stagnation in mining and manufacturing is only partly true."[4]

In the subsequent pages we shall examine the evidence concerning migration and industrial conditions in an effort to determine the accuracy of the a priori reasoning and of the opinions just cited. Does the volume of migration ebb and flow with industry? Do some elements in immigration show the readier response? Is this response imperfect?

First let us turn our attention to the earlier period for which the evidence is less detailed and the picture consequently less clear-cut.

The Periods Selected.

For convenience of analysis the years for which immigration data are available for the United States (1820 to date) are divided in this study into four main periods—namely, the seventy years from 1820 to 1889, inclusive; the pre-war quarter century, 1890 to 1914; the war period, 1914 to 1918; and the post-war years, 1919 to 1923. This division, although somewhat arbitrary, finds justification partly in essential differences in the character of migration and employment movements in the several periods, and partly in variations in the adequacy of the available statistical data.

However, in the following analysis there has been no rigid adherence to the chronological boundaries just mentioned. These somewhat arbitrary limits have been ignored whenever it has appeared that the objects of our inquiry would be furthered by extending the analysis of a particular phase beyond the termination of the period in which the analysis begins.

[3]United States Industrial Commission, *Reports, Vol. XV, Immigration*, p. 305.
[4]J. W. Jenks and W. Jett Lauck, *The Immigration Problem*, third edition, p. 208.

Characteristics of the Period Prior to 1890.

The period prior to 1890 may appropriately be designated as the agricultural frontier period, in that the existence of great areas of tillable free land doubtless affected materially the character of immigration during these decades. The data for analysis of this period are restricted to annual or, at best, quarterly statistics of immigration, with only such evidence of emigration as is afforded by statistics of the annual totals of outgoing passengers, virtually no statistics of employment, and only limited statistics of production. Also these seventy years are characterized by the predominance of immigrants from northern and western Europe who early in the following period, even before the close of the nineties, were outnumbered by those from southern and eastern Europe.[5] It is to this period prior to 1890 that we shall first turn our attention.

Imports of Men and of Merchandise.

A preliminary survey of the approximate relation between immigration and business conditions over the entire period for which data are available will afford a convenient starting point for the more precise and detailed analysis which is possible for the shorter periods for which there are more adequate data. In the earlier decades of the nineteenth century there are no employment statistics and few records of industrial activity, but statistics of the value of annual imports of merchandise are available and, inasmuch as these vary with industrial activity in the importing country,[6] except in war years, they furnish an approximate measure of industrial conditions.

In Table 18 and Chart 10, we have the cycles in the annual statistics of immigration and of merchandise imports. The curves represent deviations from seven-year moving averages, and hence picture the condition in a given year relative to the three immediately preceding and three following years. For convenience in comparison the deviations are divided by the standard or typical deviation for the respective series.

An examination of the evidence afforded by the fluctuations of immigration and imports for the whole period appears to support the preliminary hypothesis reached on a priori grounds; namely, that the current of immigration is markedly susceptible to changes in industrial conditions.

[5]See Chart 4 on page 41.
[6]For similarity of fluctuations in imports to those in pig iron production, for example, see Charts 6 and 7 in Chapter III.

An examination of Chart 10 reveals that, on the whole, particularly after the Civil War, each of the marked swells or troughs in the
import curve is accompanied, in the same year or within the succeeding year or two, by a somewhat similar fluctuation in immigration. This fact may be made more obvious by concentrating
our attention on those periods which are customarily designated as
depression years.

CHART 10

CYCLES IN IMPORTS OF MEN AND OF MERCHANDISE: 1820-1923.

Unit = one standard deviation

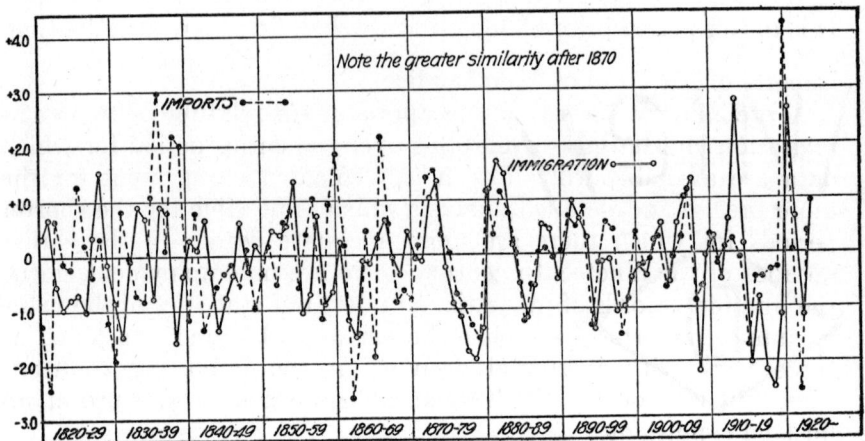

.Numerical data in Table 18.

The discussion of periods of prosperity and depression in the
United States in the following paragraphs, and in European countries in subsequent sections of this report, rests chiefly upon the
recently published *Business Annals* compiled by Dr. Willard L.
Thorp, of the staff of the National Bureau of Economic Research.
The first period of dullness after 1820 comes in 1826, following
the crisis of 1825. Both immigration and imports declined in 1826,
and imports continued to decline in 1827. The ready interpretation
of the evidence, however, is rendered somewhat difficult by the
fact that in this period neither the immigration nor import data
refer to years ending December 31st.[7]

[7]See footnote (c) to Table 18.

TABLE 18.—CYCLES OF IMMIGRATION AND OF IMPORTS OF MERCHANDISE,
BY YEARS, 1820-1923

Percentage deviations from seven-year moving averages, expressed in multiples of their standard deviations (26.62 per cent for immigrants, and 12.25 per cent for imports).

YEAR	IMMI-GRANTS[a]	IM-PORTS[b]	YEAR	IMMI-GRANTS	IM-PORTS	YEAR	IMMI-GRANTS	IM-PORTS
1820	......	−1.25[d]	1855	−1.05	−0.60	1890	.00	+0.06
1821	......	−2.44	1856	−0.71	+0.39	1891	+0.98	+0.69
1822	......	+0.64	1857	+0.71	+1.04	1892	+0.64	+0.50
1823	−0.98[c]	−0.13	1858	−0.90	−1.18	1893	+0.30	+0.85
1824	−0.79	−0.21	1859	−0.68	+0.91	1894	−1.39	−1.32
1825	−0.71	+1.29	1860	+0.23	+1.84	1895	−0.15	−0.18
1826	−1.01	+0.21	1861	−1.20	+0.16	1896	−0.11	+0.56
1827	+0.34	−0.38	1862	−1.50	−2.64	1897	−1.05	+0.42
1828	+1.54	+0.31	1863	−0.11	−1.44	1898	−0.98	−1.48
1829	−0.15	−1.20	1864	−0.15	+0.42	1899	−0.45	−0.83
1830	−0.86	−1.92	1865	+0.30	−1.89	1900	−0.23	+0.38
1831	−1.47	+0.81	1866	+0.64	+2.17	1901	−0.41	−0.20
1832	−0.08[c]	−0.02	1867	−0.04	+0.55	1902	+0.23	−0.11
1833	+0.90[c]	−0.73	1868	−0.38	−0.87	1903	+0.53	+0.29
1834	+0.68	−0.82	1869	+0.41	−0.68	1904	−0.53	−0.64
1835	−0.79	+1.09	1870	−0.08	−0.82	1905	+0.53	−0.07
1836	+0.90	+2.98	1871	−0.11	+0.17	1906	+1.01	+0.28
1837	+0.79	+0.10	1872	+1.05	+1.40	1907	+1.35	+1.12
1838	−1.58	−2.19	1873	+1.35	+1.53	1908	−2.18	−0.88
1839	−0.38	+2.03	1874	−0.23	+0.37	1909	−0.04	−0.60
1840	+0.27	−1.17	1875	−0.90	+0.02	1910	+0.30	+0.32
1841	+0.10	+0.78	1876	−1.13	−0.72	1911	−0.49	−0.20
1842	+0.65	−1.36	1877	−1.77	−0.92	1912	+0.60	+0.10
1843	−0.30[c]	d	1878	−1.92	−1.30	1913	+2.78	+0.24
1844	−1.36[c]	−0.58	1879	−1.35	−1.51	1914	+0.15	−0.10
1845	−0.77	−0.31	1880	+1.20	+1.16	1915	−2.03	−1.71
1846	−0.37	−0.16	1881	+1.69	+0.36	1916	−0.83	−0.45
1847	+0.60	−0.56	1882	+1.47	+1.14	1917	−2.18	−0.45
1848	−0.30	+0.10	1883	+0.15	+0.74	1918	−2.48	−0.32
1849	+0.19	−0.97	1884	−0.53	+0.02	1919	−1.16	−0.27
1850	−0.04	−0.34	1885	−1.16	−1.21	1920	+2.63	+4.17
1851	+0.45[c]	+0.18	1886	−0.56	−0.55	1921	+0.65	+0.02
1852	+0.38	−0.53	1887	+0.53	+0.02	1922	−1.16	−2.53
1853	+0.53	+0.60	1888	+0.45	+0.10	1923	+0.94	+0.37
1854	+1.35	+0.81	1889	−0.45	−0.07			

[a]Computed from data given in Table 1.
[b]Computed from data published in the *Monthly Summary of Commerce and Finance*, and the *Statistical Abstract of the United States*.
[c]From 1820 to 1831, the immigration data cover years ending September 30th; from 1833 to 1842, December 31st; from 1844 to 1850, September 30th; from 1851 to 1923, December 31st. The figures for 1832 and 1843 are estimated from data for fifteen and nine months, respectively.
[d]Prior to 1843, the import figures are for years ending September 30th; after 1843, for years ending June 30th.

The marked depression year 1837 shows a sharp decline of imports but immigration does not show a substantial decline until 1838. The dullness from 1840 to 1842 and again in 1846 is evident in imports in 1840, 1842, and 1846, but is only tardily reflected in immigration by slumps in 1845 and 1848, respectively.

Imports and immigration both show a substantial decline in 1855 and 1858, which may have been due to the brief depressions following the panics of 1854 and 1857, respectively.

The evidence considered in the preceding paragraphs, though fragmentary and scarcely adequate for conclusive judgments, suggests that prior to the Civil War, although the relation between industrial conditions in this country and the fluctuations in immigration is not obviously close, there is, nevertheless, some tendency for the effects of a depression to be evident in immigration after a period of time somewhat irregular in duration.

Of course, as long as free land was the chief lure to immigration, one would not expect so close a relation between immigration and business conditions as later when the chief incentive became the chance of employment and good wages.

The Civil War interfered with both the imports of men and of merchandise, but for both there was a recovery to a peak in 1866. The influence of the depression of 1866-1867 is seen in a decline in both immigration and imports in 1867 and 1868.

The great depression of the seventies, precipitated by the September panic of 1873, is accompanied in both imports and immigration by the most severe and prolonged slump in the entire period, except that immigration fell off even more decisively during the Great War. The decline in both immigration and imports is evident in the annual data by 1874, and both curves show a recovery in 1879 (fiscal year for imports, calendar year for immigration).

The industrial boom of the early eighties, culminating in 1882, is accompanied by a similar boom in immigration, and the subsequent depression, which became acute by May of 1884, is accompanied by a continuous decline in both imports and immigration to a lowpoint in 1885.

The period after the Civil War, and particularly the years subsequent to 1889, is dealt with in more detail in succeeding chapters, but we may profitably note here the major features of these recent decades by continuing our comparison of immigration with imports of merchandise as shown in Chart 10.

The mild crisis of 1890 does not find reflection in the movement either of imports or immigrants, but the long depression of the middle nineties finds a counterpart in a prolonged slump in immigration, with only temporary recovery movements until a long upward swell begins in 1899.

Suggestions of the effect of the minor business uncertainties of 1900 and 1901 are found in the slight reaction in imports in the year ending June 30, 1901, and in immigration in the year ending December 31, 1901.

In the depression of 1903-1904, both curves show a decline in 1904, and a strikingly close similarity in movement appears in the years 1904 to 1912, inclusive. The deep depression of 1908, following the panic of 1907, is accompanied by a sharp decline in immigration and imports, and the minor depression of 1911 is also evident.

The marked boom in immigration in 1913 is unique, in that while the second half of 1912 is marked by industrial activity and by indications of labor scarcity, it can scarcely be said that it is obvious that the degree of increase in industrial activity affords an adequate explanation of the unusual increase in immigration.

The slumps in immigration during the Great War and following the depression of 1921, which are evident on Chart 10, will receive more detailed attention later.

Wholesale Price Fluctuations.

By linking together the indexes compiled by various investigators, an index of wholesale prices from 1820 to date was prepared, but is not shown in the charts in this chapter because upon examination it appeared that the movement of the value of merchandise imports, which includes prices as one element, affords a better basis for comparison with immigration, particularly in the early decades, and for more recent decades more directly pertinent data than either prices or imports are available in the form of production and employment statistics.

The Annual Production of Pig Iron.

The comparison made in the previous pages between imports and immigration is necessarily somewhat sketchy, not only because it rests merely on annual data, but also because imports are, at best, only a partially adequate measure of industrial activity. A somewhat more direct measure is found in the annual production of pig iron. Ordinarily, as noted in Chapter III, the production of pig iron fluctuates in close sympathy with the volume of industrial operations and is consequently considered a good barometer of industrial activity. Monthly estimates of pig iron production are not available until in the eighties, but annual production figures are given for the years beginning with 1854 and hence afford additional evidence concerning industrial conditions in the period during and following the Civil War.

CHART 11

CYCLES OF PIG IRON PRODUCTION AND IMMIGRATION: 1860-1919.

Unit = one standard deviation

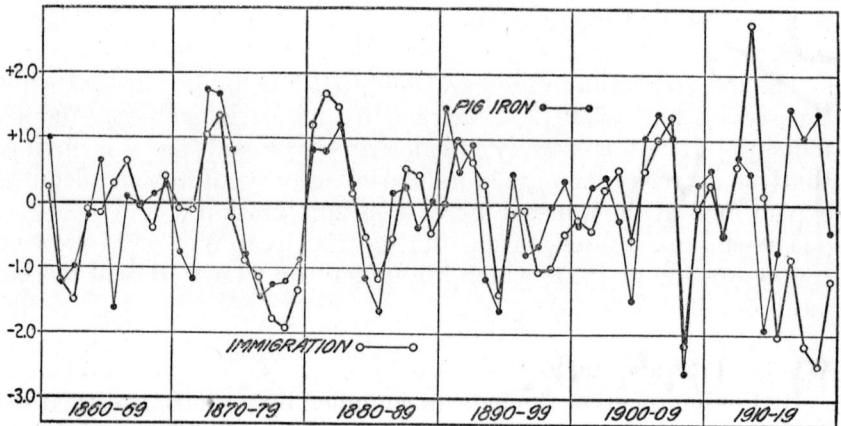

ªNumerical data in Tables 14 and 18.

In Chart 11 we have a comparison of the cyclical fluctuations in annual pig iron production and total immigration from 1860 to 1919. On close examination it will be seen that, aside from a few striking exceptions such as the marked fall in pig iron in 1865 and in the period of the Great War, the two series exhibit approximately the same succession of peaks and troughs, but that these do not always exactly coincide in time. This observation leads us to inquire to what extent the fluctuations in immigration lag behind the fluctuations in industrial activity.

The Lag.

With only annual data it is impossible to make a close computation of the extent of such lag as may exist, but it is possible to determine the probable maximum and minimum limits of the typical lag. An examination of the curve of imports from 1820 to date (on both the calendar year and fiscal year basis after 1870) and a comparison with the curve for total immigration, indicates that immigration probably lags behind imports a few months, the period evidently being nearer six months than a full year and possibly less than six months.

A similiar scrutiny of the pig iron and immigration curves from 1854 to date reveals a similiar tendency for some lag in immigration of an apparent length of less than one year, as evidenced by the fact that, in about half of the instances, the troughs and peaks are reached in the same year by the immigration and pig iron curves, and, in the other half, the annual immigration movement reaches the corresponding maximum or minimum a year later than pig iron.

It remains to examine the question of lag more closely with the aid of quarterly and monthly data and by numerical computation of the allowance for lag which gives the highest degree of correlation between immigration and industrial activity.

Numerical Computation of the Typical Lag.

In the usual statistical terminology, the arithmetic evidence of the lag giving the closest correspondence between the curves may be expressed by the following summary:

Period compared	Correlation coefficient when the given number of years lag is imputed to immigration as compared with pig iron.		
	No lag	One year	Two years
1857-1914	+.64	+.35	—.15
1857-1919	+.51	+.27	—.18
1872-1914	+.78	+.48	—.11

This numerical interpretation of the statistical evidence, in terms of the coefficient of correlation, indicates that the closest relationship is found between pig iron and immigration when the years between the Civil War and the Great War are selected for study and it is assumed that such lag as may exist is less than one year.

COMPARISONS BASED UPON QUARTERLY DATA: 1868-1889

Male Immigration.

Quarterly immigration data are available by sex beginning with the quarter ending September 30, 1856. For reasons previously discussed, male immigration is of greatest significance for our purpose, and, consequently in the more detailed analysis based upon quarterly and monthly data, we have, where convenient, made use of the statistics of male immigration rather than of the totals for both sexes.

Adjustment for a Variable Seasonal.

In analyzing the fluctuations of quarterly male immigration, the typical seasonal element has been, so far as practicable, eliminated and the adjusted fluctuations expressed as deviations from a twenty-

CHART 12

CYCLES IN QUARTERLY IMPORTS OF MERCHANDISE AND IN MALE IMMIGRATION: 1868-1889.

Adjusted for typical seasonal variation

Unit = one standard deviation

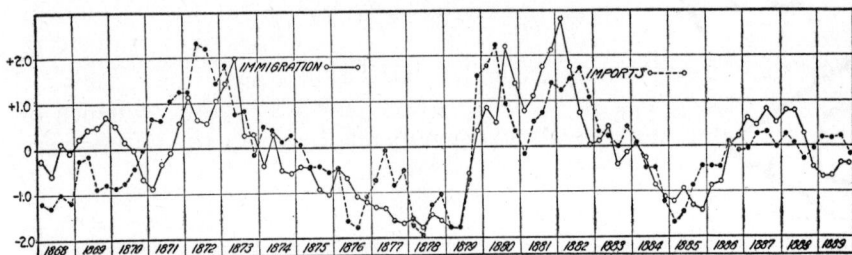

ªNumerical data in Table 19.

eight quarter moving average. In thus correcting for seasonal variation, allowance was made for a seasonal influence which varies at different stages in the cycle, in order to conform to the fact, revealed by examination of the raw data, that the seasonal fluctuation experiences somewhat regularly a damping down in the depression period of each cycle. In other words, the seasonal is itself subject to a cyclical variation.

Inasmuch as during most of the period prior to 1890 quarterly figures on production or employment are not available, we have used quarterly statistics of merchandise imports as a rough measure of industrial activity in the years 1868 to 1889. The import figures, like the immigration data, have been adjusted for a changing normal seasonal variation and expressed as deviations from a twenty-eight quarter moving average.

General Similarity.

The cyclical curves for quarterly imports of men and of merchandise, exhibited in Chart 12, reveal marked similarities in their major swings. Both show a marked boom in the early seventies,

TABLE 19.—CYCLES IN MALE IMMIGRATION AND IMPORTS OF MERCHANDISE, BY QUARTERS, 1868-1889[a]

Percentage deviations from trend, corrected for seasonal variation and expressed in terms of the standard deviations (29.77 per cent for male immigration and 12.05 per cent for imports).

YEAR	MALE IMMIGRATION				MERCHANDISE IMPORTS			
	QUARTER ENDING				QUARTER ENDING			
	MAR. 31	JUNE 30	SEPT. 30	DEC. 31	MAR. 31	JUNE 30	SEPT. 30	DEC. 31
1868	—0.24	—0.59	+0.10	—0.11	—1.21	—1.31	—1.00	—1.20
1869	+0.21	+0.42	+0.47	+0.70	—0.27	—0.17	—0.90	—0.80
1870	+0.50	+0.14	—0.05	—0.69	—0.88	—0.76	—0.44	—0.04
1871	—0.89	—0.35	—0.10	+0.56	+0.66	+0.61	+1.05	+1.24
1872	+1.13	+0.64	+0.57	+1.04	+1.24	+2.32	+2.20	+1.43
1873	+1.42	+1.98	+0.28	+0.30	+1.82	+0.75	+0.80	—0.15
1874	—0.40	+0.29	—0.50	—0.57	+0.47	+0.38	+0.11	+0.26
1875	—0.42	—0.43	—0.92	—1.03	+0.04	—0.43	—0.42	—0.56
1876	—0.47	—0.69	—1.11	—1.21	—0.48	—1.64	—1.78	—1.10
1877	—1.32	—1.36	—1.62	—1.69	—0.74	—0.10	—0.85	—0.53
1878	—1.59	—1.79	—1.50	—1.63	—1.76	—1.96	—1.30	—1.06
1879	—1.79	—1.77	—0.60	+0.35	—1.78	—1.78	—0.73	+1.56
1880	+0.86	+0.53	+2.20	+1.39	+1.78	+2.24	+0.92	+0.34
1881	+0.79	—1.12	+1.76	+2.14	—0.17	+0.53	+0.73	+1.39
1882	+2.81	+1.76	+0.74	+0.04	+1.23	+1.48	+1.71	+1.07
1883	+0.13	+0.44	—0.38	—0.13	+0.32	+0.22	—0.01	+0.41
1884	+0.07	—0.24	—0.85	—1.12	+0.09	—0.49	—0.47	—1.22
1885	—1.21	—0.92	—1.31	—1.41	—1.68	—1.46	—0.87	—0.43
1886	—0.86	—0.78	+0.02	+0.23	—0.44	—0.44	+0.09	—0.11
1887	+0.62	+0.48	+0.83	+0.53	—0.07	+0.27	+0.31	—0.02
1888	+0.78	+0.79	+0.28	—0.46	+0.26	—0.06	—0.29	—0.08
1889	—0.69	—0.65	—0.36	—0.38	+0.18	+0.16	+0.19	—0.20

[a]Computed from quarterly statistics of male immigrants in Table I of appendix, and from statistics of imports published by the U. S. Bureau of Foreign and Domestic Commerce in the *Monthly Summary o Commerce and Finance*. For methods of adjusting for seasonal variation and trend, see Chapter IV.

followed by a long decline; another boom in 1880, followed by a short recession and a new peak in 1882; then a decline to a low in 1885 and a recovery in the late eighties. The import recovery in 1877, however, finds no comparable movement in immigration.

The Lag.

The movements in quarterly male immigration and merchandise imports are not, however, exactly coincident. From 1869 to 1873 immigration clearly lags from two to four quarters behind the turns in imports. The lag, if any, in the depression of the seventies is not obvious; and thereafter, while evident at times, does not appear to be so great as in the first part of the period, ranging from no lag in the short depression of 1881 to about three quarters in the depression of 1885.

CHAPTER SUMMARY

In this chapter we have first taken a bird's-eye view of the relation of immigration to industrial activity by comparing the annual statistics of immigration with those for imports of merchandise over the entire century beginning in 1820, and with the annual production of pig iron in the period beginning with 1860. From these comparisons it is clear that, particularly after the Civil War, the cyclical fluctuations in immigration are to a large extent a reflex of industrial conditions in the United States, the effect upon immigration evidently becoming apparent in something less than a year.

Then we have subjected the period from 1868 to 1889 to a somewhat more detailed scrutiny by comparing quarterly cycles of male immigration and imports of merchandise, both corrected for their typical seasonal variations. This comparison strengthens our preliminary conclusions based upon annual data, and indicates a lag in the effect of industrial conditions upon immigration of from two to four quarters in the early part of the period and a somewhat shorter lag in the latter part of the period.

In the following chapter we turn our attention to an examination of the more detailed data available for the years following 1889.

CHAPTER V

THE PRE-WAR QUARTER CENTURY: 1890-1914

Characteristics of the Period.

The twenty-five years from 1890 to the outbreak of the World War include a most fascinating period of American industrial history, and one which in many ways affords the richest field for study of the relations of migration to industrial activity. The decade of the eighties witnessed the virtual passing of the frontier with an abundant area of free and fertile land available for the homesteader. While railroad construction activities did not in the following decades reach the magnitude which they had attained in the eighties, and though the first years of the nineties were characterized by prolonged depression and business uncertainty, toward the end of the decade there began a sharp recovery in industrial activity, accompanied by an equally remarkable increase in the volume of immigration, which reached its peak in the calendar year 1913 with a recorded total of 1,387,318 immigrant aliens and 229,585 nonimmigrant aliens. It will be remembered, also, that it is in the nineties that the "old" immigration from northern and western Europe ceased to be the predominating element in the immigrant stream, yielding in numbers to the rising tide of immigrants from southern and eastern Europe.

Data Available for Quantitative Analysis.

This quarter century also affords much more adequate data for the purposes of our study than are available for the earlier decades. While the years during and following the Great War have witnessed a remarkable development in the variety and adequacy of statistics of production and employment, even in the preceding quarter century to which we now wish to turn our attention we find at hand statistics which facilitate the close study of cyclical movements in industry. Monthly estimates of pig iron production, usually considered a good index of industrial activity, are available in some form throughout the entire period; and, as noted in a previous chapter, it has been possible to weld together a monthly index of factory employment in one or more states which are notable immigrant centers. Monthly statistics of immigration, classified by country of origin beginning in July, 1888, and by sex from July, 1892, are available; and toward the end of the pre-war period the monthly immigration statistics become more and more detailed, so that for the last five or six years of the period they are available by race, country of origin, occupation, and other bases of classification. Also, beginning in July, 1907, monthly statistics of emigration were published, so that it becomes possible thereafter to give a relatively complete picture of the net movement of migration.

With its relative abundance of immigration statistics, accompanied by reasonably adequate measures of industrial activity and with little in the way of war or legal restriction to interfere with the free interplay of industrial forces and immigration, the quarter century from 1890 to 1914 affords an exceptional opportunity for the analysis of these phenomena.

Method of Analysis.

The approach in this chapter is, first, by comparisons over the entire quarter century between the cyclical fluctuations in the monthly statistics of male immigration on the one hand and pig iron production and factory employment on the other. Then, to facilitate the study of certain significant details which are apt to be unduly subordinated in comparisons covering as long a period as a quarter century, and particularly to make possible the satisfactory analysis of emigration series which are not available prior to July, 1907, the entire period from 1890 to 1914 has been broken up into shorter segments, each of which includes at least one major or minor industrial depression and one or two years of the preceding period of prosperity and of the succeeding period of recovery. These selected depression periods are: the severe depression of 1894, the depression of 1904, the major depression of 1908, the minor depression of 1911, and the decline beginning in 1913.

This concentration upon short periods facilitates the focusing of attention upon certain details in the reaction of migration to employment which are apt to be overlooked in the more inclusive picture. In the last three of these short periods we introduce comparisons with emigration and with the net results of immigration and emigration. The analysis, however, of the movement of various separate elements in the immigrant current, such as studies by race or occupation, is largely postponed to a subsequent chapter.

As will be noted more in detail in connection with the immediate discussion of each period, the method of analysis differs somewhat from period to period in order to make the most profitable use of data available.

QUARTER-CENTURY COMPARISONS

In Chart 13 we have depicted the fluctuations of *male immigration and factory employment*. Both series represent deviations from computed trends with the normal seasonal movement eliminated, and hence represent the cyclical fluctuations to the extent that these can be statistically isolated. In plotting these curves the scale unit for each curve is the typical measure of its fluctuations, or the standard deviation, so that the curves are brought into convenient form for comparison of the timing of the cyclical fluctuations. It should be remembered, however, in interpreting these curves, that the method used conceals the fact that the fluctuations in the migration curve are relatively more violent. An approximate measure of the relative violence of fluctuation of the two series is found in their average deviations from trend, which are, respectively, 24.74 per cent for male immigration and 3.40 for employment.

Immigration Fluctuations Lag Behind Employment Changes.
These series and others subsequently discussed have been examined for the degree of consistency in their timing by two methods. In the first place a graphic comparison was made by plotting the curves on separate sheets and superimposing them over an illuminated chartbox with varying degrees of lag assigned to the migration curve. Then, in significant cases, coefficients of correlation have been calculated as one means of testing the conclusions reached from the graphic comparisons.

It is quite obvious upon a brief examination of Chart 13 that in general contour the fluctuations of male immigration and factory employment bear a marked resemblance. Both show a decided depression in 1894, a checkered recovery through the late nineties, a mild depression in 1904, a boom in 1906 and 1907, followed by the severe depression of 1908, a new high in early 1910, and a sharp decline in 1914.

There are also a few striking differences which challenge attention. The sharp drop in immigration in the latter part of 1892, a temporary crest in the latter part of 1904 and the first months of 1905,

CHART 13

CYCLICAL FLUCTUATIONS IN MALE IMMIGRATION AND FACTORY EMPLOYMENT: 1890-1914ᵃ

Three-month moving averages of deviations from trend, corrected for seasonal variation. Unit = one standard deviation

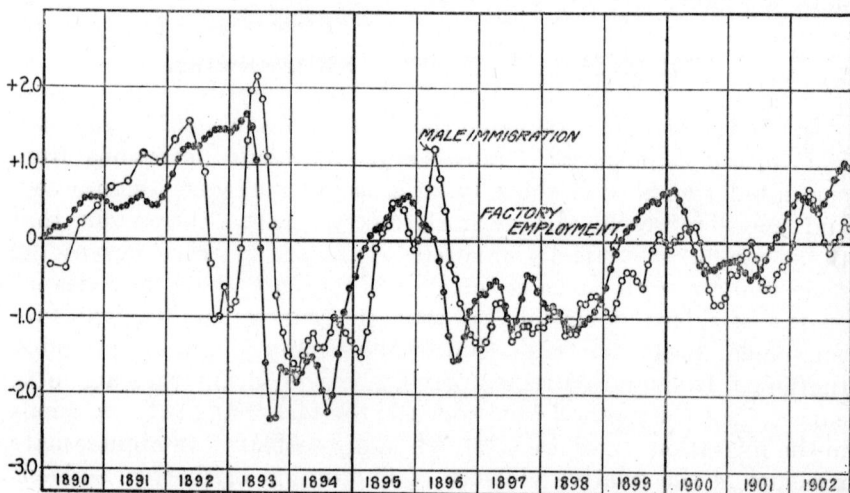

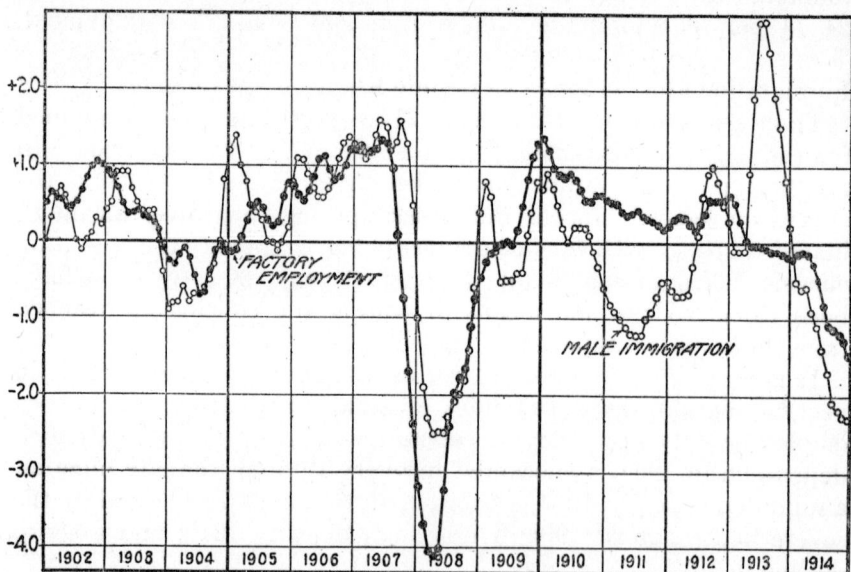

ᵃThe numerical data for the male immigration curve are in Appendix Table III. The employment curve represents a three-month moving average of data in Appendix Table V, expressed in multiples of their standard deviation, 4.55 per cent.

and the marked boom in 1913 find no close counterparts on the employment curve. Also the depression of 1911 is more clearly defined on the immigration curve. Various minor irregularities may also be detected, but none of these differences appear sufficient to overcome the presumption raised by the general similarity in movement, that fluctuations in the two series are to a large extent cause and effect or are dominated by common causes.

When the curves are closely examined to determine the extent to which the major turns in the two curves coincide, it appears that they agree most closely when it is assumed that the fluctuations in immigration lag from two to four months after the corresponding fluctuations in the employment curve. This statement is not, of course, to be interpreted as meaning that the lag is always from two to four months. For example, the high points in 1893 and the low points in 1908 appear to be approximately simultaneous.[1]

Indexes of Industrial and Commercial Activity.

The employment curve used in the above comparison is constructed from limited material and, as noted, there are some relatively large fluctuations in migration, notably in 1892, 1905, 1909, 1911, and 1913, for which the factory employment curve does not afford adequate explanation.

Pig Iron Production.

For additional evidence we turn first to a comparison with an index of pig iron production corrected for computed trend and seasonal variation by methods described in Chapter III. In Chart 14 this series is plotted together with the male immigration curve for the quarter century 1890-1914. As in the comparison with the factory employment curve, in most of their major movements the two curves agree, especially in the second half of the period. The immigration curve appears to lag at the major turn from one to four months, although there are a number of instances, particularly at the turning points of moderate booms or depressions, where the immigration curve turns first.[2]

An examination of the pig iron curve affords some explanation of certain immigration fluctuations which we noted as contrary to

[1]The conclusion reached from visual inspection of the charts is supported by the mathematical computation of coefficients of correlation with various intervals of lag. When it is assumed that there is no lag, a coefficient of +.66 is obtained; when immigration is assumed to lag two months, the coefficient is +.76; four months, +.72; and six months, +.55.

[2]With no lag assumed, the correlation of the monthly indices is +.63 ± .02.

the course of the employment curve. A drop in the pig iron curve in 1892 suggests a recession in industrial activity which may account for the immigration slump later in that year; also, pig iron production shows a decline in 1911 which harmonizes well with the migration slump in that year.

In some respects pig iron production is a better index of employment opportunity than our index of factory employment. Iron is basic to many industries, including, for example, building construction, for which we have no adequate direct statistics of

CHART 14

CYCLICAL FLUCTUATIONS IN MALE IMMIGRATION AND PIG IRON
PRODUCTION: 1890-1914ᴬ

*Three-month moving averages of deviations from trend, corrected for
seasonal variation. Unit = one standard deviation*

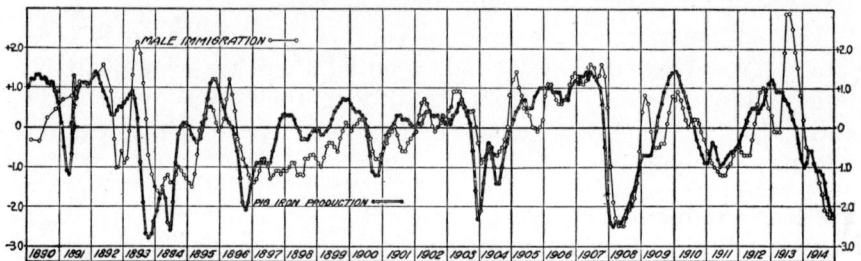

ᴬThe numerical data for the male immigration curve are in Appendix Table III; the pig iron curve represents a three-month moving average of the data in Appendix Table VI, expressed in multiples of their standard deviation, 17.13 per cent.

employment. It also has a wider geographic scope than the employment index. The evidence, therefore, of similarities to the pig iron curve should strengthen the conclusion previously reached to the effect that male immigration fluctuates in rather close sympathy with employment, but lags somewhat, though apparently only two to four months.

Clearings index.

A comparison was also made between male immigration and an index of business prepared by Mr. Carl Snyder of the Federal Reserve Bank of New York.[3] This index is based on bank clearings outside of New York deflated by a general index of prices designed

[3] *Journal of the American Statistical Association*, September, 1924, p. 335.

to represent the best estimate of the course of prices of those goods and services which constitute the bulk of clearings. Mr. Snyder has demonstrated that this curve may be interpreted as a measure of the volume of trade and ordinarily anticipates the fluctuation of production.

This index does not differ materially from those for factory employment and pig iron production, though the lag between its changes and those in migration is somewhat greater. The maximum correlation, judging from visual inspection, is obtained when a lag of about four months is assigned to immigration.

SHORT-PERIOD IMMIGRATION AND EMIGRATION STUDIES

The Period from 1892 to 1902, inclusive.

This period was marked by a prolonged depression, with a temporary recovery in 1895, followed toward the end of the decade by the beginning of an era of industrial expansion, accompanied by rising immigration. Aside from the growth movement, which has been approximately eliminated by the device of expressing the data as deviations from an eighty-four month moving average, the features just mentioned may be observed by reference to Chart 13 on page 92.

We have previously noted the approximate similarity in the general contour of the immigration and the factory employment curves. While immigration evidences a slump in the latter part of 1892 and early in 1893 which is not shown on the employment curve, it quickly recovers and reaches a high point in 1893 about two months after the employment curve reaches its crest. Both show clearly the decline in 1893 and the subsequent depression. Both recover in 1895 and decline again in 1896, but the migration decline begins about five months later than the employment decline and continues for about five months later. Both series experience a long rise beginning in 1898.

The Depression of 1893-1894.

Because of the relatively scant data upon which comparisons of industrial activity and immigration are based in the nineties, too much importance should not be attached to conclusions reached by a study of this period until they are substantiated by reference to the more complete information available in later years. However, the depression of 1893-94 affords an opportunity to illustrate and compare various available methods of analysis and presentation.

CHART 15

DEPRESSION OF 1893-94[a]

Four Methods of Comparing Immigration and Economic
Conditions

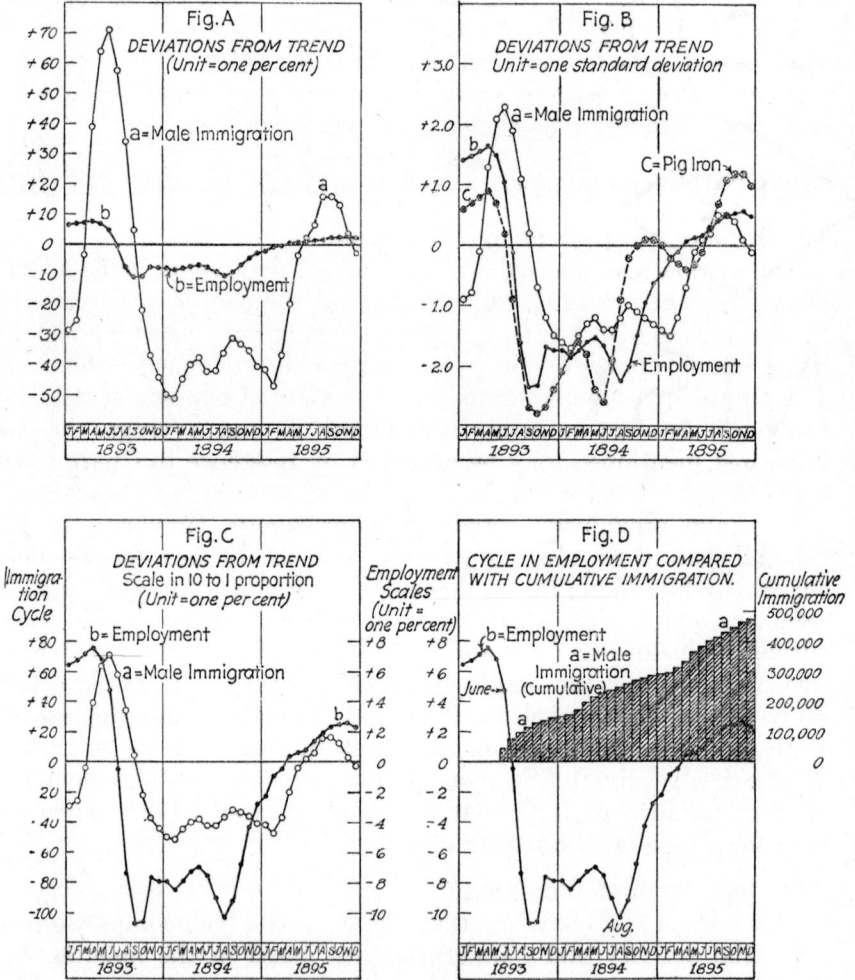

Fig. A
DEVIATIONS FROM TREND
(Unit = one per cent)
a = Male Immigration
b
b = Employment

+70 +60 +50 +40 +30 +20 +10 0 −10 −20 −30 −40 −50

JFMAMJJASOND JFMAMJJASOND JFMAMJJASOND
1893   1894   1895

Fig. B
DEVIATIONS FROM TREND
Unit = one standard deviation
a = Male Immigration
b
c
C = Pig Iron
Employment

+3.0 +2.0 +1.0 0 −1.0 −2.0

JFMAMJJASOND JFMAMJJASOND JFMAMJJASOND
1893   1894   1895

Fig. C
DEVIATIONS FROM TREND
Scale in 10 to 1 proportion
(Unit = one per cent)
b = Employment
a = Male Immigration
b

Immigration Cycle
+80 +60 +40 +20 0 20 ·40 −60 −80 −100

Employment Scales (Unit = one per cent)
+8 +6 +4 +2 0 −2 −4 −6 −8 −10

+8 +6 +4 +2 0 −2 −4 −6 −8 −10

JFMAMJJASOND JFMAMJJASOND JFMAMJJASOND
1893   1894   1895

Fig. D
CYCLE IN EMPLOYMENT COMPARED
WITH CUMULATIVE IMMIGRATION.
b = Employment
a = Male Immigration (Cumulative)
June
a
a
Aug.

Cumulative Immigration
500,000 400,000 300,000 200,000 100,000 0

JFMAMJJASOND JFMAMJJASOND JFMAMJJASOND
1893   1894   1895

[a]Based upon data in Table 20 and Appendix Table VI.
Fig. A=Percentage deviations from trend (Unit= one per cent).
Fig. B=Deviations from trend (Unit=one standard deviation).
Fig. C=Deviations from trend (Adjusted scales, ratio 10 to 1).
Fig. D=Deviations of employment from trend, and cumulative immigration.

TABLE 20.—FACTORY EMPLOYMENT AND MALE IMMIGRATION IN THE DEPRESSION
OF 1893-1894

YEAR AND MONTH	THREE-MONTH MOVING AVERAGE OF PERCENTAGE DEVIATIONS FROM TREND[a]		NUMBER OF IMMIGRANTS[b] (THOUSANDS)	
	FACTORY EMPLOYMENT	IMMIGRATION	IN SPECIFIED MONTH	TOTAL NUMBER SINCE JUNE, 1893
1893				
Jan........	+6.4	—28.7	8.8	.....
Feb.......	+6.7	—25.6	8.2	.....
Mar.......	+7.1	— 3.7	28.7	.....
Apr.......	+7.5	+39.1	51.8	.....
May......	+6.8	+63.8	65.2	.....
June......	+4.7	+71.0	43.6	.....
July......	—0.5	+57.7	29.4	73.1
Aug.......	—7.4	+33.9	23.3	96.3
Sept......	—10.7	+4.8	16.9	113.3
Oct.	—10.6	—21.9	14.4	127.6
Nov.......	—7.7	—37.0	10.6	138.3
Dec.......	—7.9	—44.1	7.3	145.6
1894				
Jan.......	—7.9	—49.7	5.9	151.4
Feb.......	—8.5	—51.0	6.3	157.7
Mar.......	—7.9	—44.8	13.1	170.8
Apr.	—7.3	—39.9	24.4	195.2
May	—7.0	—37.5	19.7	214.9
June	—7.5	—42.1	12.8	227.6
July	—9.0	—41.8	9.6	237.2
Aug.......	—10.3	—36.0	8.9	246.1
Sept.......	—9.2	—31.1	11.5	257.6
Oct........	—6.8	—32.9	12.5	270.1
Nov.......	—4.3	—35.2	8.2	278.3
Dec.......	—2.8	—40.4	8.3	286.6
1895				
Jan.......	—2.2	—41.6	5.5	292.1
Feb.......	—0.9	—46.8	6.3	298.5
Mar.......	—0.5	—36.6	11.6	310.1
Apr.	+0.4	—19.8	26.3	336.4
May......	+0.6	— 3.6	28.9	365.3
June......	+0.8	+ 2.4	19.6	384.9
July......	+1.4	+66.4	15.4	400.3
Aug.	+1.9	+15.9	14.5	414.8
Sept.......	+2.3	+16.0	17.3	432.1
Oct.......	+2.5	+13.3	16.1	448.2
Nov.......	+2.6	+ 3.8	13.6	461.8
Dec.......	+2.3	— 2.6	10.8	472.7

[a]Computed from Tables II and IV (in appendix) by methods described in Chapter III.
[b]Compiled from Table II (in appendix).

In Chart 15 we have the relation of factory employment to male immigration in the three years 1893 to 1895 presented in four different ways. These four charts, though based on the same fundamental data, do not look closely similar nor do they convey the same impression.

In Fig. A, the series are expressed as percentage deviations from their computed trends. The impression received from this section of the chart is that fluctuations in employment are relatively minor as compared with those of immigration. This is literally correct, but the resulting impression is misleading, for the chart conveys no suggestion of the fact that a one per cent fluctuation in employment involves a much larger number of men than a one per cent change in immigration. Nor is it easy to determine from Fig. A whether the fluctuations of the two series are substantially similar in timing and direction. Ease of comparison in timing and direction of movement is obtained by presentation in the form shown in Fig. B; that is, with the data expressed as deviations from their trends measured in terms of the typical deviation of each respective series. This latter method, which has been used in several of the charts in this book, has the distinct advantage of throwing the curves close together and thus facilitating comparison of their changes in direction, but, to avoid false impressions, it should be noted that the numerical significance of a given change is almost entirely concealed. On such a curve the change in immigration may appear exactly equal to that in employment, but we cannot tell from the curve whether the number of men represented by the change in employment is equal to the number affected by the change in immigration or, possibly, one hundred times as great.

For reasons which will be more obvious as we note the many possible bases of comparison, it is practically impossible to select scales which will give a precise and unquestionably true impression of the relative numerical importance of the changes in employment and immigration. However, if we are turning our attention to the relation of changes in the *volume* of employment and immigration, in terms of the number of persons affected, rather than to the timing and direction of such changes, then a more accurate impression is probably obtained by the use of charts similar to those found in Fig. C and Fig. D of Chart 15.

In Fig. C the fluctuations in employment are emphasized by the use of a larger scale than that used for immigration, so that a deviation of one per cent in employment appears as great as a ten per cent deviation in immigration. This ratio of ten to one is somewhat arbitrarily chosen,[4] nor could the correct ratio be determined without full knowledge of the number of immigrants destined for gainful employment as compared with the number of persons employed in the occupations and geographical areas affected by immigration. However, the visual impression received from Fig. C probably comes closer to a correct interpretation of the relative numbers involved than is furnished by either of the two methods first considered.

But another question arises which is not answered by any of the three graphs so far considered; that is, what is the cumulative immigration during the period of declining employment? In Fig. D we have a comparison between the employment curve shown in Fig. C and a bar chart showing the cumulative number of male immigrants beginning in June, 1893, the first month in which the employment curve shows a decided cyclical drop. Though, as just noted, the employment curve begins to drop sharply in June, immigration continues to some extent, and, while it also declines sharply, in no month of these three years were there less than five thousand immigrant males arriving. By the end of September, 1894, when the employment curve first begins to show a decided recovery, over 270,000 males had immigrated. Obviously, even such a severe depression as that of 1893-1894 did not operate to check immigration completely, and it seems unquestionable that some of these 270,000 newly arrived immigrants from June, 1893, to September, 1894, found employment with great difficulty or replaced others who were forced into the ranks of the unemployed.

However, in interpreting the significance of cumulative immigration in depression periods, it should be noted that, as in Chart 15, the cycle curves ordinarily represent deviations from an upward trend, and this trend in employment may be more than sufficient to offset such upward trend as is present in the available number of workers other than immigrants. In such case, at least part of the cumulative immigration is absorbed by the trend in employment.

In the following pages no one of the four methods of graphic comparison illustrated in Chart 15 has been used exclusively; but in each case the method of presentation has been determined by the

[4]Based upon consideration of the fact that in the early nineties the number of persons engaged in manufacturing was between 4,000,000 and 5,000,000 and the annual immigration then averaged somewhat less than ten per cent of that number; hence the number of persons represented by a one per cent change in factory employment was roughly approximate to the number involved in a ten per cent change in immigration.

character of the data and the particular aspect of the problem which is under consideration. If the reader will note the type of chart used in each instance, it will facilitate his interpretation of the facts portrayed.

Emigration during the Depression of 1893-1894.

In the preceding discussion of the depression of 1894, we have made no allowance for the fact that there is an outgoing as well as an incoming stream of aliens. Prior to 1907 there were no official statistics of this movement, but something of its extent can be indicated by comparing the movement of incoming male immigrants with the number of outgoing male passengers in steerage, the great bulk of whom were doubtless alien emigrants. In the fiscal year 1892 (ending June 30, 1892) 96,834 male steerage passengers are reported as having departed, or twenty-five for each one hundred male immigrants arriving; in 1893, the proportion is 28 to 100; in 1894, 61 to 100; and in 1895, 79 to 100. While these figures do not give us an exact measure of the numbers of emigrants, they are adequate to indicate that the volume of net immigration was materially reduced by the departure of aliens. We return to these data concerning outgoing passengers at a later point in this chapter.

Depression of 1904.

As a background for analysis of the fluctuations of migration in the depression of 1904, we have plotted in Chart 16 immigration and factory employment for the five years from 1902 to 1906, inclusive. In so far as the two curves for male immigration and employment, respectively, are concerned, this chart is practically a reproduction of a section of Chart 13 to which we turned our attention earlier in the chapter, except that in this case the minor irregularities of the employment curve have not been smoothed out by reducing them to a three-month moving average, after the correction for trend and seasonal variation was made.

As in the depression of 1894, we again note a general similarity in the cyclical movements of the two series, with a few months lag on the part of immigration, the exact extent of which is rendered less obvious by the minor irregularities of the curves. It will be noted that the effect of the decline in employment which begins at the close of 1902 is not clearly revealed in the immigration curve until June of 1903; but that the first recovery movement in 1904 begins almost simultaneously in the two series, although employment suffers a relapse in the middle of the year.

As to the cumulative immigration during the period under consideration, whether we start to cumulate from the time the decline in employment begins in April, 1903, and continue until the lowest point in the employment curve is reached in August, 1904, or

CHART 16

DEPRESSION OF 1904

Cumulative Male Immigration and Cycles in Employment and Male Immigration[a]

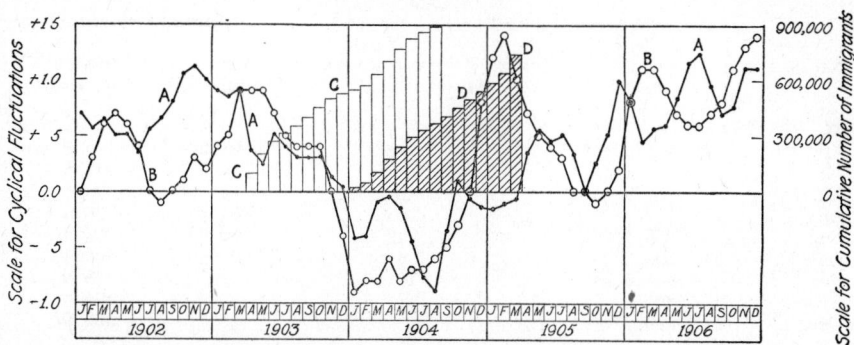

[a]*Explanation of curves and sources of numerical data*:

A=Factory employment, cyclical fluctuations (Appendix Table V).
B=Male immigration, cyclical fluctuations, three-month averages (Appendix Table III).
C=Cumulative male immigration from beginning of employment decline (number of immigrants). See Table 21.
D=Cumulative male immigration during period employment was below trend (number of immigrants). See Table 21.

cumulate from January, 1904, to March, 1905, during which period employment was in all months except one below its computed trend—in either case we find that the cumulative number of male immigrants mounts into the hundreds of thousands, as graphically represented by the vertical bars in Chart 16.

That this gross immigration was probably offset to a considerable extent by emigration is suggested by the fact that in the year ending June 30, 1904, the number of outgoing male steerage passengers was approximately 209,000.

The years covered by the immediately preceding discussion were included in a study of cyclical fluctuations made by Professor Alvin

H. Hansen.   He correlated various monthly series with wholesale prices in the United States, and found the maximum correlation of prices with immigration ($+$.696) to occur when no lag is assigned to either series, but that the maximum correlation of employment and prices is obtained when unemployment changes are assumed to precede prices by three months.   He makes the surmise that this earlier movement in employment "may possibly be explained in part at least by the fact that the building series precedes the in-

TABLE 21.—CUMULATIVE NUMBER OF MALE IMMIGRANTS DURING THE DECLINE AND DEPRESSION PERIOD OF 1903-1904[a]

Thousands of Persons

YEAR AND MONTH	NUMBER ARRIVED		YEAR AND MONTH	NUMBER ARRIVED	
	SINCE MARCH, 1903[b]	SINCE DEC., 1903[c]		SINCE MARCH, 1903	SINCE DEC., 1903
1903			1904 (con.)		
Apr......	100.3	.....	Apr......	698.9	175.2
May.....	200.1	.....	May.....	768.5	244.8
June.....	268.2	.....	June.....	817.3	293.6
July.....	312.1	.....	July.....	854.3	330.6
Aug......	353.1	.....	Aug......	890.9	367.2
Sept......	399.9	.....	Sept......	.....	406.4
Oct......	451.1	.....	Oct......	.....	448.9
Nov.....	495.0	.....	Nov......	.....	495.5
Dec.....	523.7	.....	Dec......	.....	539.9
1904			1905		
Jan......	543.2	19.5	Jan......	.....	582.4
Feb......	567.5	43.8	Feb......	.....	634.9
Mar.....	629.6	105.9	Mar......	.....	736.7

[a]Compiled from Table II, in appendix.
[b]The data in this column cover the period of declining factory employment.
[c]The data in this column cover the period during which factory employment was below its computed trend.

dustrial group by several months.   The slackening of building operations would affect unemployment."

While Professor Hansen did not compute directly the correlation of immigration with pig iron and imports, his correlation with prices would suggest that the maximum degree of correlation between immigration and pig iron would be reached with immigration lagging one month, and likewise for imports.

It may be mentioned in passing that other students of cyclical fluctuations in the first decade or so of the present century have found a close relation between immigration and industrial activity. The Brookmire service, in analyzing various cyclical phenomena preparatory to the construction of an index of business conditions, puts immigration with the Business Group, which includes clearings, pig iron production, pig iron prices, commodity prices, imports, building, and railroad earnings; Babson groups immigration with new building, commercial failures, and clearings; and Persons, with pig iron production, prices, etc.

Departing Steerage Passengers.

In examining the depression periods of 1894 and 1904, we have noted incidentally that the volume of departing steerage passengers furnishes a rough index of emigration. Also, beginning in July, 1907, official statistics of emigration are available; hence, before we turn to a comparison of employment and migratory movements in the depression of 1908, it will be of advantage to note the chief characteristics of the emigration movement and its relation to immigration.

As previously noted, official statistics of emigration are lacking prior to July, 1907, but for most of the years subsequent to the Civil War there are statistics of the number of departing passengers, made available to the Government by the courtesy of the steamship companies. These data are classified as "cabin" and "other than cabin" or steerage passengers, and also by sex. The male steerage passengers probably afford the best index of the departures of alien workers from this country. The ratio of the number of departing male steerage passengers to the number of incoming male immigrants affords an approximate measure of the response of the net migration of workers to employment opportunity in this country. This ratio is not to be taken as representing the exact numerical relation of incoming immigrants to departing emigrants, for the numerator of the ratio, male immigrants, does not include those coming for a temporary sojourn (the non-immigrant group); while the denominator, "other than cabin" passengers, is not, in all probability, a complete count of emigrant aliens, though it doubtless includes some nonemigrant aliens and some citizens of the United States. For example, in the years (fiscal) 1908 and 1909 the number of departing male steerage passengers was 578,097 and the number of officially recorded male emigrant aliens was 501,892. However, it is probable that such differences are relatively constant, and hence when the ratio of departing steerage passengers to incoming immigrants is low it is an indication that emigration is light as compared to immigration. If the ratio is high when industrial

depression exists and relatively low in boom times, this may be
taken as evidence that net immigration is closely correlated with
employment conditions.

In Table 22 and Chart 17 we have this ratio of male steerage passengers departing to male immigrants arriving, compared with the
deviations of pig iron production from its trend (seven-year
moving average).   In interpreting this chart, it must be remembered

CHART 17

RELATION BETWEEN CYCLES IN PRODUCTION OF PIG IRON AND
RATIO OF DEPARTING ALIEN MALE STEERAGE PASSENGERS TO
MALE IMMIGRANTS: 1870-1909[a]

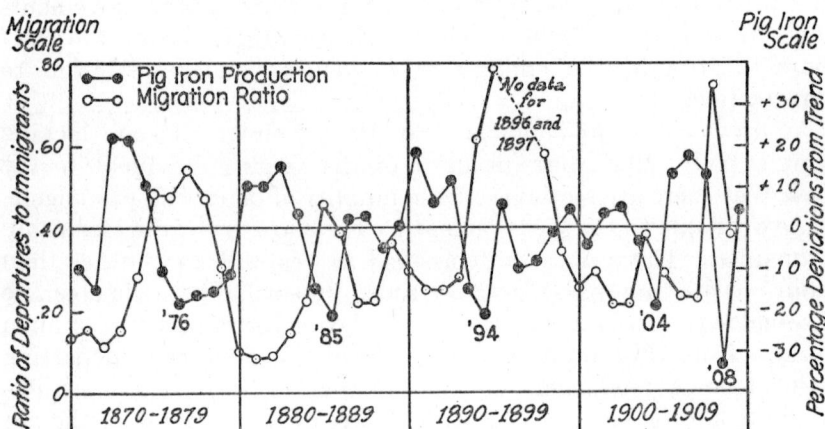

[a]The pig iron curve is computed from data in Table 12-A; the data for the migration
ratio curve are in Table 22.

that the pig iron figures are for calendar years, but the migration
ratios are for years ending June 30th; so that, for example, the low
point in pig iron production in 1908 represents the pig iron production for the twelve months ending December 31st, and the 1908
migration ratio refers to the twelve months ending June 30, 1908.

Though the limitations of the data prevent precise comparisons,
it is obvious from an examination of Chart 17 that there is a high
degree of inverse correlation between industrial conditions as
measured by pig iron production and the ratio of departing male
steerage passengers to male immigrants.   When pig iron production
is at low ebb, as in the late seventies, the middle eighties, the middle
nineties, and in 1904 and 1908, then the outgoing flow is large
relative to the incoming flow.

TABLE 22.—RATIO OF DEPARTING MALE STEERAGE PASSENGERS TO MALE IMMIGRANTS: 1870-1909[a]

	A	B	C		A	B	C
YEAR ENDING JUNE 30	MALE IMMI-GRANTS (THOUS-ANDS)	MALE STEERAGE PASSEN-GERS (THOUS-ANDS)	RATIO $B \div A$	YEAR ENDING JUNE 30	MALE IMMI-GRANTS (THOUS-ANDS)	MALE STEERAGE PASSEN-GERS (THOUS-ANDS)	RATIO $B \div A$
1870	235.6	31.9	.135	1890	281.9	83.1	.295
1871	190.4	29.9	.157	1891	354.1	89.0	.251
1872	240.2	27.2	.113	1892	385.8	96.8	.251
1873	275.8	42.1	.153	1893	315.8	88.3	.280
1874	189.2	53.2	.281	1894	184.0	112.9	.614
1875	140.0	67.6	.483	1895	157.3	123.8	.787*
1876	111.8	53.3	.477	1896	212.5	....b	....
1877	92.0	49.7	.540*	1897	135.1	....b	....
1878	86.3	40.8	.473	1898	135.7	78.6	.579
1879	111.9	33.9	.303	1899	227.1	78.1	.344
1880	287.6	28.8	.100	1900	304.1	78.2	.257
1881	410.7	33.9	.082	1901	331.1	96.8	.292*
1882	498.8	45.5	.091	1902	466.4	100.0	.214
1883	363.9	53.7	.147	1903	613.1	132.9	.217
1884	308.5	68.9	.223	1904	549.1	209.2	.381*
1885	226.4	104.0	.459*	1905	724.9	210.3	.290
1886	200.7	78.5	.391	1906	764.5	179.9	.235
1887	306.7	67.1	.219	1907	930.0	215.0	.231
1888	345.4	77.8	.225	1908	506.9	378.2	.746*
1889	263.0	95.7	.364*	1909	520.0	199.9	.384

[a]From U. S. Bureau of Statistics, *Arrivals of Alien Passengers and Immigrants into the United States from 1820-1892* (pamphlet); the Monthly Summary of Commerce and Finance, June, 1903, pp. 4362-64; and the *Statistical Abstract of the United States.*
[b]No data published for 1896 and 1897.
*Peaks in the ratio.

Let us turn to the more detailed picture of emigration afforded by the monthly statistics of emigration which are available for the period beginning with July, 1907.

Net Alien Arrivals, by Months.

In Chart 18 we have a representation of the net increase or decrease in population through the arrival or departure of aliens, both immigrant and nonimmigrant, emigrant and nonemigrant. The net movement for both sexes is shown by the solid silhouette—that for alien males only, by the double line which traverses the silhouette and occasionally falls below it. Broadly speaking, this curve reveals the tendency of the net movement to correlate directly

CHART 18*

NET ALIEN MOVEMENT
(Arrivals less Departures)
By Months

Black = Both Sexes
White Line = Males

Both Sexes   Alien Males

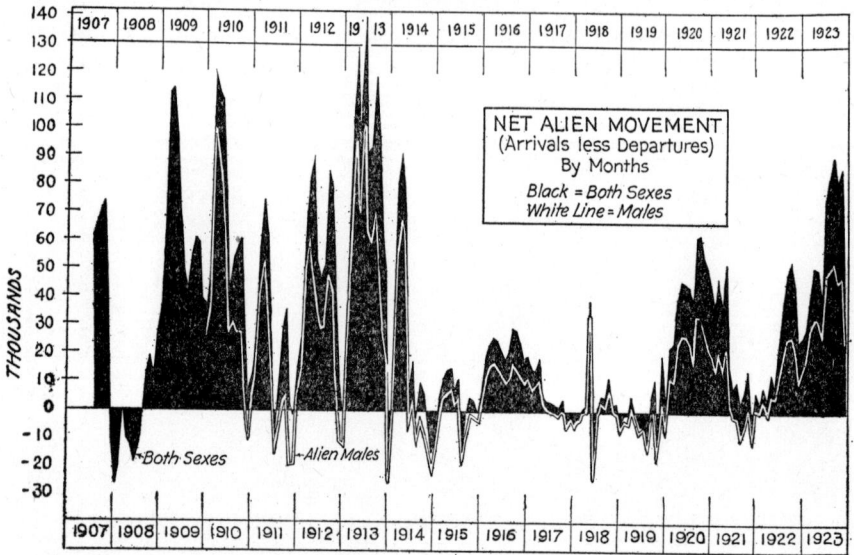

*Numerical data in Tables 23 and 24.

TABLE 23.—NET ALIEN ARRIVALS, BY MONTHS, JULY, 1907, TO DECEMBER, 1923*

Alien immigrants and nonimmigrants less alien emigrants and nonemigrants, of both sexes.
Thousands of persons.

Year	Total for Year	Jan.	Feb.	Mar.	Apr.	May	June	July	Aug.	Sept.	Oct.	Nov.	Dec.
1907	......	......	......	......	......	......	......	61.3	66.8	71.6	73.7	38.2	d11.3
1908	d41.2	d27.2	d20.4	*	d10.5	d13.0	d19.4	d14.4	d 8.0	12.8	18.8	12.4	27.7
1909	802.7	36.9	66.9	112.5	114.1	95.9	68.3	50.0	43.5	55.1	61.5	58.9	39.0
1910	763.9	37.2	48.4	121.1	113.0	110.1	79.7	43.1	54.3	57.4	61.1	31.4	7.0
1911	326.0	12.8	24.5	58.1	74.4	62.5	25.4	d8.1	10.8	28.4	35.7	1.7	d0.2
1912	646.7	15.6	25.6	67.8	80.9	90.3	53.3	47.7	51.4	85.2	79.3	38.0	11.8
1913	1018.0	d1.8	41.2	90.4	129.7	102.3	140.3	91.9	93.6	118.8	98.5	63.1	50.1
1914	262.9	d16.1	21.4	80.1	92.0	69.1	6.9	17.1	d 2.9	9.9	5.8	d 5.4	d15.1
1915	43.0	d10.9	4.5	11.2	14.1	14.7	7.0	11.1	d14.3	d 2.0	4.9	3.3	d 0.6
1916	263.9	7.3	19.4	23.8	26.1	24.7	22.2	18.2	21.4	29.3	28.3	24.2	18.8
1917	80.7	19.6	14.7	14.1	18.8	5.3	3.6	2.8	2.2	1.7	3.8	d 4.5	d 1.5
1918	41.5	d 4.1	d 3.7	0.6	1.5	39.3	d19.6	0.4	5.6	4.8	12.0	2.3	2.4
1919	4.6	d 5.1	d 1.4	d 1.2	5.5	d 0.3	d 4.1	d 5.7	d 9.3	4.9	11.3	d 9.8	19.9
1920	495.1	3.2	22.6	24.2	40.2	46.3	45.8	44.5	36.7	62.3	63.2	54.8	51.3
1921	280.1	45.9	37.9	47.9	38.0	52.6	16.9	8.6	10.4	3.1	7.0	15.0	d 3.2
1922	277.4	7.0	3.2	8.8	4.2	13.7	9.3	22.4	35.5	49.8	53.4	44.9	25.2
1923	706.8	26.8	29.9	42.7	51.4	50.5	40.5	76.3	83.2	91.3	82.4	86.9	44.9

*A portion of the above table is compiled from unpublished statistics made available by the courtesy of the U. S. Bureau of Immigration; the balance is based upon data also compiled by the Bureau of Immigration and appearing in the following publications: U. S. Bureau of Immigration and Naturalization, *Immigration Statement and Inward Passenger Movement* (July, 1907, to February, 1909, inclusive); *Immigration Bulletin* (March, 1909, to December, 1917, inclusive); *U. S. Immigration Service Bulletin* (April 1, 1918, to August 1, 1919); and the *Annual Reports* of the Commissioner General of Immigration. For some portions of the post-war period the monthly data were obtained from the U. S. Bureau of Labor Statistics, *Monthly Labor Review.*

d—excess of departures over arrivals.
*—Less than 50.

TABLE 24.—NET MALE ALIEN ARRIVALS, BY MONTHS, JANUARY, 1910, TO DECEMBER, 1923*

Male alien immigrants and nonimmigrants less male alien emigrants and nonemigrants

Thousands of Persons

YEAR	TOTAL FOR YEAR	JAN.	FEB.	MAR.	APR.	MAY	JUNE	JULY	AUG.	SEPT.	OCT.	NOV.	DEC.
1910	503.8	26.1	37.3	99.1	90.0	82.5	56.5	26.4	31.3	27.5	27.7	8.4	d 9.2
1911	112.5	4.0	14.0	41.9	51.9	37.6	11.5	d 14.5	d 3.5	3.0	5.8	d 19.7	d 19.5
1912	367.4	5.0	14.4	48.6	56.7	60.7	35.5	29.4	30.1	47.6	41.9	8.2	d 10.7
1913	638.3	d 13.0	25.4	64.0	95.9	71.9	101.5	63.7	59.8	69.8	51.5	29.7	18.2
1914	89.5	d 24.7	9.5	57.2	67.1	42.0	d 4.8	2.5	d 11.5	d 3.5	d 8.5	d 14.6	d 21.1
1915	d 24.0	d 14.1	0.2	4.5	6.5	7.8	2.0	4.5	d 17.9	d 9.3	d 2.2	d 2.2	3.8
1916	152.1	3.2	11.9	15.7	17.0	15.5	13.1	9.8	11.5	17.3	14.6	13.0	9.4
1917	32.8	11.7	7.9	8.7	11.3	2.7	0.5	d 0.1	d 0.6	d 1.5	0.4	d 5.4	2.9
1918	8.6	d 5.5	d 3.3	d 1.4	d 0.1	35.4	d 24.7	d 1.6	2.6	1.0	6.7	d *	d 0.4
1919	d 61.1	d 6.5	d 3.4	d 4.3	1.0	d 3.6	d 7.7	d 7.9	d 12.5	d 3.8	0.6	15.9	4.0
1920	255.4	d 6.6	11.9	10.6	24.5	27.3	27.1	24.9	17.5	34.2	33.4	28.0	22.4
1921	70.0	19.6	15.1	21.4	15.1	22.1	2.7	d 1.8	d 2.0	d 8.1	d 5.2	0.8	d 9.6
1922	132.4	0.9	d 0.1	3.5	d 0.9	6.0	5.0	13.1	18.6	25.9	27.0	22.1	11.2
1923	428.4	15.0	18.8	29.5	33.4	33.1	26.8	48.5	51.3	53.1	45.7	48.8	24.4

*For sources of data see Table 23.
d =excess of departures over arrivals.
* =less than 50.

with business conditions. The depression periods of 1907 to 1908, 1911, 1913 to 1914, 1919, and 1921 to 1922, all show a net emigration, preceded, except in 1919, by a relatively large net immigration. The seasonal movement is not eliminated from this chart and, consequently, some of the lower points toward the end of each year are largely due to the normal coincidence of low immigration and high emigration in the late fall.

Before endeavoring to make a more refined analysis of the relation of net immigration to employment conditions, let us note briefly the characteristics of the cyclical fluctuations in monthly male emigration in the few years prior to the war for which such data are available.

Male Emigration: 1910-1914.

The cyclical fluctuations in emigration are the inverse of the cyclical fluctuations in immigration. When industry booms, immigration increases and emigration decreases; when industry is dull, immigration declines and emigration increases. This inverse correlation of the inflow and outflow of aliens may be illustrated by comparing the monthly data in Chart 19 for male immigrants, male emigrants, and pig iron production, all three series being adjusted so as to eliminate the typical influence of seasonal factors.

Through 1910 immigration and production are, on the whole, declining, and emigration increasing. In 1911 production recovers temporarily, declines again, and then begins a steady recovery; immigration exhibits a clear depression, from which recovery begins in September; while emigration shows a distinct boom, with a decided decline in September. In 1912 and 1913 the inverse relation-

CHART 19

CYCLICAL MOVEMENTS IN EMIGRATION, IMMIGRATION, AND PIG IRON PRODUCTION

Three-month moving average

Unit = one standard deviation

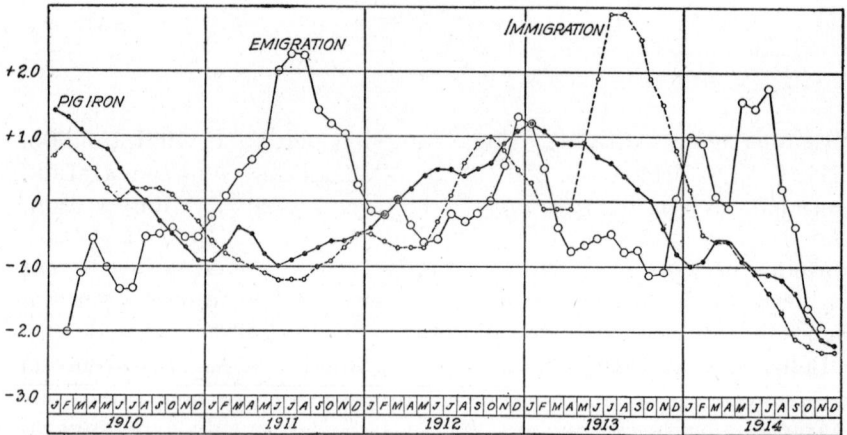

a The numerical data for the immigration curve are in Appendix Table III; for the emigration curve, in Table 25; and the data for the pig iron curve are computed from Appendix Table VI. The immigration and pig iron curves represent deviations from trends; the emigration curve, deviations from the mean for the period.

ship, though still evident, is less perfect. In 1912 both production and immigration rise, but immigration suffers a setback at the close of the year, while emigration after a mild decline in the first part of the year rises toward the close. In 1913 production declines steadily, immigration rises to a sharp but briefly maintained peak, while emigration declines until about the end of the year. In 1914 immigration is low and emigration high during the first seven months, after which, under war conditions, both decline.

TABLE 25.—CYCLES IN MALE EMIGRATION, BY MONTHS: 1910-1914ᵃ

Three-month moving average of percentage deviations from the mean for the period, expressed as multiples of their standard deviation (19.1 per cent).

YEAR AND MONTH	DEVIATION	YEAR AND MONTH	DEVIATION
1910		1912	
Jan.............	....	July...........	—0.2
Feb............	—2.0	Aug............	—0.3
Mar...........	—1.1	Sept...........	—0.2
Apr............	—0.6	Oct............	.0
May...........	—1.0	Nov...........	+0.6
June..........	—1.4	Dec............	+1.3
July..........	—1.3	1913	
Aug.	—0.5		
Sept...........	—0.5	Jan............	+1.2
Oct.	—0.4	Feb............	+0.5
Nov...........	—0.6	Mar...........	—0.4
Dec...........	—0.5	Apr...........	—0.8
		May...........	—0.7
1911		June	—0.6
Jan............	—0.2	July	—0.5
Feb...........	+0.1	Aug............	—0.8
Mar...........	+0.4	Sept...........	—0.7
Apr.	+0.6	Oct............	—1.1
May..........	+0.9	Nov...........	—1.1
June	+2.0	Dec............	+0.1
July..........	+2.3	1914	
Aug.	+2.3	Jan.	+1.0
Sept...........	+1.4	Feb............	+0.9
Oct............	+1.2	Mar...........	+0.1
Nov...........	+1.0	Apr...........	—0.1
Dec...........	+0.3	May..........	+1.6
		June..........	+1.5
1912		July	+1.8
Jan............	—0.2	Aug...........	+0.2
Feb...........	—0.2	Sept...........	—0.4
Mar...........	.0	Oct............	—1.6
Apr...........	—0.4	Nov...........	—1.9
May..........	—0.6	Dec............	.....
June..........	—0.6		

ᵃComputed from monthly emigration statistics in the U. S. Bureau of Immigration and Naturalization, *Immigration Bulletin* (monthly).

The Volume of Unemployment and the Volume of Immigration.

The analysis in the preceding sections has indicated rather clearly that fluctuations in both emigration and immigration are closely related to employment conditions in this country.

The question next arises as to the extent to which the volume of immigration is numerically comparable with the contemporaneous volume of unemployment. It is obvious that the inadequacy of the data available makes a precise answer to this question impossible, particularly for the earlier years.   However, the available estimates are probably accurate enough to establish within reasonable limits of error the volume relation between migration and unemployment.

Professor Hornell Hart has made an estimate of the numbers unemployed in non-agricultural occupations by months from 1902 to 1917, which will serve for a preliminary comparison of the volume of immigration and the estimated volume of unemployment.[5] There is, as suggested above, necessarily a considerable margin of error in these estimates and consequently they should be looked upon, not as giving a refined measure of the volume of unemployment, but as an approximation probably sufficiently close to the truth to permit rough comparisons to be made with a reasonable degree of accuracy.

Upon what basis should the volume of immigration and employment be compared?

Immigration is Appropriately Compared with Changes in the Volume of Employment.

Immigration represents an addition to the supply of labor over a period of time, and, as to numerical volume, is logically comparable, not so much with the amount of unemployment existing at a given time, as with the change in the number unemployed over the same period of time.   This principle may be illustrated by making the assumption that the domestic labor supply is kept regularly employed, with no seasonal or cyclical unemployment.   Under such conditions, any changes in the volume of employment would represent additions to or subtractions from the labor supply by migration.   Thus, with migratory workers as the sole fluctuating element in employment, there would be perfect correlation between the fluctuations in migration and those in employment.   An increase of 100,000 in the number employed would be accompanied by a net immigration of 100,000; a decrease of 50,000 in employment, by a net emigration of 50,000.

But under conditions as they actually exist, employment changes do not correlate perfectly in numbers with migration, and the discrepancy represents either a failure of the immigrants to obtain employment or a change in the number of domestic workers employed.   If the net migration is always less than the employment change, but in the same direction—for example, if an excess of

[5]For a somewhat fuller description of this estimate, see Chapter III.

emigrants over immigrants is concurrent with an increase in the number unemployed—then migration is clearly an alleviation rather than a primary direct cause of fluctuations in unemployment in the host country. On the other hand, if the net migration of workers exceeds in number the employment change, or is contrary in direction, it is clearly a disturbing factor.

Net migration is obviously the most significant basis for volume comparisons; but, particularly where emigration is not known, the volume of arrivals is important as indicating the magnitude of the absorption task as compared with the current tendencies in employment. Even if the number of arriving immigrants is balanced by an equal number of departing emigrants, it is scarcely to be assumed that the necessary employment adjustments are made without considerable loss of time to the worker and disturbance to industry.

But over what period shall the change in employment and migration be compared? A week, a month, a quarter year, a year, a decade, the period of decline in employment, or the duration of a depression? The answer will depend upon the particular purpose to be served. If the purpose is to show the adjustment of migration to seasonal variations in employment, or to the combined effects of cyclical, seasonal, and other forces, a month-to-month comparison may be pertinent. If it is desired to eliminate in part the erratic month-to-month fluctuations, and yet to restrict the analysis to the effect of relatively current immigration, a three-month comparison is appropriate. If from January to March, inclusive, employment falls off 50,000, and 100,000 working immigrants arrive, it is obvious that their arrival is not well timed and apt to aggravate the unemployment situation. To eliminate seasonal factors, comparisons over twelve-month periods are suitable. In considering a given depression period, it would appear worth while to ascertain the cumulative volume of migration either during the period of decline, or, to change the point of view somewhat, during the depression period—defined herein, ordinarily, as the period during which employment is below its computed trend. It would be somewhat unduly dogmatic to insist that any one of the bases of comparison just mentioned is, in all cases, the most logical. It is worth noting what results are obtained from the use of each of them, and consequently, in the various volume comparisons in this chapter, no invariable basis of cumulation has been adhered to. Accordingly, the reader should in each case take into consideration the basis upon which the given comparison rests.

In Chart 20, we have a comparison on a twelve-month basis;

CHART 20

CUMULATIVE MIGRATION AND HART'S ESTIMATE OF CHANGES IN UNEMPLOYMENT IN NON-AGRICULTURAL OCCUPATIONS[a]

Totals for twelve months ending in given month

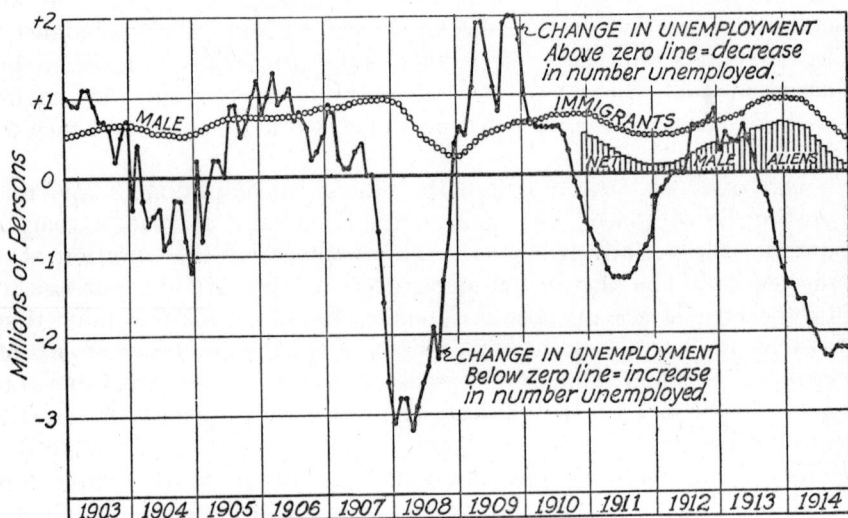

[a]Sources: Male immigrants computed from Appendix Table II.
Net alien arrivals computed from Table 24.
Unemployment change, computed from estimates made by Professor Hornell Hart, see Chapter III.

that is, each point on the male immigration curve represents the aggregate immigration of the preceding twelve months (including the given month) and each point on the unemployment curve represents the *increase* or *decrease* in the number unemployed in non-agricultural pursuits, as estimated by Professor Hart. For example, in the twelve months ending in January, 1903, unemployment is estimated to have decreased one million and in the same twelve months 527,000 male immigrants arrived. It should be noted that on this chart when the unemployment curve is below the line, it represents an increase in unemployment; when above, a decrease.

Net Male Immigration.

Male emigration statistics are available beginning with January, 1910. Beginning in December, 1910, the vertical bars in Chart 20 show, for each twelve-month period ending with the given month, the excess of arriving over departing male aliens (including both permanent and temporary migrants), hereinafter referred to as net alien male arrivals.

What conclusions can be drawn from the facts shown in Chart 20 concerning the volume relation between unemployment and migration?

In the first place, gross male immigration, disregarding emigration, ordinarily numbered several hundred thousand each twelve months, even in periods like 1911 when unemployment was increasing, and hence represents a volume of immigration which, if not offset by emigration, is large enough to materially aggravate the unemployment situation.

Secondly, the net arrivals of alien males, cumulated over twelve-month periods, show always an excess of arrivals over departures, even in 1911 when the twelve-month change in unemployment shows increases in the numbers unemployed; that is, in each of the twelve-month periods in which unemployment had increased and data on net arrivals are available, migration was evidently aggravating the situation by adding to the number of available workers.

Lastly, in other twelve-month periods, unemployment is decreasing while there is a net excess of arrivals, and in these periods it may be that immigration should be looked upon as increasing in response to an increasing demand for labor. For example, for the twelve-month periods ending in the latter part of 1912 and the early part of 1913, a substantial net immigration is accompanied by a decrease in unemployment.

With this preliminary consideration of the relative volume of unemployment and immigration for the years 1903 to 1914 in mind, let us now return to a consideration of the conditions existing during selected depression periods, beginning with that of 1908.

Depression of 1908.

The depression of 1908 affords the first opportunity for a close study of the *net* movement of migration during a business cycle, inasmuch as the publication of emigration statistics by months

began in July, 1907, shortly before the signs of the depression began
to be evident.

Chart 21 portrays the movement of gross and net immigration

CHART 21

COMPARISON OF CUMULATIVE IMMIGRATION AND EMIGRATION WITH
FACTORY EMPLOYMENT IN THE 1908 DEPRESSION*

*Number arriving or departing while employment curve is below its
trend*

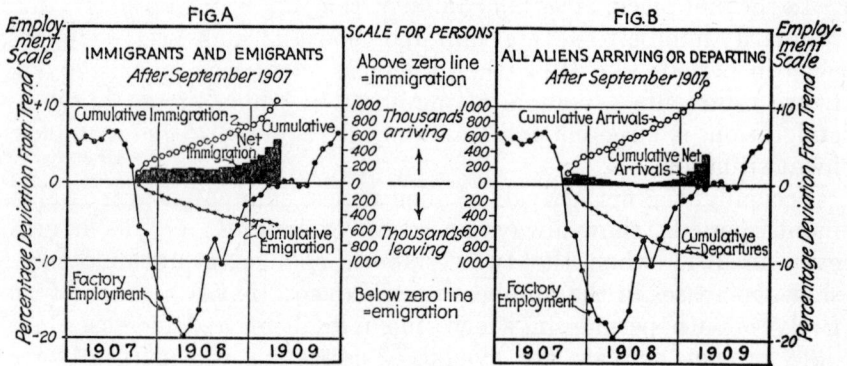

*Plotted from numerical data in Table 26 and computations based upon Appendix
Table IV.

during the period of the depression, which is defined as the period
during which our factory curve remained below its computed trend,
or from October, 1907, to February, 1909, inclusive. In addition
to the employment cycle curve, the left-hand section of the chart
shows the total number of alien immigrants arrived after September, 1907, to the end of each respective month, and also the net
alien immigration when the number of emigrants is deducted from
the cumulative total for immigration. Too much importance should
not be assigned to the apparent relative magnitude of the employment and migration fluctuations as the scales are necessarily somewhat arbitrary. They are so chosen that the vertical unit for 100,000
persons is the same as that for a one per cent deviation of employment from its computed trend.

The right-hand section of the chart is similar to the left-hand
section, except that the movement of all aliens, both immigrant
and non-immigrant, emigrant and non-emigrant, is shown.

TABLE 26.—CUMULATIVE MIGRATION DURING THE 1908 DEPRESSION[a]

(Thousands)

YEAR AND MONTH	A IMMI-GRANTS	B EMIGRANTS	C NET A-B	D ALL ALIEN ARRIVALS	E ALL ALIEN DEPART-URES	F NET D-E
1907						
Oct.	111.5	28.6	+ 82.9	129.6	55.8	+ 73.7
Nov.	229.0	78.0	+151.0	262.2	150.3	+111.9
Dec.	295.6	124.0	+171.6	339.3	238.7	+100.6
1908						
Jan.	322.8	161.6	+161.1	372.4	298.9	+ 73.4
Feb.	346.2	191.4	+154.8	402.6	349.6	+ 53.0
Mar.	378.7	217.0	+161.7	446.2	393.1	+ 53.1
Apr.	420.0	255.8	+164.1	501.4	458.8	+ 42.6
May	456.3	287.7	+168.6	549.6	520.1	+ 29.5
June	488.2	320.6	+167.7	590.7	580.6	+ 10.2
July	515.8	351.3	+164.5	627.9	632.1	− 4.2
Aug.	543.6	379.8	+163.8	667.5	679.7	− 12.2
Sept.	581.8	404.7	+177.1	724.1	723.5	+ 0.6
Oct.	622.8	428.0	+194.8	784.8	765.5	+ 19.4
Nov.	659.9	449.0	+210.9	835.8	804.1	+ 31.7
Dec.	705.9	465.4	+240.5	896.9	837.5	+ 59.4
1909						
Jan.	749.8	475.9	+273.9	951.9	855.5	+ 96.3
Feb.	816.9	484.5	+332.4	1033.9	870.6	+163.2
Mar.	929.9	498.6	+431.4	1168.9	893.2	+275.7
Apr.	1046.7	513.1	+533.6	1307.3	917.5	+389.8

[a]Defined as from October, 1907, to April, 1909, during which period our index of factory employment in selected states was below its computed trend. For sources of the data in this table, see Table 23. Employment is only slightly below trend in March and April of 1909.

Comparison of Fluctuations.

Immigration, while partially checked, never ceased during the depression of 1907-1908. From October, 1907, to February, 1909, the depression period as delimited by us, over 800,000 immigrant aliens arrived, half of them while employment was still on the decline. On the other hand, emigration greatly increased after the depression set in, reducing the net migration during the fifteen months under consideration to 332,000.

The statistics just cited deal only with those officially classified as immigrants and emigrants. In the right-hand section of the chart a more complete picture is shown by including the alien non-immigrant and nonemigrant groups, a large proportion of which are in this country for employment though they are not classed as being here for a permanent sojourn. The noteworthy difference in the two sections of Chart 21 is that when nonemigrants are included the departures of aliens were so numerous from December, 1907, to August, 1908, inclusive, that there was practically a continuous excess of alien departures over arrivals, suggesting that the temporary element in the alien population is more susceptible to changes in employment conditions than those aliens officially classified as immigrants.

The Depression of 1911.

The year 1910 was marked by a gradual decline into a mild depression in 1911, and dullness continued through the first few months of 1912. In 1911 crops were very poor, but in 1912 they were much better, and the industrial dullness in the early months of that year gave way to a great activity in the latter part of the year, accompanied by reports of labor scarcity. The depression of 1911 is not marked in the Federal Reserve Bank's clearings index, nor does it appear as a below-trend period in our three-state index of factory employment, though this index does show a relatively continuous decline from the peak in January, 1910, to the middle of 1912. The movement is shown more distinctly as a depression in the fluctuations of pig iron production and in the male immigration curve.

Net Male Alien Arrivals and Changes in the Number Unemployed.

In the depression of 1911 we have an opportunity for the first time to study the net immigration of males by months. In Table 27 and Chart 22 we have a comparison designed to make clear the numerical proportion between changes in the number unemployed in non-agricultural pursuits, as estimated by Professor Hart, and the net additions to the working population through migration. For this purpose the number of alien male immigrants and nonimmigrants combined, less the number of alien male emigrants and nonemigrants, has been taken to represent the industrially significant net immigration. It will be recalled that somewhat similar comparisons have been made with the same data for twelve-month periods from 1903 to 1914 (Chart 20). The present discussion merely presents the same data in a different manner.

In the left-hand section of Chart 22 the comparison is between the net arrivals for three-month periods and the net change in numbers unemployed in the same three-month periods. In this chart unemployment is inverted, that is to say, a decrease in unemployment is represented by a bar above the line; whereas an excess of arrivals is plotted above the line, an excess of departures, below. Hence, if an increase in unemployment is accompanied by an excess of departures, the two sets of bars will be found on the same side of the zero line, if by an excess of arrivals, on opposite sides. For example, in the three months ending in March, 1911,

CHART 22

NET ARRIVALS OF ALIEN MALES COMPARED WITH CHANGES IN THE
NUMBER UNEMPLOYED IN NON-AGRICULTURAL OCCUPATIONS:
1911-1912 DEPRESSION[a]

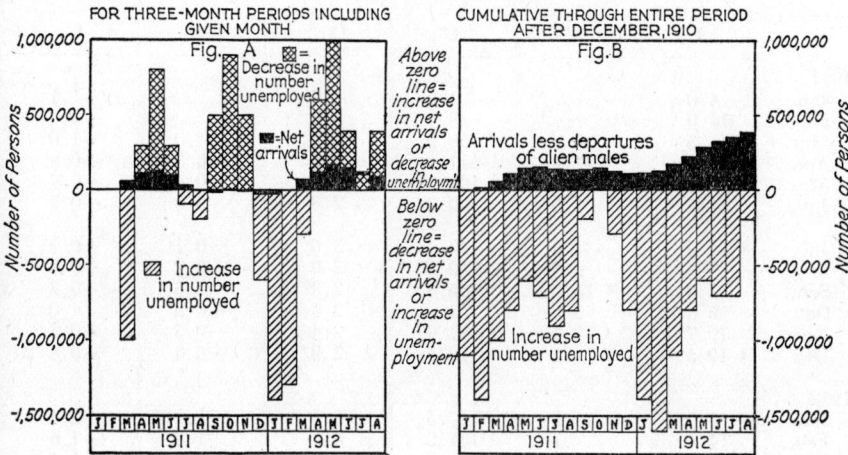

[a]Numerical data in Table 27.

the net immigration of alien males was about 60,000, but in the same period unemployment increased by about 1,100,000 and hence is represented by a bar projecting below the zero line.

In nine of the eleven three-month periods in which there is shown a decrease in the number unemployed, there was a net excess of arrivals over departures; in four of the seven periods in which unemployment increased, there was a net excess of departures over arrivals. To this extent the direction of the net movement in immigration may be considered as responsive to changes in employment conditions. But only in the period ending in July, 1912, are the numbers of net arrivals substantially equal to the net change

in the number unemployed. On the whole, in these three-month
periods, the volume of net immigration is much smaller than the
contemporaneous changes in the number unemployed.

TABLE 27.—NET ALIEN MALE MIGRATION AND CHANGE IN NUMBER EMPLOYED
IN NON-AGRICULTURAL OCCUPATIONS: DEPRESSION OF
1911-1912

YEAR AND MONTH	NET MIGRATION OF ALIEN MALES (THOUSANDS)[a]			HART'S ESTIMATE OF NUMBER UNEMPLOYED IN NON-AGRICULTURAL OCCUPATIONS (MILLIONS)[b]		
	IN SPECIFIED MONTH	SPECIFIED AND TWO PRECEDING MONTHS	TOTAL AFTER DEC. 1910	IN SPECIFIED MONTH	CHANGE IN 3 MONTHS ENDING IN SPECIFIED MONTH	CHANGE AFTER DEC. 1910
	A	B	C	D	E	F
1911						
Jan.	4.0	.....	4.0	3.2	.....	+1.1
Feb.	14.0	.....	18.0	3.5	.....	+1.4
Mar.	41.9	59.9	59.9	3.1	+1.0	+1.0
Apr.	51.9	107.7	111.8	2.9	—0.3	+0.8
May	37.6	131.3	149.3	2.7	—0.8	+0.6
June	11.5	101.0	160.9	2.8	—0.3	+0.7
July	d 14.5	34.6	146.4	3.0	+0.1	+0.9
Aug.	d 3.5	d 6.5	142.8	2.9	+0.2	+0.8
Sept.	3.0	d 15.0	145.8	2.3	—0.5	+0.2
Oct.	5.8	5.2	151.6	2.1	—0.9	.0
Nov.	d 19.7	d 10.9	131.9	2.4	—0.5	+0.3
Dec.	d 19.5	d 33.4	112.5	2.9	+0.6	+0.8
1912						
Jan.	5.0	d 34.1	117.5	3.5	+1.4	+1.4
Feb.	14.4	d .1	131.9	3.7	+1.3	+1.6
Mar.	48.6	68.0	180.4	3.2	+0.3	+1.1
Apr.	56.7	119.6	237.1	2.9	—0.6	+0.8
May	60.7	166.0	297.8	2.7	—1.0	+0.6
June	35.5	152.9	333.3	2.8	—0.4	+0.7
July	29.4	125.6	362.7	2.8	—0.1	+0.7
Aug.	30.1	95.0	392.8	2.3	—0.4	+0.2

[a]From data in Table 24. Columns B and C computed from A.
[b]From Hornell Hart, *Fluctuations in Unemployment in Cities of the United States, 1902 to 1917*, Studies
rom the Helen S. Trounstine Foundation, Volume I, Number 2.
    Columns E and F were computed from D.
    d = Excess of departures over arrivals.

In the right-hand section of Chart 22 there is shown, by months,
the cumulated number of net arrivals of male aliens beginning with
January, 1911, and the change in the number unemployed in non-
agricultural pursuits in the given month as compared with De-

cember, 1910. In both cases, we are dealing with the raw data uncorrected for trend or seasonal variation. It is obvious from this chart that during this period, in which the number of unemployed is estimated to have been, on the average, several hundred thousand greater than in December, 1910, the number of arriving male aliens exceeded those leaving by nearly 400,000.

The Pre-War Decline of 1913 and 1914.

Prior to the outbreak of the Great War, employment had been on the decline continuously, aside from brief recovery movements, since the early part of 1913. On the other hand, during several months in 1913 immigration was unusually large; but it also began to decline sharply toward the end of 1913. A statement of the cumulative number of arrivals, and also of arrivals less departures, is given in Table 28, beginning in March, 1913, when the employ-

TABLE 28—THE PRE-WAR DECLINE OF 1913-1914

Cumulative number of arrivals and departures since February, 1913*

(Thousands)

YEAR AND MONTH	ALIEN ARRIVALS				ALIEN ARRIVALS LESS DEPARTURES			
	MALE IMMIGRANTS	MALE NON-IMMI-GRANTS	TOTAL MALES	TOTAL BOTH SEXES	MALE IMMIGRANTS LESS EMIGRANTS	MALE NON-IMMI-GRANTS LESS NON-EMI-GRANTS	TOTAL MALES	TOTAL BOTH SEXES
	A	B	C	D	E	F	G	H
1913								
Mar.	69.2	18.6	87.7	121.2	56.9	7.1	64.0	90.4
Apr.	168.9	49.2	218.1	296.4	142.4	17.5	159.8	220.0
May	266.3	70.0	336.2	461.1	225.9	5.8	231.7	322.4
June	391.1	86.5	477.6	659.6	334.6	—1.3	333.3	462.6
July	485.8	98.2	584.0	814.2	410.3	—13.4	396.9	554.5
Aug.	570.4	109.0	679.4	956.8	477.6	—20.9	456.7	648.1
Sept.	657.4	120.4	777.8	1113.5	549.7	—23.2	526.5	766.9
Oct.	740.3	130.7	871.0	1266.6	611.1	—33.1	578.0	865.3
Nov.	805.8	138.5	944.3	1383.6	653.3	—45.6	607.7	928.4
Dec.	864.9	146.0	1010.9	1490.3	685.4	—59.5	625.9	978.5
1914								
Jan.	893.4	151.9	1045.3	1543.5	683.4	—82.2	601.3	962.5
Feb.	924.2	158.5	1082.7	1599.6	700.0	—89.2	610.7	983.8
Mar.	991.3	170.4	1161.7	1708.5	756.3	—88.5	667.9	1064.0
Apr.	1079.2	187.2	1266.3	1850.7	826.4	—91.5	734.9	1156.0
May	1149.0	200.9	1349.9	1977.6	878.8	—101.9	776.9	1225.0
June	1189.9	209.9	1399.8	2062.6	891.1	—119.0	772.2	1231.9
July	1222.8	217.4	1440.3	2134.7	902.9	—128.2	774.6	1249.0

*Compiled from U. S. Bureau of Immigration and Naturalization, *Immigration Bulletin* (monthly).

ment curve first shows a substantial decline, and continuing until the outbreak of the war. The first column gives the cumulative number of male "immigrants"; the second column, male "nonimmigrants"; the third column, the total of the first two columns; and the fourth column, a similar total for both sexes combined. In like manner, the right-hand half of the table gives, for the same four groups, the net movement, that is, arrivals less departures. Of these several series, the most important with reference to its bearing on the contemporaneous employment situation is probably the net movement of males, including temporary migrants, as given in Column G. It will be noted that in the seventeen months of this period, the net contribution of migration to the number of alien males in the United States was approximately three-quarters of a million. If nonimmigrants and nonemigrants are excluded from consideration, the net immigration is even greater, exceeding, slightly, nine hundred thousand males. This large volume of net immigration is chiefly due to unusually heavy immigration and light emigration during several months of 1913; but even in 1914 it is only in January and June that there is an excess of departing over arriving male aliens. It would appear that immigration, in the year before the war, contributed materially to the growing volume of unemployment as portrayed in Charts 13 and 20 on preceding pages of this chapter.[a]

CHAPTER SUMMARY[a]

The present chapter has dealt with the quarter century immediately preceding the Great War, which is, in many respects, the most significant period for the purposes of this study. The

[a]Director's Comment.—Col. M. C. Rorty, a director of the National Bureau of Economic Research, comments as follows: It would hardly seem that the fact that there is frequently, if not usually, a net immigration during periods of declining employment would, in itself, justify the conclusion that such immigration contributes to, or accentuates, unemployment. If there should be a static population in the United States, with no immigration or emigration whatever, and other economic factors were unchanged, we should presumably have business booms and depressions of the same character and intensity as we would have with a population growing at a uniform rate. Furthermore, for any uniform rate of increase in population, it would seem to be a matter of relative (economic) indifference whether the resulting annual increase in the number of (potential) workers was derived from the natural growth of the native population, or from immigration, or from a combination of the two. Immigration might involve a gradual shifting of the native-born workers from unskilled to skilled or semi-skilled occupations, but such a process, if continuous and uniform, should not involve economic disturbances of serious character.

If the preceding arguments are sound—and they appear to be supported by experience as well as by economic theory—then it might very well be argued that the effect of immigration is almost always to reduce the severity of periods of unemployment, since it is rather clear that the net movements so vary that they tend in practically all cases to *reduce the rate of increase* of the working population during periods of depression.

There are undoubtedly flaws in this last argument as well as in the opposing one. Nevertheless the nature of the problem can be made clearer in some respects by considering whether periods of unemployment would be made more or less severe in the United States if the free movement of workers between the several states should be restricted. Is there, for example, any indication, or reason to believe, that the western states have suffered more severely from business depressions and unemployment than they would if they had not received a steady influx of population from the eastern states?

The preceding points of view are in no way intended as an argument for unrestricted immigration. They are brought forward simply to suggest that an increase in unemployment is not necessarily one of the evils to be charged against it.

The preceding comments apply to several other portions of the text.

major conclusions reached in the chapter may be summarized as follows:

Sensitiveness of Migration to Business Conditions.

1. A comparison of data pertaining to male immigration, pig iron production, and factory employment, in the pre-war period, reveals the fact that cyclical fluctuations in male immigration are ordinarily associated with prior changes, in the same direction, in production and employment.

Inasmuch as good employment conditions would presumably encourage the prospective immigrant and also increase the instances in which friends and relatives in this country would remit funds for the journey, we may reasonably assume that the observed close relation is not a mere coincidence but that business conditions are in fact a dominating determinant of cyclical fluctuations in immigration.

2. The influence of a major cyclical change in industrial conditions is usually apparent in immigration within less than a half year.

3. The cyclical movements in emigration are inversely correlated with those of immigration and employment, with large emigration in depression periods and relatively small emigration in boom periods.

4. The fluctuations of *net* immigration exhibit a high degree of sensitiveness to employment conditions in the United States. This is evident when immigration and emigration are jointly considered, either in terms of the ratio of emigration to immigration, or in terms of the numerical excess of arrivals over departures or of departures over arrivals.

Relative Volume of Migration and Changes in Employment.

When we turned from a consideration of the direction and timing of turns in the cycles of immigration and emigration to the somewhat more concrete problem of the relation between the volume of immigration, gross or net, expressed in number of persons, and the concurrent change in the number employed or unemployed, we found, partly because of the diversity of the possible bases of comparison, a somewhat less secure basis upon which to form unequivocal conclusions. For example, the conclusions reached in comparing cumulative immigration with the change in employment or unemployment are materially affected by the length of the period over which the comparison is made. However, the following suggestions are worthy of note:

1. When relative numbers are under consideration, the volume of migration should be compared with the *change* in the number employed.

2. The number of incoming immigrants is sufficiently large, even in depression periods, to suggest that, even though there may be extensive emigration in the same period, the adjustment of the recent immigrant to industry is an ever-present and serious problem.

3. The cumulative volume of net immigration is seldom equal in numbers to the concurrent change in employment when periods as short as three months are considered, but in some instances is contrary in direction,—that is, an increase in unemployment is accompanied by an excess of immigrants over emigrants (Chart 22, Fig. A).

4. When cumulated over long periods, as for twelve months (Chart 20) or during the duration of a depression (Charts 21 and 22, Fig. B), it was found that only in the severe depression of 1908, and then for a brief time only, was there an excess of departures; and that in many parts of such periods there was a substantial excess of arriving over departing aliens, with a probable aggravation of the unemployment situation. The burden of such unemployment probably falls in part on the newly-arrived immigrants and in part on resident workers who are replaced by immigrants willing to work for lower wages.

CHAPTER VI

THE WAR AND POST-WAR PERIOD

The principal emphasis in this study has been placed, for somewhat obvious reasons, upon the years preceding the Great War. The pre-war period is particularly significant for our purpose because at that time, on this side of the Atlantic at least, there were fewer legal or unusual barriers to the free flow of migration in accordance with the pull of economic motives.

On the other hand, the decade just past is not to be entirely neglected. Despite the restraint and distortion due to unusual political conditions and restrictive legislation, to a considerable extent it is possible to clear away the results of such extraneous influences, and to throw still further light on the influence upon migration of cyclical variations and other economic phenomena.

THE WAR PERIOD: 1914-1918

For our purpose, the years from the outbreak of the war to the conclusion of the armistice are relatively inconsequential. Ordinary migratory movements were hindered by the hazards of ocean travel, the restraints placed upon their nationals by the belligerent countries, and similar obstacles to the normal movement of migrants.

The net result of these influences is shown in Table 29 giving the number of alien arrivals, alien departures, and the net alien movement in the war period and in a few years immediately preceding and succeeding the war.

It is evident that even before our entry into the war, the number of arrivals had shrunk to less than a third of the 1913, or peak year, total, and reached a still lower ebb in 1917 and 1918. Departures also decreased during the war, but, after the armistice, recovered more quickly than arrivals, and in 1919 the number of alien departures was within a few thousand of the number of arrivals. In fact, if we consider male aliens only, we find that the departures exceeded the arrivals by 24,045 in 1915 and by 61,090 in 1919. We must not conclude that there were no migratory movements

123

actuated by economic motives in this period. Prior to our entry into the war, a considerable fraction of the usual flow continued from neutral countries, and even from the allied countries; and the number of "immigrants" recorded from British North America increased, exceeding one hundred thousand in each of the fiscal years 1915-16, and 1916-17. The numbers from Mexico also increased, particularly if we include those admitted during and immediately following the war period by special provision waiving the literacy test and admitting for temporary conditional sojourn to help meet the demand for labor.

TABLE 29.—EFFECT OF THE WAR UPON ALIEN MIGRATION[a]

Thousands of Persons

CALENDAR YEAR	ALIEN ARRIVALS	ALIEN DEPARTURES	EXCESS OF ARRIVALS OVER DEPARTURES[b]
1913	1,617	599	1,018
1914	848	585	263
1915	328	285	43
1916	429	165	264
1917	212	131	81
1918	225	184	41
1919	397	393	5
1920	918	423	495
1921	694	414	280
1922	520	242	277
1923	906	199	707
1924	527	232	295

[a]Compiled from the publications of the United States Bureau of Immigration. Both permanent and temporary migrants are included.
[b]Apparent discrepancies of one thousand in this column compared with the difference of the first two columns is due to the fact that the differences were computed from the original data before reduction to thousands.

THE POST-WAR PERIOD

The history of migration subsequent to the armistice presents many peculiar features. Over the greater part of the period unusual forces were operating to distort fluctuations in migration from their characteristic pre-war types.

In the fiscal year ending June 30, 1919, the greater part of emigration was to Canada, Mexico, Italy, and Greece, but emigration to Europe trebled in the following immigration year, ending June 30, 1920.

On the return of transportation to something akin to normal conditions, thousands of foreign-born residents of the United States who had been forced by war conditions to postpone a trip to their former home sailed for Europe. Among these were many returning because of changed political conditions. For example, in the three fiscal years 1920, 1921, and 1922, the emigrant aliens destined to reconstituted Poland numbered over 90,000, most of them of the Polish race.

Obviously, the emigration movements of the early post-war period, at least, need close analysis for other influences before the role played by economic conditions in this country can be ascertained.

Tardy Recovery of Immigration.

Immigration, likewise, was somewhat slow to recover, not quite reaching the two hundred and fifty thousand mark in 1919 (calendar year). The incoming movement, however, exhibited a growing momentum and reached a total of over seven hundred thousand in the calendar year 1920, not including nonimmigrants; and even in 1921, despite industrial depression, did not drop below 50,000 per month until June, 1921, by which time the three per centum quota law had gone into effect.

This law was apparently due, in part at least, to the fear that the volume of immigration in 1920 was but an indication of the growing momentum of a flood of immigrants which had been dammed up by war conditions and which now, spurred by actual or impending economic and political chaos in Europe, threatened to inundate this country with an unprecedented volume of aliens.

Whatever the facts may be concerning the probability of the expected inundation, steps were taken in the law of May, 1921, which make the disentanglement of the economic trends in the subsequent period more than usually difficult. Because the quotas began to be available in July, and twenty per cent of the quota of any country could be admitted in a single month, the law has tended to concentrate the arrivals in the second half of the calendar year, thus creating a seasonal movement materially different from that characteristic of the pre-war period, and obscuring the effects of industrial prosperity and depression except for those countries which were obviously falling short of the quota or, like Canada and Mexico, were not subject to the law.

Male Immigration.

The course of male immigration during the war and post-war period and, for the sake of comparison, a few of the pre-war years, is shown in Chart 23. The curve in this chart represents the

CHART 23

MALE IMMIGRATION: 1910-1924.

Three-month moving average of index, adjusted for seasonal variation, with base 1910 = 100

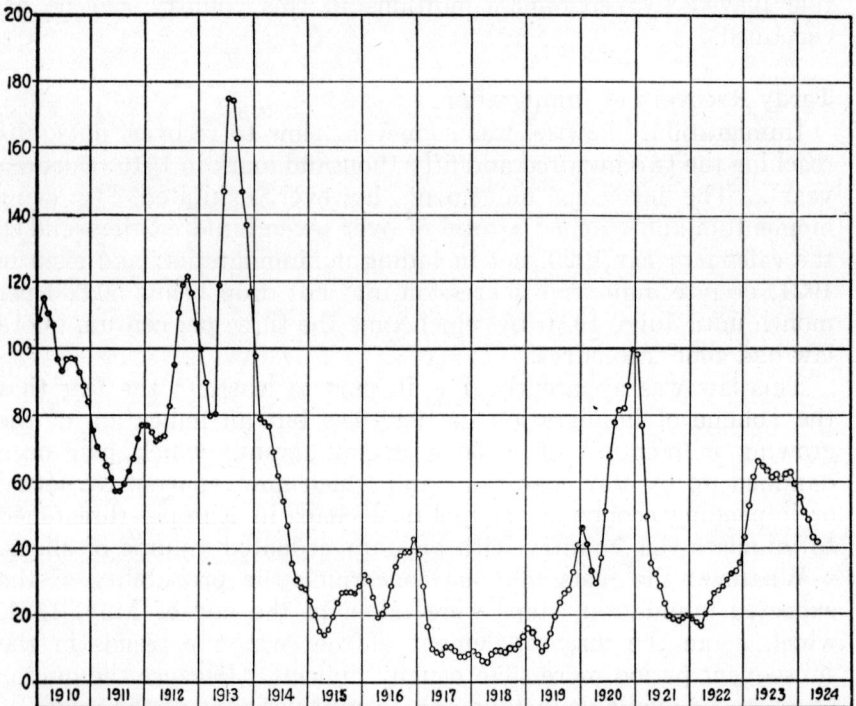

.Numerical data in Table 30.

changes in the numbers of those officially recorded as male immigrants, after adjustment has been made for the typical seasonal variation. The tendency for the quota law to concentrate the greater part of immigration in the months of July to November required the computation of a special seasonal correction for the years beginning in July, 1921, in order that the curve as shown might be free as far as possible from mere seasonal fluctuations.

The depression of 1911, the long decline just before and in the early part of the war, the low ebb during the war, the recovery beginning in 1919 and gaining momentum in 1920, the sharp decline in 1921, and the subsequent recovery in 1923, modified doubtless by the quota restrictions—all show up clearly on this chart.

Chart 23 furnishes the general picture of the war and post-war period. The details of the movement of migration from 1919 to 1923 are set forth more clearly in subsequent paragraphs.

TABLE 30.—CYCLES IN MALE IMMIGRATION: 1910-1924[a]

Three-month moving average of index corrected for seasonal variation: 1910=100

YEAR	JAN.	FEB.	MAR.	APR.	MAY	JUNE	JULY	AUG.	SEPT.	OCT.	NOV.	DEC.
1910	109.1	115.0	110.5	107.1	96.8	93.5	96.8	97.3	96.9	93.2	88.9	84.0
1911	75.4	70.5	68.0	65.3	61.1	57.4	57.4	59.7	63.3	67.0	73.4	76.9
1912	77.0	74.9	71.9	73.0	73.9	82.9	95.4	110.6	119.2	121.5	116.5	107.7
1913	99.9	89.8	90.1	90.1	118.7	147.2	174.7	174.3	163.1	147.1	136.7	116.9
1914	97.9	79.2	77.9	76.5	69.0	61.9	54.1	46.8	35.6	30.4	28.3	27.8
1915	24.3	20.0	15.3	14.2	15.8	19.5	23.8	26.6	26.9	27.1	26.7	29.3
1916	32.1	30.5	25.5	19.4	20.4	22.9	28.8	34.6	38.0	39.2	39.1	43.0
1917	38.4	28.7	16.6	10.0	9.1	8.6	10.4	10.4	9.6	7.9	7.8	8.6
1918	9.6	8.2	6.4	6.1	8.4	9.5	9.6	9.2	10.2	10.3	11.7	13.9
1919	16.2	14.7	12.0	9.6	11.1	14.7	19.9	23.9	26.6	27.8	33.3	41.4
1920	46.5	41.6	33.5	29.7	37.3	51.2	67.7	77.8	81.8	82.2	89.2	99.9
1921	98.3	77.6	49.7	35.6	32.4[b]	28.7	23.7	19.9	19.1	18.6	19.0	19.9
1922	19.1	18.0	17.4	20.1	23.8	26.6	27.5	28.4	30.8	32.3	33.3	35.7
1923	43.5	53.2	61.8	66.1	64.9	63.6	61.6	62.2	61.3	62.3	62.6	59.8
1924	55.5	51.0	48.6	43.7	42.0	....	....	....	....	....	....	....

[a]Computed from the data in Table II, Appendix.

[b]For the period subsequent to April, 1921, a special computation of the typical seasonal variation was made to allow for the change in the seasonal movement caused by the quota limit law.

Employment and Production Data in Post-War Period.

We have just noted that only certain elements in the migratory movement since the war have escaped material modification by non-economic forces. However, the statistical data concerning industrial conditions available for comparison are more nearly adequate than in any previous period. The years since the war have witnessed unusual activity in statistical compilation and analysis. New index numbers of employment, production, and the volume of trade have been developed; and while some of these have been extended back into earlier years, the data are most adequate for the period beginning with 1919. Also, we have in this period one severe depression period, affording an interesting basis for comparison with migratory movements.

Of the several indices of employment conditions in the years
1919 to 1923, one of the most significant for our purposes is the
"labor market" index, described in the following paragraph.

Immigration and the State of the Labor Market.

For the years 1919 to 1923, the Federal Reserve Board has published an index of the state of the labor market, based upon the
ratio of jobs to applicants in the operations of the public employment

CHART 24

CYCLES OF EMPLOYMENT AND OF MALE IMMIGRATION IN THE POST-
WAR PERIOD: 1919-1923[a]

*Deviations from the average for the period 1919-1922, seasonally
adjusted*

Unit = one standard deviation

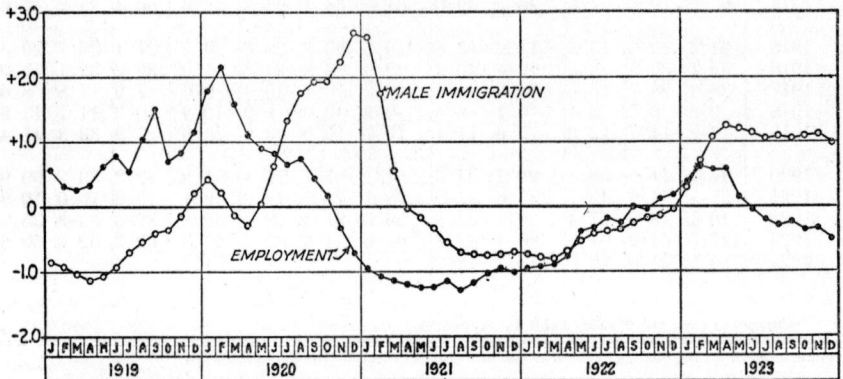

[a]Numerical data in Table 31. The employment index is computed from the ratio
of jobs to applicants in public employment offices in six states.

offices in six states: New York, Pennsylvania, Massachusetts,
Ohio, Illinois, and Wisconsin.[1]   In the period from July 1, 1918, to
June 30, 1923, over half of the total number of immigrants named
one of these six states as their intended destination.   This index is
of special interest, not only because the states in question are those
to which a large proportion of newly arrived immigrants are destined,
but also because the business of the public employment offices is
with the common laborer to a large extent, and not only with
factory labor but with construction labor as well.

[1]*Federal Reserve Bulletin*, February 1924, p. 87.

TABLE 31.—CYCLES IN THE LABOR MARKET AND IN MALE IMMIGRATION:
1919-1923

Percentage deviations from mean for 1919 to 1922, corrected for seasonal variation
and expressed in multiples of their standard deviations.

YEAR AND MONTH	LABOR MARKET[a]	MALE IM- MIGRATION[b]	YEAR AND MONTH	LABOR MARKET	MALE IM- MIGRATION
1919			**1921 (con.)**		
January....	+0.58	−0.85	July	−1.14	−0.54
February...	+0.32	−0.92	August.....	−1.29	−0.70
March.....	+0.27	−1.03	September..	−1.18	−0.73
April.......	+0.33	−1.13	October	−1.03	−0.75
May.......	+0.62	−1.07	November..	−0.96	−0.73
June.......	+0.79	−0.92	December ..	−1.01	−0.70
July	+0.55	−0.70	**1922**		
August.....	+1.04	−0.53	January....	−0.95	−0.73
September..	+1.50	−0.41	February...	−0.92	−0.78
October....	+0.70	−0.36	March	−0.90	−0.80
November..	+0.83	−0.13	April.......	−0.77	−0.69
December ..	+1.16	+0.21	May........	−0.39	−0.53
			June.......	−0.32	−0.41
1920					
January....	+1.79	+0.43	July	−0.18	−0.38
February...	+2.15	+0.22	August.....	−0.24	−0.34
March.....	+1.58	−0.12	September..	0.00	−0.24
April.......	+1.10	−0.28	October....	−0.04	−0.17
May	+0.90	+0.04	November..	+0.12	−0.13
June	+0.82	+0.62	December ..	+0.18	−0.03
July.......	+0.66	+1.32	**1923**		
August	+0.74	+1.75	January....	+0.38	+0.30
September..	+0.43	+1.92	February...	+0.62	+0.71
October....	+0.17	+1.93	March	+0.57	+1.07
November..	−0.32	+2.23	April.......	+0.58	+1.25
December ..	−0.71	+2.68	May	+0.14	+1.20
			June	−0.04	+1.15
1921					
January	−0.96	+2.61	July	−0.20	+1.06
February...	−1.07	+1.74	August	−0.29	+1.09
March.....	−1.13	+0.56	September..	−0.23	+1.05
April.......	−1.20	−0.03	October	−0.36	+1.09
May.......	−1.24	−0.17	November..	−0.33	+1.11
June	−1.24	−0.33	December ..	−0.50	+0.99

[a]*Federal Reserve Bulletin*, February, 1924, p. 87. Based upon the ratio of jobs to applicants in public employment offices.
[b]Computed from the index given in Table 30.

In Table 31 and Chart 24, the fluctuations of male immigration
and of the labor market, as computed by the Federal Reserve
Board, are compared. Both curves are corrected for typical seasonal
variation, but not for trend, and are expressed in terms of the

standard deviation from the average of the four years, 1919-1922;
hence the curves are useful only for the study of timing and not for
comparing the volume of unemployment with the volume of migration.

Lag.

The male immigration curve, it will be noted, continues to
rise for ten months after the employment curve begins to fall
early in 1920. It is true there is a temporary slump in immigration
in the early part of 1920, but it may be equally plausible to interpret
this as a reflection of some of the erratic movements of 1919 rather
than as a prompt reaction to the current decline in employment.
On the downward swing of the cycle, although the evidence is less
emphatic, immigration again seems to reach low ebb six or seven
months later than the labor market, but on the upward movement,
in the attainment of the 1923 high and the commencement of the
subsequent decline, the labor market leads immigration by only a
couple of months.

Doubtless the cyclical movement of migration after the middle
of 1921 is influenced by the quota restrictions, but no small part of
the immigration of these years came from Canada and Mexico,
which are not subject to the quota limitations. In a subsequent
section, we return to an examination of the movement of immigration from Canada.

Post-War Cyclical Movements in Male Emigration.

The post-war fluctuations in male emigration, as in immigration,
are somewhat abnormal. In 1919 emigration increased, not so
much because employment conditions were discouraging as because
many who would otherwise have returned to Europe during the
war years found in 1919 their first opportunity to revisit their native
lands. In 1920 the emigrant movement declined somewhat from
the high point reached toward the close of 1919 and the beginning
of 1920, but this decline was temporarily checked by the depression
of 1921. Since 1921, emigration has been consistently low, not
only because of the industrial recovery from the depression conditions of 1921-1922, but also because of the fact that the restriction
of the incoming flow, and the fear of those who are here that they
may be unable to return readily if they once leave, combined with
the deterring effect of unsettled political conditions and industrial
depression in European countries, have kept emigration to a minimum.

The Comparative Volume of Migration and Changes in Employment in the Depression of 1921

The major depression of the post-war period is the depression of 1921. The recession phase of this period began in 1920, and the depression continued into 1922, but for the sake of brevity we shall designate it as the depression of 1921. The delimitation of its exact duration depends upon the slope of the trend assigned to the indexes of production and industrial activity, but the satisfactory determination of trends for the short period since the war is indeed difficult. In our index of factory employment in New York and Massachusetts, the cycle of employment reached its high point in March, 1920, declined thereafter to its lowest point in January, 1921, and remained below the estimated trend until December, 1922.

Employment in the nine quarters from the first quarter of 1920 to the first quarter of 1922, inclusive, is covered by the special investigation conducted by the National Bureau of Economic Research for the President's Conference on Unemployment. The computations made by Dr. W. I. King on the basis of this investigation give the estimated average number of employees in each quarter, not only in manufacturing but also in other major industries. The estimated total number employed in the extraction of minerals, construction, and manufacturing affords the best basis of comparison with migration. These are the industries in which the great bulk of new immigrants engage.

In Table 32 and Chart 25, Fig. A, are presented data concerning the change from quarter to quarter in the average number employed in the given industries and also the net additions to the alien male population of the United States in the same period, obtained by subtracting the recorded number of outgoing males, both emigrant and nonemigrant, from the recorded number of alien male arrivals, both immigrant and nonimmigrant. Each comparison, then, is between the net alien male migration in the given quarter and the increase or decrease from the previous quarter in the number employed.

Lag.

A sharp decline in employment appears in the fourth quarter of 1920, but arrivals continue to exceed departures through that and the following two quarters. Only in the last two quarters of 1921 does the net movement of male aliens show an excess of departures.

The relatively tardy response of migration to the employment decline in 1920 and 1921, as shown in Charts 24 and 25, may be in part due to the desire of prospective immigrants to enter before the threatened restriction became effective.

CHART 25

CHANGES IN THE NUMBER EMPLOYED IN SELECTED INDUSTRIES COMPARED WITH ALIEN MALE ARRIVALS LESS DEPARTURES: DEPRESSION OF 1921ᵃ

Fig. A: During Stated Quarter.
Fig. B: Cumulatively from October 1, 1920.

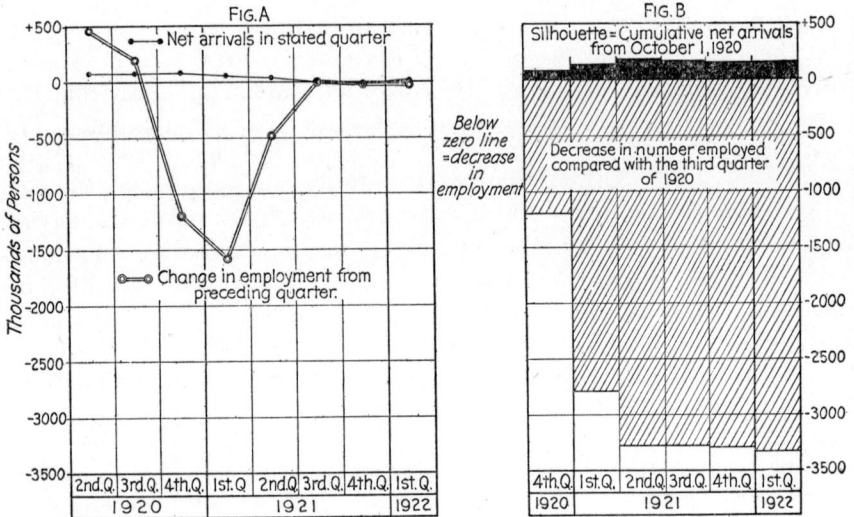

ᵃNumerical data in Table 32.

Comparative Volume.

In most of the eight quarters under consideration the volume of alien male net migration is relatively small in comparison to the concurrent change in employment. On the average, the quarterly change in employment is ten times as great as the corresponding net alien male migration.

Similarly, if we take the high quarter in 1920, that is, the third quarter, as our starting point, and compare the total net immigration of alien males after that quarter with the total change in the number employed, (Fig. B of Chart 25) we find that by the first quarter of 1922 there had been a decrease of about 3,300,000 in the number employed in mining, construction, and manufacturing, accompanied by a total net immigration after the third quarter of 1920 of 158,000.

Clearly, in the depression of 1921 the available evidence indicates that migration was a factor aggravating unemployment to some extent but was not sufficiently large in volume to be considered a major cause of unemployment.

TABLE 32.—NET MALE MIGRATION AND CHANGES IN THE VOLUME OF EMPLOYMENT IN SELECTED INDUSTRIES IN THE DEPRESSION OF
1921-1922

Unit = one thousand persons

YEAR AND QUARTER	ARRIVALS LESS DEPARTURES OF ALIEN MALES[a]		CHANGE IN NUMBER EMPLOYED[b]	
	IN GIVEN QUARTER	AFTER THE THIRD QUARTER OF 1920	FROM PRECEDING QUARTER	AFTER THE THIRD QUARTER OF 1920
1920				
1st quarter....	....	......	......	......
2d quarter.....	+79	......	+ 462	......
3rd quarter....	+77	......	+ 192	......
4th quarter....	+84	+ 84	—1,199	—1,199
1921				
1st quarter.....	+56	+140	—1,587	—2,786
2d quarter.....	+40	+180	— 485	—3,271
3d quarter.....	—12	+168	— .0	—3,271
4th quarter....	—14	+154	— 21	—3,292
1922				
1st quarter	+ 4	+158	— 38	—3,330

[a]Computed from Table 24.
[b]Based on estimates of the total number of employees on the payrolls of all establishments in the extraction of minerals, construction, and factory industries, published in *Employment Hours and Earnings in Prosperity and Depression*, Vol. 5 of the publications of the National Bureau of Economic Research, Inc.

Immigration from Canada.

The post-war movement of immigration from Canada is of special interest because the 1921 quota law did not apply to natives of Canada or to persons born in other countries who had resided there for five years, and also because the volume of immigration from that country, as shown by the official statistics of theUnited States Bureau of Immigration, reached such dimensions in this period that it aroused considerable discussion in the Canadian press.

Leaving out of consideration citizens and nonimmigrants and including only the "immigrant alien" group, the immigration in calendar years from Canada and Newfoundland[2] to the United States is recorded as follows:

Table 33

IMMIGRATION FROM CANADA

1919	81,179
1920	85,249
1921	52,929
1922	63,089
1923	182,369

When adjusted for typical seasonal variation, the curve of immigration from Canada (Chart 26) exhibits a substantial decline during the greater part of 1921; in fact, through most of 1920 a

CHART 26

CYCLES IN IMMIGRATION FROM CANADA AND IN EMPLOYMENT CONDITIONS: 1919-1923.

Unit= one standard deviation

•Numerical data in Tables 31 and 34.

slight tendency to decline is evidenced in immigration from Canada, though the general movement of immigration from all countries is still on the upgrade (See Chart 24), suggesting that the decline in

[2]At other points in our discussion of these data, we have used the term "Canada" as inclusive of all British North America.

industrial activity in the United States affected immigration from Canada more quickly than from Europe.

In Chart 26, the fluctuations of immigration into the United

TABLE 34.—EMPLOYMENT CONDITIONS IN CANADA AND IMMIGRATION THEREFROM TO THE UNITED STATES: 1919-1923

Deviations from monthly average, 1919-1923, corrected for seasonal variations, and expressed in multiples of their standard deviations.

YEAR AND MONTH	IMMIGRA-TION FROM CANADA[a]	EMPLOY-MENT IN CANADA[b]	YEAR AND MONTH	IMMIGRA-TION FROM CANADA	EMPLOY-MENT IN CANADA
1919			**1921**		
Jan.......	—0.45	+1.02	July	—0.91	—1.92
Feb......	—0.28	+0.71	Aug.....	—0.96	—2.15
Mar......	—0.39	+0.71	Sept.....	—0.97	—2.19
Apr.......	—0.43	+0.70	Oct......	—1.01	—1.06
May......	—0.65	+0.82	Nov.	—1.03	—0.78
June.....	—0.46	+0.87	Dec.....	—1.00	—1.07
July.......	0	+0.75	**1922**		
Aug......	—0.03	+0.75	Jan.	—0.97	—0.81
Sept......	+0.04	+0.90	Feb....	—0.97	—0.33
Oct.......	—0.02	+0.97	Mar.....	—0.93	—0.23
Nov.......	—0.04	+0.92	Apr.....	—0.85	—0.68
Dec......	0	+0.93	May....	—0.83	—0.45
			June....	—0.82	—0.04
1920					
Jan......	—0.21	+1.00	July	—0.72	+0.08
Feb......	—0.14	+0.96	Aug.....	—0.67	+0.12
Mar......	+0.01	+1.09	Sept.	—0.54	+0.43
Apr.......	—0.10	+1.14	Oct......	—0.13	+0.26
May......	—0.05	+1.13	Nov.....	—0.04	+0.32
June.....	—0.16	+1.01	Dec.....	+0.29	+0.54
July......	—0.25	+0.79	**1923**		
Aug.......	—0.18	+0.67	Jan.	+0.54	+0.31
Sept......	—0.22	+0.22	Feb....	+0.52	+0.49
Oct.	—0.11	—0.56	Mar.....	+0.63	+0.34
Nov.......	—0.15	—0.60	Apr.	+1.27	+0.66
Dec.......	—0.25	—0.69	May....	+1.86	+0.60
			June....	+2.13	+0.59
1921					
Jan.......	—0.18	—0.65	July....	+2.09	+0.56
Feb......	—0.48	—1.40	Aug.....	+2.09	+0.75
Mar......	—0.60	—1.63	Sept.....	+1.89	+0.80
Apr......	—0.72	—2.04	Oct.	+1.88	—0.08
May......	—0.75	—2.15	Nov.....	+3.07	+0.32
June.....	—0.86	—2.67	Dec.....	+3.16	+0.39

[a] Computed from monthly statistics prepared by the U. S. Bureau of Immigration and published in the *Monthly Labor Review*.
[b] Obtained by reversing the signs of an index of unemployment, computed from percentages of unemployment in trade unions, published in the *Canada Year Book* for 1921, 1922, and 1923, and the *Canada Labor Gazette* for February and November, 1924.

States from Canada, adjusted to eliminate the influence of typical seasonal variation, are compared with employment conditions in the United States and Canada, respectively. Employment conditions in Canada are represented by the percentage of unemployment among trade union members (with the signs reversed so that severe unemployment is represented by a depression in the curve and vice versa). Employment in the United States is represented by the "labor market" index previously described.

The major depression of 1921 and the lesser decline in 1923 are common to employment in both countries. Both are above average in 1919 and the first half of 1920, begin to decline in 1920 to a low point in 1921, with a recovery beginning in 1921 and continuing through 1922 and part of 1923, followed by a moderate decline. In 1920, the downturn in employment came about three months later in Canada than it did in the United States.

To summarize, in the years from 1919 to 1922, inclusive, immigration from Canada tended to be greatest when employment was good in both countries and to be low when employment was at a minimum. For Canada in these years, it would appear that it is good prospects in the country receiving the immigration, rather than distress in the home country of the prospective immigrant, which cause cyclical fluctuations in immigration. However, the upward movement of Canadian immigration in 1923 is not consistent with this principle, inasmuch as employment in the United States evidences a cyclical decline subsequent to April of that year. In Chapter VIII, we return to this problem of the relative influence of conditions in the country of immigration and the country of emigration.

CHAPTER SUMMARY

Fluctuations in migration in the war and post-war periods are dominated by non-economic influences to a much larger extent than in the pre-war period. Nevertheless when the effect of the economic factors has been as far as possible isolated, we find in the post-war period much the same relation between employment and migration as in the pre-war years. An increase in employment is reflected, somewhat later, in an increase in immigration and a decrease in emigration.

CHAPTER VII

CYCLICAL FLUCTUATIONS OF SELECTED ELEMENTS IN MIGRATION

The evidence presented in the preceding chapters indicates a pronounced tendency for cyclical fluctuations in immigration to, and emigration from, the United States to be determined primarily by cyclical fluctuations in industrial activity in this country. The nature of this relationship may be made clearer by comparing the cyclical movements of selected elements in migration.

For this purpose we shall make comparisons between immigrants and nonimmigrants, males and females, and laborers and other occupational groups.

PERMANENT AND TEMPORARY MIGRATION

Immigrants and Nonimmigrants.

The official statistics, as we have previously noted, distinguish between alien immigrants and alien nonimmigrants, the latter comprising aliens entering the United States for a temporary stay or returning here after a temporary sojourn abroad. Most of the popular and scientific discussion of immigration problems deals solely with the relatively permanent "immigrant" group. To the extent that the nonimmigrant group is made up of tourists and other persons not seeking employment we should expect it to show less responsiveness to cyclical changes than the "immigrant" group proper; but, on the other hand, if we could segregate those nonimmigrants who, despite a declared intention of temporary sojourn, enter for purposes of employment, we should expect the fluctuations of this working element to show, particularly as to the exodus during depression periods, even greater sensitiveness to cyclical conditions than the more permanent migration.

Prior to the present century, the recorded number of arriving aliens other than those listed as immigrants was relatively small. In the nineteenth century, the number of recorded alien nonimmigrants never exceeded fifty thousand and exceeded ten per cent

of the total number of arriving aliens only in the depression years
ending June 30, 1876, 1877, 1878, 1879, and 1894.

The ratio of nonimmigrants to total aliens, in the years ending
June 30, 1900 to 1924, is given in Table 35. Two features of this

TABLE 35.—RATIO OF NONIMMIGRANTS TO TOTAL ARRIVING ALIENS:
1900-1924[a]

Years ending June 30

YEAR	PERCENTAGE RATIO	YEAR	PERCENTAGE RATIO	YEAR	PERCENTAGE RATIO
1900	5.4[b]	1909	20.4	1917	18.6
1901	5.8	1910	13.1	1918	47.8
1902	4.4	1911	14.7	1919	40.5
1903	3.2	1912	17.6	1920	30.8
1904	3.3	1913	16.1	1921	17.7
1905	3.8	1914	13.2	1922	28.4
1906	5.6	1915	24.8	1923	22.3
1907	10.6	1916	18.5	1924	19.6
1908	15.3				

[a]Computed from data given in the annual reports of the U. S. Commissioner General of Immigration
and in the *Statistical Abstract of the United States*. See Table 36 for 1905-1924.
[b]For some of the years from 1900 to 1905, two sets of figures have been published for the number of
non-immigrants, and the figures here used are the lower of the two sets, selected because they appeared
more consistent from year to year. Hence it is not safe to conclude that the ratio of nonimmigrants to immigrants actually increased after 1906 to the extent suggested by the data in this table.

ratio are noteworthy. First, in the last two decades the proportion
of recorded nonimmigrants to total arrivals substantially increased,
even before the war; and secondly, the ratio is relatively high in
and immediately following depression years, and also in the war
years, suggesting that war and depression both tend to exercise a
greater check on the flow of immigrants than of nonimmigrants.

In the depression year 1908 (fiscal), for example, the number of
immigrants declined 39.1 per cent, as compared with a decline of
only 7.4 per cent in the number of nonimmigrants. On the other
hand, the number of nonimmigrants declined more than the number
of immigrants in 1914, but in 1922 the latter movement again exhibited the greater sensitiveness to industrial depression. Taken as
a whole, therefore, the nonimmigrant group seems to be less sensitive to cyclical changes than the immigrant element. These tentative conclusions may be verified by reference to Chart 27, which
appears on page 139 and shows the relative fluctuations in the
number of male and female immigrants and nonimmigrants, respectively, in the years 1905 to 1924, inclusive.

CHART 27

RELATIVE FLUCTUATIONS IN NUMBER OF IMMIGRANTS AND NON-
IMMIGRANTS, CLASSIFIED BY SEX: 1905-1924[a]

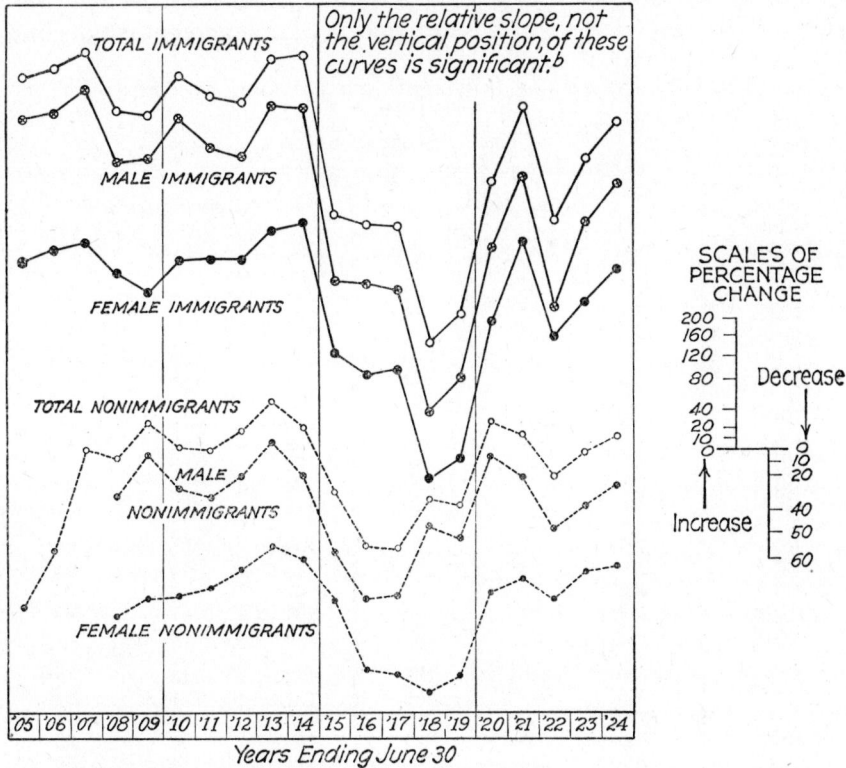

[a]Numerical data in Table 36.
  [b]All of the curves shown in the above chart have been plotted to the same ratio scale, so that equal vertical distances measured upward indicate the same percentage increase; and equal distances measured downward, the same percentage decrease, as shown by the Scales of Percentage Change accompanying the chart. But, to avoid confusing recrossing, each curve has a different base line; hence in interpreting this chart only the slope, or vertical change, and not the vertical position of a curve, should be considered.

Method of Charting.

The method of charting used in Chart 27 may not be familiar to the reader, and as there are several charts in this and the following chapter which are similar in principle a few words of explanation are pertinent.   These are so-called "ratio" or "rate-of-change" charts, with a logarithmic vertical scale and also with a different

base line for each curve. The effect of the "ratio" scale is that the
relative amount of increase or decrease in any year-to-year change is
graphically represented by the relative slope of the connecting lines,
that is, by the vertical change from one year to the next. If, for
example, two series experience the same percentage decline, the
slope of the two curves will be the same. A large percentage decline

TABLE 36.—NUMBER OF IMMIGRANTS AND NONIMMIGRANTS, BY SEX,
1905-1924[a]

Thousands of persons

YEAR ENDING JUNE 30	IMMIGRANTS			NONIMMIGRANTS		
	TOTAL	MALE	FEMALE	TOTAL	MALE	FEMALE
1905	1,026	725	302	41	...	..
1906	1,101	764	336	66	...	..
1907	1,285	930	355	153	...	..
1908	783	507	276	142	103	38
1909	752	520	232	192	148	44
1910	1,042	736	306	156	111	45
1911	879	570	309	152	103	48
1912	838	530	308	179	123	56
1913	1,198	808	390	229	162	68
1914	1,218	799	420	185	123	61
1915	327	187	140	108	65	43
1916	299	182	117	68	44	24
1917	295	174	121	67	45	23
1918	111	62	49	101	81	20
1919	141	83	58	96	73	23
1920	430	248	182	192	145	46
1921	805	449	356	173	121	52
1922	310	150	160	123	79	44
1923	523	308	215	150	96	55
1924	707	423	284	172	114	58

[a]From the *Statistical Abstract of the United States*, 1921, p. 103, and the annual reports of the U. S.
Commissioner General of Immigration.

is shown by a sharp drop; a small percentage decline, by a slight
drop. Hence the relative variability of the series represented can
be approximated visually by comparison of the shapes of the curves.
The steadier the series represented, the less the curve deviates from
a straight line or smooth curve. To facilitate an approximation of
the percentage change in any year, scales for percentage increases
and decreases are given at the right of the chart.

Also, although all the curves are drawn to the same scale, to avoid
confusing crossing of the lines each curve has been plotted from a

separate base line. The result is that the curves are more conveniently placed for use in comparing the degree of year-to-year
change but the vertical position of a curve ceases to be significant
and the numerical amounts represented by a given point thereon
cannot be read from the chart. This type of chart is appropriate
for the one purpose for which it is here used—as a visual aid to the
comparison of year-to-year changes—but care should be taken to
avoid the errors of interpretation which may arise if the limitations
of this form of chart are overlooked.

Emigrants and Nonemigrants.

There is no marked difference in the degree to which the cyclical
movements of the number of emigrants and of nonemigrants are
affected by employment conditions.[1] One bit of evidence leading
to this conclusion is afforded by the data in Table 37, showing the
ratio of nonemigrants to total departing aliens in each of the calendar
years, 1908 to 1924.

TABLE 37.—RATIO OF NONEMIGRANTS TO TOTAL ALIENS DEPARTED:
1908-1924[a]

YEAR ENDING JUNE 30TH	ALIENS DEPARTED		PERCENTAGE RATIO
	TOTAL	NONEMIGRANT	
1908	714,828	319,755	44.7
1909	400,392	174,590	43.6
1910	380,418	177,982	46.8
1911	518,215	222,549	42.9
1912	615,292	282,030	45.8
1913	611,924	303,734	49.6
1914	633,805	330,467	52.1
1915	384,174	180,100	46.9
1916	240,807	111,042	46.1
1917	146,379	80,102	54.7
1918	193,268	98,683	51.1
1919	216,231	92,709	42.9
1920	428,062	139,747	32.6
1921	426,031	178,313	41.9
1922	345,384	146,672	42.5
1923	200,586	119,136	59.4
1924	216,745	139,956	64.6

[a]Compiled from the annual reports of the Commissioner General of Immigration, U. S. Bureau of
Immigration.

[1]However, our study of the depression of 1908, in Chapter V, suggested that the
effect of that depression was most marked upon net migration when the temporary
element was included.

Prior to 1914, it will be noted, the ratio of nonemigrants to the total fluctuated within the narrow range of 42.9 to 49.6 per cent; and after 1914, shows no striking changes except a general increase during the war period, and a sharp decline in 1920, followed in 1923 and 1924 by a marked increase. Probably the 1920 decline may be attributed to the fact that the preceding years had not been favorable to the arrival of large numbers of temporary immigrants and, consequently, most of those who made up the rising tide of emigration in 1920 were aliens who had established a relatively permanent residence in the United States and were consequently classified as emigrants rather than nonemigrants if they were leaving for a permanent sojourn abroad. In 1923 and 1924 there is a rise in the proportion of nonemigrants, due, in part at least, to the fact that certain classes of temporary emigrants are not subject to the quota limit law and hence pass in and out of the country in much the same volume as before the law was passed.

Graphic Comparison of Departing Aliens, by Sex and Permanency of Migration.

As in the case of all alien departures, there is much general similarity observed in the cyclical fluctuations when outgoing emigrants and nonemigrants are classified by sex. The fluctuations in the annual data for total, male, and female emigrants, respectively, and for total, male, and female nonemigrants, respectively, are shown in Chart 28, which, like most of the charts in this chapter, is a "rate-of-change" chart, appropriate for comparison of relative rates of change but not capable of being used for comparison of the actual numbers involved. The reader who is interested in the actual number of emigrants of the given type should turn to Table 38, which contains the data from which this chart is plotted.

While the six curves in Chart 28 show a pronounced general resemblance, there are noteworthy differences in detail.

Emigrants and Nonemigrants.

In the comparison between emigrants and nonemigrants in Chart 28 we again find that, although the fluctuations in the nonemigrant element are somewhat less violent, there are no persistent marked differences between the permanent and temporary elements. The male nonemigrant curve is quite similar to the emigrant curve, except that it reaches a peak in 1914 as compared with 1912 for emigrants, shows a spurt in 1918, reaches a peak in 1921 as compared with 1920 for male emigrants, and does not decline so much after restriction becomes effective.   The 1918 spurt is largely due to the inclusion in the number of nonemigrants of thousands of Chinese in transit across the United States for work behind the battle lines in France.

CHART 28

RELATIVE FLUCTUATIONS IN NUMBER OF EMIGRANTS AND NON-EMIGRANTS, CLASSIFIED BY SEX: 1908-1924.[a]

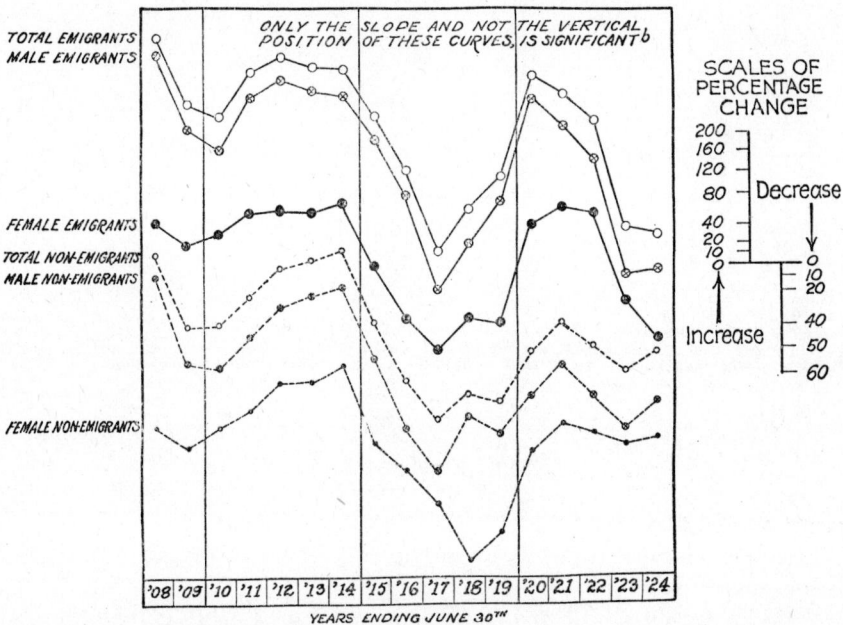

[a]Numerical data in Table 38.
[b]For a more complete discussion of the method of constructing the above chart, see footnote (b) to Chart 27.

The fluctuations in the number of emigrant and nonemigrant females, respectively, are also not markedly dissimilar, except that when immigration restriction became effective the accompanying decline in departures was more pronounced in the emigrant curve.

TABLE 38.—NUMBER OF EMIGRANTS AND NONEMIGRANTS, BY SEX, 1908-1924[a]

Thousands of persons

YEAR ENDING JUNE 30TH	EMIGRANTS			NON-EMIGRANTS		
	TOTAL	MALE	FEMALE	TOTAL	MALE	FEMALE
1908	395	343	52	320	266	54
1909	226	183[b]	43[b]	175	129	45
1910	202	155	48	178	125	53
1911	296	239	57	223	161	61
1912	333	276	57	282	205	77
1913	308	252	56	304	226	78
1914	303	242	61	330	241	89
1915	204	168	36	180	134	46
1916	130	107	23	111	74	37
1917	66	48	18	80	52	28
1918	95	71	23	99	82	17
1919	124	101	22	93	71	22
1920	288	238	51	140	97	43
1921	248	189	59	178	125	53
1922	199	143	55	147	97	49
1923	81	55	27	119	74	45
1924	77	57	19	140	93	47

[a]From the annual reports of the U. S. Commissioner General of Immigration and the Statistical Abstract of the United States.
[b]Estimated on the assumption that the sex distribution of about 30,000 emigrants via the Canadian border, for whom sex is not known, is the same as that among the 196,000 emigrants for whom sex is known.

RELATIVE CYCLICAL FLUCTUATIONS IN MALE AND FEMALE MIGRATION

Immigration by Sex.

In periods of industrial boom the proportion of males among the immigrants is high; in periods of depression it is low. This is as would be expected, for in a smaller proportion of cases is employment the immediate objective of female immigration and hence the time of this immigration is less dependent upon the current condition of industry than is the immigration of males. This greater susceptibility of male immigration to the state of employment is indicated in Chart 3, which appears in Chapter II, page 38. Upon examination of this chart, it will be noted that in 1885, 1894-1895, 1904, 1908, and 1922 (fiscal years), all of which were in depression periods, the proportion of males to females was appreciably smaller than in the preceding and following years.

This tendency may also be illustrated by the accompanying

table, showing the percentage decline in the depression years ending
June 30, 1904, 1908, 1911, and 1922, respectively, as compared with
the number of arrivals in the relatively high years immediately
preceding.

Table 39

PERCENTAGE CHANGE IN DEPRESSION YEARS

Year ending June 30	Male immigration	Female immigration
1904	—10.4	+ 8.1
1908	—45.5	—22.3
1911	—22.6	+ 1.0
1922	—66.7	—55.1

In 1904 and 1911, the immigration of females even increased
slightly, and in each of the other two depression years the decrease
was less than that in male immigration of the corresponding period.

The greater stability of the movement of incoming alien females
is further illustrated in Chart 27, on an earlier page in this chapter.
The fluctuations in neither "female immigrants" nor "female nonimmigrants" are as decided as the corresponding fluctuations in the
number of arriving male aliens. This fact is particularly noticeable
prior to the war.

Emigration by Sex.

The number of outgoing females is somewhat less variable than
that of males. For example, in 1909, when industrial conditions in
the United States were improving, the decline in the number of
departing females is relatively smaller; likewise in 1917, and again
in 1921 and 1922.

The less pronounced movement of female emigration is illustrated
by the curves in Chart 28, on page 143. All the curves—male and
female emigrant and male and female nonemigrant—fell sharply
during the war, but in both the pre-war and post-war periods, the
fluctuations in female departures are somewhat less violent than
those of male departures. There are exceptions to this tendency,
such as the decline in "emigrant" females in 1924.

Inasmuch as ordinarily there are no marked differences in direction
in the fluctuations of the emigration of the sexes, and as males are
numerically the larger element in the total, for both emigrants and
nonemigrants the curves for the combined numbers of males and
females closely resemble the curves for males alone, although their
fluctuations are toned down slightly by the lesser fluctuations of
the female element.

OCCUPATIONAL COMPARISONS

That the wage-earning element in migration is most susceptible to depressions in this country may be illustrated by the fact that in severe depression years the ratio of laborers (farm laborers plus general laborers) to total immigration decreases, while the "no occupation" group becomes a larger fraction of the total. The fiscal years 1904, 1908, 1911, 1914, and 1922 correspond with industrial depressions, and in each one of these years, as shown in Table 40, the "laborers" group, in terms of percentages of the total, decreases relatively and the "no occupation" group increases.

TABLE 40.—THE EFFECT OF DEPRESSIONS UPON THE OCCUPATIONAL DISTRIBUTION OF IMMIGRANTS[a]

YEAR ENDING JUNE 30	PER CENT OF TOTAL IMMIGRATION	
	LABORERS AND FARM LABORERS	NO OCCUPATION
1902	49.8	23.6
1903	46.5	23.3
1904[b]	36.4	26.4
1905	41.9	22.6
1906	42.3	25.9
1907	47.8	23.7
1908[b]	36.4	31.0
1909	46.0	29.4
1910	48.3	25.0
1911[b]	37.8	28.0
1912	38.2	27.6
1913	45.2	24.8
1914[b]	42.2	26.3
1920	22.6	40.3
1921	24.0	37.4
1922[b]	14.0	42.3
1923	20.9	36.6
1924	19.2	39.3

[a]Computed from statistics compiled by the United States Bureau of Immigration.
[b]Depression years.
[c]The war period is omitted.

Comparison between the cyclical fluctuations in the immigration of various occupational groups may also be made by means of the relative decline in depression years, as in the accompanying summary in Table 41.

TABLE 41.—RELATIVE DECLINE IN DEPRESSION YEARS OF THE IMMIGRATION
OF SELECTED OCCUPATIONAL GROUPS

OCCUPATION OF IMMIGRANTS	PERCENTAGE CHANGE FROM THE PRECEDING YEAR ENDING JUNE 30TH			
	1904	1908	1911	1922
Unskilled (general and farm laborers)	—25.6	—53.7	—34.0	—77.6
Servants	+13.2	—26.0	+10.9	—56.5
Professional	+89.5	—12.1	+16.5	—24.9
Skilled	+22.1	—35.0	+ 7.4	—60.9
No occupation	+ 7.5	—20.4	— 5.4	—56.5

In these four depression years, including both mild and severe employment slumps, the greatest drop in each case is evidenced in the number of unskilled workers, while the other groups in some instances even show an increase.

A more complete picture of the relative fluctuations in the several occupational groups is given in Chart 29, covering the fiscal years 1899 to 1914 and 1920 to 1924.

The effect of the minor depressions of 1901, 1904, 1911, and 1914 are evidenced in most of the occupational groups by a decline, or at least a slackening of the rate of increase; all series declined sharply in 1908 and some series continued this decline in 1909; all series rose in the boom of 1913. After the war, a strong upward movement is evident in all groups through 1919, 1920, and 1921, followed by a sharp decline in 1922, with a decided recovery in 1923 and 1924, despite the restrictive influence of the quota law.

While similarities in the movements of the several groups are more striking than differences, yet on close examination of the separate curves in Chart 29 exceptions from the general tendencies do become apparent. The "no occupation" and professional groups evidence relatively less complete and less prompt reaction to depression conditions than the other groups. For example, in 1908 these groups decline, but not so much as the general decline, and they continue to decline in 1909. The skilled and servant groups show somewhat greater responsiveness than the two just mentioned, but also do not reach bottom until 1909. The farm laborers, general laborers, and farmers appear to move more nearly in accord with industrial ups and downs.

CHART 29

RELATIVE FLUCTUATIONS IN IMMIGRATION, BY OCCUPATION:
1899-1924[a]

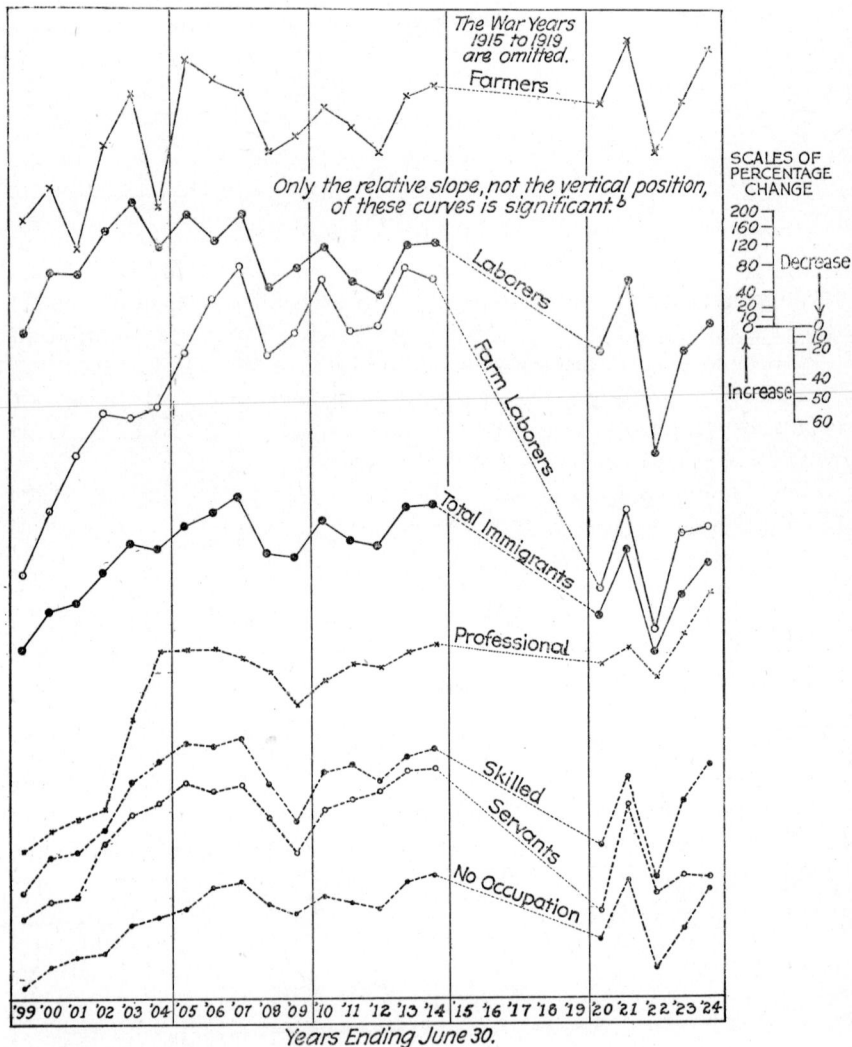

The War Years 1915 to 1919 are omitted.

Farmers

Only the relative slope, not the vertical position, of these curves is significant.[b]

Laborers

Farm Laborers

Total Immigrants

Professional

Skilled

Servants

No Occupation

SCALES OF
PERCENTAGE
CHANGE

```
200 —
160 —
120 —
 80 — Decrease
 40 —            ↓
 20 —           0
  0 —          10
              20
              40
Increase  50
              60
```

'99 '00 '01 '02 '03 '04 '05 '06 '07 '08 '09 '10 '11 '12 '13 '14 '15 '16 '17 '18 '19 '20 '21 '22 '23 '24
Years Ending June 30.

[a]Numerical data in Table 42.
[b]For a more complete discussion of the method of constructing the above chart, see footnote (b) to Chart 27.

TABLE 42.—NUMBER OF IMMIGRANTS, BY SELECTED OCCUPATIONAL GROUPS
1899-1924[a]

Thousands of persons

YEAR ENDING JUNE 30	TOTAL IMMIGRANT ALIENS	LABORERS	FARM LABORERS	FARMERS	SERVANTS	SKILLED	PROFESSIONAL	NO OCCUPATION
1899	311.7	92.0	17.3	4.0	34.1	44.0	2.0	109.4
1900	448.6	163.5	31.9	5.4	40.3	61.4	2.4	134.9
1901	487.9	161.9	54.8	3.0	42.0	64.5	2.7	148.7
1902	648.7	242.7	80.6	8.2	69.9	79.8	2.9	153.2
1903	857.0	320.6	77.5	13.4	92.7	124.7	7.0	199.7
1904	812.9	210.4	85.8	4.5	104.9	152.2	13.3	214.7
1905	1,026.5	287.4	142.2	18.5	125.5	180.1	13.6	232.0
1906	1,100.7	226.3	239.1	15.3	116.0	177.1	13.8	285.5
1907	1,285.3	291.1	323.9	13.5	121.6	190.3	12.6	304.7
1908	782.9	146.1	138.8	7.7	89.9	123.6	11.1	242.7
1909	751.8	174.8	171.3	8.9	64.6	87.2	8.1	221.3
1910	1,041.6	214.3	288.7	11.8	96.7	138.6	10.3	260.0
1911	878.6	156.0	176.0	9.7	107.2	148.9	12.0	246.0
1912	838.2	135.7	184.2	7.7	116.5	127.0	11.7	231.1
1913	1,197.9	221.0	320.1	13.2	140.2	160.1	13.5	297.2
1914	1,218.5	226.4	288.1	14.4	144.4	173.2	14.6	320.2
1915	326.7	48.4	24.7	6.5	39.8	55.6	12.3	116.9
1916	298.8	55.8	26.2	6.8	29.3	45.5	9.8	104.8
1917	295.4	51.1	22.3	7.8	31.9	48.8	8.4	104.4
1918	110.6	14.7	4.5	2.6	7.8	21.6	4.6	45.0
1919	141.1	18.3	4.4	3.9	6.3	27.5	6.3	58.3
1920	430.0	81.7	15.3	12.2	37.2	70.0	12.4	173.1
1921	805.2	160.6	32.4	22.3	102.5	131.8	14.6	301.1
1922	309.6	32.7	10.5	7.7	44.5	51.6	11.0	131.0
1923	522.9	83.6	25.9	12.5	52.2	106.2	16.5	191.6
1924	706.9	108.0	27.5	20.3	51.7	150.7	24.8	277.9

[a]Compiled from the annual reports of the Commissioner General of Immigration, U. S. Bureau of Immigration.

Emigration of Various Occupational Groups.

A study of the fluctuations in the number of emigrants of the principal occupation groups (Chart 30) leads to conclusions similar to those obtained from the study of immigration. On the whole, the emigrant groups of laborers and farmers show the most marked tendency to be large in depression years and low in boom years, though the differences are not completely uniform or very striking. The professional group shows relatively the least adjustment to industrial conditions.

CHART 30

RELATIVE FLUCTUATIONS IN EMIGRATION, BY OCCUPATION:
1908-1924[a]

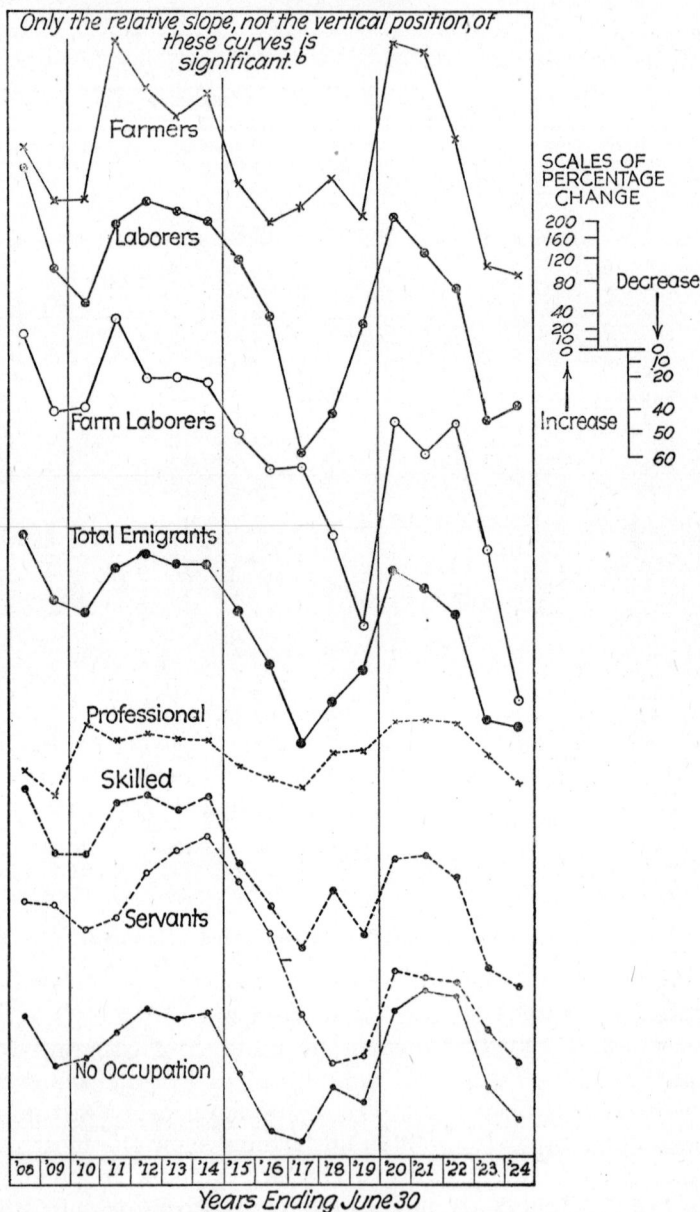

Only the relative slope, not the vertical position, of these curves is significant.[b]

Farmers

Laborers

Farm Laborers

Total Emigrants

Professional

Skilled

Servants

No Occupation

SCALES OF
PERCENTAGE
CHANGE

200
160
120
80   Decrease

40
20
10
0
10
20

40   Increase
50
60

'08 '09 '10 '11 '12 '13 '14 '15 '16 '17 '18 '19 '20 '21 '22 '23 '24

Years Ending June 30

[a]Numerical data in Table 43.
[b]For a more complete discussion of the method of constructing the above chart, see footnote (b) to Chart 27.

That the volume of emigration, like that of immigration, of unskilled laborers is more dependent upon industrial conditions than is the "no occupation" group is further indicated by comparing the fluctuations in the monthly data for these two series corrected for seasonal variation (Chart 31). The curve for the "no occupation" group follows a fairly steady course, while that for the unskilled element shows an erratic tendency. The depression of 1911, for

TABLE 43.—NUMBER OF EMIGRANTS, BY SELECTED OCCUPATIONAL GROUPS
1908-1924[a]

Thousands of persons

YEAR ENDING JUNE 30	TOTAL EMIGRANT ALIENS	LABORERS	FARM LABORERS	FARMERS	SERVANTS	SKILLED	PROFESSIONAL	NO OCCUPATION
1908	395.1	279.7	5.7	4.7	10.6	37.8	2.2	46.6
1909	225.8	118.9	3.0	3.0	10.2	21.9	1.8	30.5
1910	202.4	89.4	3.1	3.0	8.3	21.6	3.3	32.5
1911	295.7	174.0	6.5	11.6	9.2	33.5	2.9	40.4
1912	333.3	209.3	4.0	7.8	13.4	35.9	3.1	49.5
1913	308.2	191.6	3.9	6.1	16.2	31.6	2.9	45.4
1914	303.3	176.6	3.8	7.4	18.2	35.2	2.9	47.8
1915	204.1	127.9	2.5	3.4	12.5	20.1	2.3	28.5
1916	129.8	78.6	1.8	2.5	8.0	13.9	2.1	17.4
1917	66.3	24.8	1.9	2.8	4.0	9.8	1.9	15.9
1918	94.6	34.6	1.1	3.6	2.7	15.9	2.6	25.1
1919	123.5	74.1	0.5	2.6	2.8	11.0	2.6	22.2
1920	288.3	183.8	2.8	11.3	5.8	20.8	3.4	48.4
1921	247.7	135.2	2.1	10.5	5.5	21.5	3.4	57.7
1922	198.7	100.1	2.7	5.0	5.2	18.0	3.3	54.9
1923	81.4	32.9	0.9	1.7	3.5	8.3	2.5	25.2
1924	76.8	37.3	0.3	1.6	2.7	7.1	2.0	19.2

[a]Compiled from the annual reports of the U. S. Commissioner General of Immigration.

example, is marked by a sharp rise in the emigration of unskilled laborers.

The post-war emigration movement is peculiar in several respects. In the prosperous year 1920, emigration, ordinarily at a low ebb in boom periods, reached the peak in all groups except the skilled classes. This large emigration is probably in part at least due to the previous interference of war and early post-war conditions with the normal emigrant movement. Then, in 1921 and 1922, despite depression in industry, emigration declines, this decline becoming even more decided in 1923 and 1924. The primary reasons for the failure of emigration to increase markedly in this depression period are probably the unsettled political and economic conditions in Europe and the anticipation of the effect of restrictive immigration laws in making it more difficult for those who left to return later.

CHART 31

SHOWING THE GREATER CYCLICAL FLUCTUATIONS IN THE EMIGRATION OF UNSKILLED LABORERS AS COMPARED WITH EMIGRANTS HAVING NO OCCUPATION*

Three-month moving average of index numbers, corrected for seasonal variation, with 1913 monthly average=100

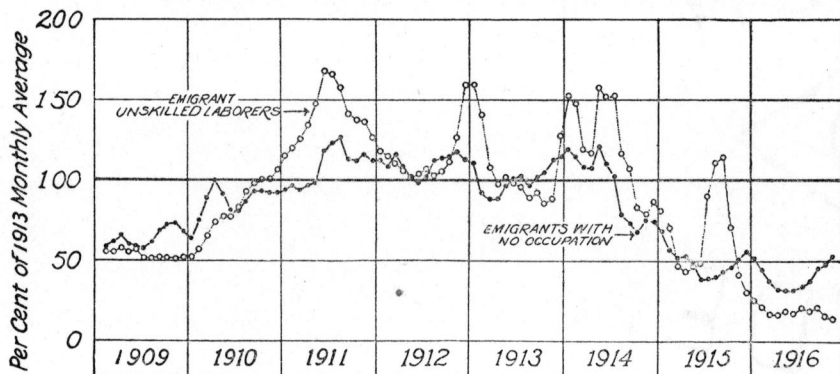

*Computed from monthly statistics compiled by the United States Bureau of Immigration.

CHAPTER SUMMARY

Briefly summarized, the evidence submitted in this chapter indicates that with reference to the degree to which they are affected by cyclical movements in industry, male migration is more susceptible than female; the immigrant and emigrant are somewhat more susceptible than the nonimmigrant and nonemigrant groups; and the unskilled immigrant and emigrant respond to industrial conditions more readily than the skilled, professional, and "no occupation" groups.

Further indications of the relative responsiveness to industrial conditions of these several elements in migration will appear in the chapter on Seasonal Movements, and the discussion of the relative cyclical fluctuations of immigrants of various races and from various countries appears in the following chapter.

CHAPTER VIII

THE INFLUENCE OF ECONOMIC CONDITIONS IN THE COUNTRIES OF EMIGRATION

To be comprehensive, an analysis of the cyclical aspects of migration should throw light on the relative influence of economic conditions in the countries of emigration and of immigration. Are fluctuations in the tide of migration due primarily to conditions at home or in the country of destination? Does the emigrant leave at a particular time because his status at home becomes intolerable or because the prospects in the "promised land" are unusually attractive?

If we had no better method of reaching a decision on this point, we should judge from a priori reasoning that the dominant cause of an unusual volume of emigration is most probably the attraction of unusual opportunities in the prospective home of the emigrant rather than the expelling force of unusually bad conditions in his former home. Particularly is this true of a common increase in emigration from several sources to a particular host country, especially if there is no similar increase in emigration from these same sources to other host countries.

An important consideration is that the passage money for many immigrants is furnished by relatives and friends in the United States and hence we should expect that increases in the immigration of this group would be particularly apt to show a close correspondence with prosperity in the United States.

On the other hand, we should expect that the time of arrival of immigrants who finance their own passage would be less influenced by conditions here. However, to the extent that business depressions in Europe and America occur at the same time—and we shall presently see that they are to a large degree concurrent—distress in the country of emigration will be accompanied by unemployment and low wages in the country of intended residence. Not only will it be difficult for both assisted and self-financed immigrants to obtain funds for their passage, but also the news from abroad will be depressing and little calculated to encourage the would-be immigrants to tear loose from their moorings.

153

An exception must be made of instances of unusual disaster in the home country. In severe famine or political oppression, even a poor chance in a new environment may appear as a relative betterment. As a result of the severe potato famines in Ireland in the late forties of the last century, great numbers of the Irish population sought escape to the newer countries, even though the conditions of transportation were wretched and during the passage many perished in fever-infested ships. Likewise, when hundreds of thousands of Armenians were driven from their homes after the collapse of the Greek campaign in 1920, they would doubtless have gladly embarked for America in large numbers had not restrictions upon immigration to the United States been imposed in 1921.

But we are concerned here, not so much with exceptional national calamities, as with the ever-recurring succession of prosperity and depression which appears to be characteristic of the modern industrial organization. In this connection, the principal questions to be considered are: to what extent are cycles in economic conditions internationally concurrent, and are they of substantially equal violence; and to what extent do fluctuations in the flow of population from countries of emigration agree? Is there a substantial uniformity in the cyclical movements of emigration or does the peak of emigration from one country coincide with the trough of emigration from another? In the following paragraphs we first turn our attention to this latter question.

COMPARISON OF CYCLICAL FLUCTUATIONS IN THE PRINCIPAL STREAMS OF IMMIGRATION TO THE UNITED STATES AND OF EMIGRATION THEREFROM

Significance of Similarities.

Are the year-to-year changes in the volume of immigration to the United States substantially the same for all countries? Or is the change in total immigration merely the non-homogeneous composite of many more or less divergent tendencies causing increases in the emigration from some countries and decreases in that from others, with no clearly predominating tendency? Such a direct comparison of the fluctuations in the immigration to the United States from the leading emigrant countries is a logical first step in determining the relative influence of economic conditions in those countries. If the flow of immigration from all countries evidences substantially the same fluctuations, a presumption is raised in favor of the theory that economic conditions in the United States are a predominating factor, particularly if business conditions in the several foreign countries are not closely parallel and these common migratory fluctuations accord well with industrial cycles in the United States.

On the other hand, if the more common phenomenon is a marked diversity in the cyclical fluctuations of the various national or racial elements in immigration, then a presumption is created in favor of the interpretation that conditions in the country of emigration are the dominant factor or that industrial prosperity and depression in the United States is itself a phenomenon so diversified in its influence upon employment that its effect is much greater upon immigration from certain countries than upon the general immigration movement.

Method of Analysis.

The facts concerning the relative fluctuations of immigration from the several countries are presented in two ways. In the first place, they are shown by means of a table (Number 44) giving the number of immigrants from each of several countries and by charts (32 and 33) to facilitate the determination of whether changes in the number of immigrants in any given year are common to the several countries. Secondly, as a means of presenting the same facts in a way which stresses the divergence of the immigration from any one country from its usual proportion to the total immigration, a table and charts are given showing the fraction of the total immigration which is represented by the number of immigrants from each of the selected list of countries. (See Table 45 and Charts 34 and 35).

Immigration from Selected Countries.

An examination of the fluctuations in the number of immigrants from leading countries of emigration in the three decades prior to the Great War (Charts 32 and 33) furnishes reasonably conclusive evidence concerning the degree of similarity in such fluctuations.

The countries included in this graphic comparison are England, Ireland, Germany, Sweden, Russia, Italy, and Austria-Hungary from 1880 to 1914; and Greece from 1891 to 1914.

In nine of the thirty-four years covered by Charts 32 and 33, the selected immigration movements either all show an increase or all

CHART 32

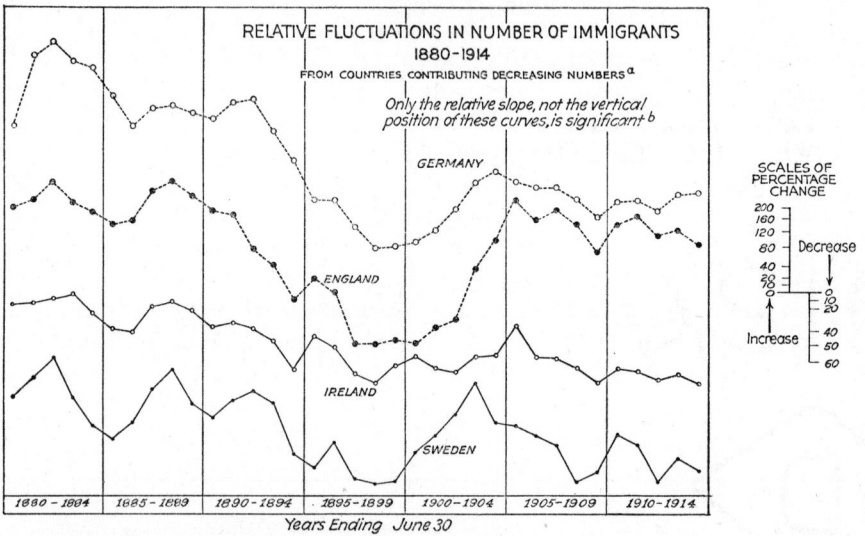

RELATIVE FLUCTUATIONS IN NUMBER OF IMMIGRANTS
1880-1914
FROM COUNTRIES CONTRIBUTING DECREASING NUMBERS[a]

Only the relative slope, not the vertical position of these curves, is significant.[b]

GERMANY

ENGLAND

IRELAND

SWEDEN

SCALES OF
PERCENTAGE
CHANGE

200
160
120
80   Decrease
40
20
10
0
10   Increase
20
40
50
60

Years Ending June 30

[a]Numerical data in Table 44.
[b]For a more complete discussion of the method of constructing the above chart, see footnote (b) to Chart 27, in Chapter VII.

CHART 33

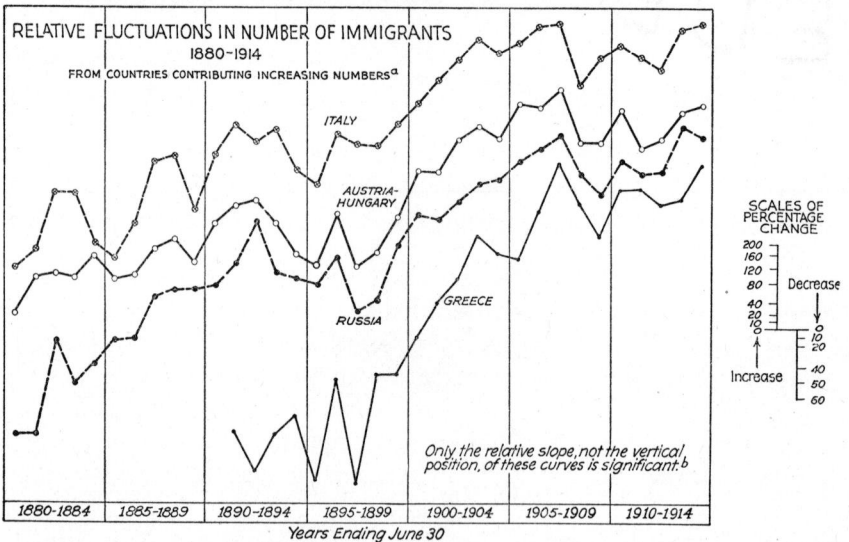

RELATIVE FLUCTUATIONS IN NUMBER OF IMMIGRANTS
1880-1914
FROM COUNTRIES CONTRIBUTING INCREASING NUMBERS[a]

ITALY

AUSTRIA-
HUNGARY

RUSSIA

GREECE

SCALES OF
PERCENTAGE
CHANGE

200
160
120
80   Decrease
40
20
10
0
10   Increase
20
40
50
60

Only the relative slope, not the vertical position, of these curves is significant.[b]

Years Ending June 30

[a]Numerical data in Table 44.
[b]For a more complete discussion of the method of constructing the above chart, see footnote (b) to Chart 27, in Chapter VII.

TABLE 44.—Recorded Number of Immigrants to the United States from Selected Countries: 1870-1914[a]

Thousands

YEAR ENDING JUNE 30	GER- MANY	ENG- LAND	IRE- LAND	SWE- DEN	ITALY	AUSTRIA HUN- GARY	RUS- SIA	GREECE
1870	118	61	57	13	3	4	1	b
1871	83	57	57	11	3	5	1	b
1872	141	70	69	13	4	4	1	b
1873	150	75	77	14	9	7	2	b
1874	87	51	54	6	8	9	4	b
1875	48	40	38	6	4	8	8	b
1876	32	24	20	6	3	6	5	b
1877	29	19	15	5	3	5	7	b
1878	29	18	16	5	4	5	3	b
1879	35	24	20	11	6	6	4	b
1880	85	59	72	39	12	17	5	b
1881	210	65	72	50	15	28	5	b
1882	251	82	76	65	32	29	17	b
1883	195	63	81	38	32	28	10	b
1884	180	56	63	27	17	37	13	b
1885	124	47	52	22	14	27	17	b
1886	84	50	50	28	21	29	18	b
1887	107	73	68	43	48	40	31	b
1888	110	83	74	55	52	46	33	1
1889	100	69	66	35	25	34	34	b
1890	92	57	53	30	52	56	36	1
1891	114	54	56	37	76	71	47	1
1892	119	34	51	42	62	77	82	1
1893	79	28	44	36	72	57	42	1
1894	54	18	30	18	43	39	39	1
1895	32	23	46	15	35	33	36	1
1896	32	19	40	21	68	65	51	2
1897	23	10	28	13	59	33	26	1
1898	17	10	25	12	59	40	30	2
1899	17	10	32	13	77	62	61	2
1900	19	10	36	19	100	115	91	4
1901	22	12	31	23	136	113	85	6
1902	28	14	29	31	178	172	107	8
1903	40	26	35	46	231	206	136	14
1904	46	39	36	28	193	177	145	11
1905	41	65	53	27	221	276	185	11
1906	38	49	35	23	273	265	216	19
1907	38	57	35	21	286	338	259	37
1908	32	47	31	13	129	169	157	21
1909	26	33	25	14	183	170	120	14
1910	31	47	30	24	216	259	187	26
1911	32	52	29	21	183	159	159	26
1912	28	40	26	13	157	179	162	21
1913	34	43	28	17	266	255	291	23
1914	36	36	25	15	284	278	256	36

[a]From reports of the U. S. Immigration Commission, *Statistical Review of Immigration: 1820-1910*; and the *Annual Report of the Commissioner General of Immigration*, 1924, pp. 115-117, U. S. Bureau of Immigration. Prior to 1906, persons entering the United States were recorded by country whence they came, thereafter by country of last permanent residence.
[b]Less than 500 recorded immigrants.

a decrease. Thus, in 1881, 1882, 1887, 1888, 1903, 1910, and 1913, immigration from all these countries shows an increase, and in 1897 and 1908 a decrease. Also, in the depression of 1885 and likewise in 1889, immigration from all the selected countries but Russia declined; in 1893, a decline from all countries but Italy and Greece occurred, and from all but Greece in 1894. With the exception of the inflow from Greece, all these immigrant streams rose in 1899, and all rose in 1902 but that from Ireland. The tendency to uniformity of movement may be summarized by noting that in twenty-one of the thirty-four years under consideration three-fourths or more of the curves show changes in the same direction. It is also noteworthy that in sixteen of these twenty-one years, an increase in immigration is preceded, to use a typical index, by an increase in pig iron production in the United States, or a decrease in immigration by a decrease in pig iron production, in the calendar year ending six months prior to the close of the given immigration year.

In the post-war years from 1920 to 1924, inclusive, which are not shown on Charts 32 and 33, the conformity in the direction of year-to-year change was even more uniform, all the selected countries showing a movement in the same direction, with the exception of Russia in 1920, Germany and Austria in 1922, Greece in 1923, and Russia and Austria-Hungary in 1924.

Differences in Degree.

It is not, of course, to be inferred that year-to-year changes in the number of immigrants, even when similar in direction for many countries, are necessarily closely similar in degree. For example, taking the severe depression of 1908 as the basis of comparison, the sharpest decline among the countries which contributed one hundred thousand or more immigrants in the year ending June 30, 1907, is found in the immigration from Hungary and Italy, countries from which immigration had been rapidly increasing. In terms of percentage decline in the year ending June 30, 1908, from the number for the preceding year, the declines were as follows: United Kingdom, 18 per cent; Russia, 40; Austria, 43; Italy, 55; and Hungary, 56.

Proportion to Total Immigration.

Further indication of variances in the fluctuations of immigration from the several countries can be obtained from Charts 34 and 35, which portray the changes in the ratio of immigration from the stated country to the total immigration for which the country of origin is known. In these charts a horizontal movement indicates that whatever the change in actual numbers, the immigration from the given country has not changed in proportion to the total. If the curve shows a drop, it means either that immigration from the

CHART 34

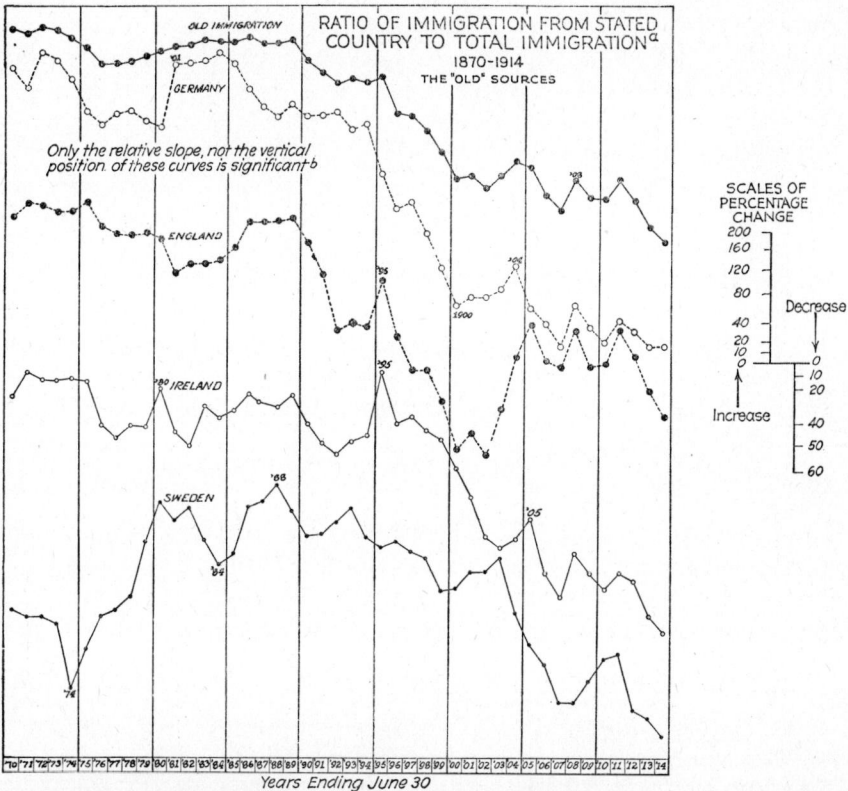

RATIO OF IMMIGRATION FROM STATED
COUNTRY TO TOTAL IMMIGRATION[a]
1870-1914
THE "OLD" SOURCES

Only the relative slope, not the vertical position of these curves is significant[b]

OLD IMMIGRATION

GERMANY

ENGLAND

IRELAND

SWEDEN

SCALES OF
PERCENTAGE
CHANGE

Years Ending June 30

[a]Numerical data in Tables 4 and 45.
[b]For a more complete discussion of the method of constructing the above chart, see footnote (b) to Chart 27, in Chapter VII.

stated country has fallen off more sharply or has not risen as rapidly as that from other countries.

Chart 34 contains curves for the leading "old" sources of immigration. It will be noted that although drawn to the same scale, these curves have been vertically shifted for convenience in plotting, so that it is only the shape of the curves and not their vertical distance from the base line which is significant. Though the movement from Sweden did not reach its peak until 1888, on the whole the proportion of total immigration contributed by each of these countries declined during the greater part of the period

CHART 35

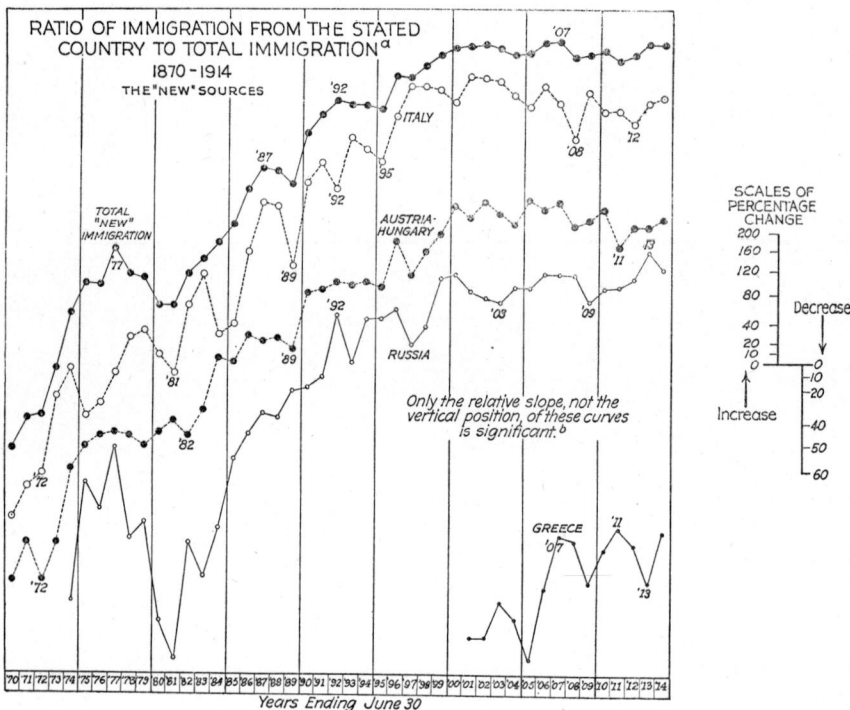

RATIO OF IMMIGRATION FROM THE STATED COUNTRY TO TOTAL IMMIGRATION[a]
1870-1914
THE "NEW" SOURCES

Only the relative slope, not the vertical position, of these curves is significant.[b]

Years Ending June 30

[a]Numerical data in Tables 4 and 45.
[b]For more a complete discussion of the method of constructing the above chart, see footnote (b) to Chart 27, in Chapter VII.

since 1870. The probable causes of substantial deviations from the general trend for any one country, such as the sharp rise in the proportion from England in 1895, from Germany in 1904, or from Ireland in 1895 and 1905, will be considered later in the chapter, when analyzing the conditions peculiar to each of the leading emigrant countries.

Chart 35 is similar to 34, except that it presents the data for the leading "new" sources of immigration. For each of these countries,

TABLE 45.—RATIO OF IMMIGRATION FROM SELECTED COUNTRIES TO TOTAL
IMMIGRATION[a]

Percentage Ratio of Immigration from Stated Country to the Total Immigration
for which Country of Origin is Known.

YEAR ENDING JUNE 30	GERMANY	ENGLAND	IRELAND	SWEDEN	ITALY	AUSTRIA HUNGARY	RUSSIA	GREECE
1870	30.5	15.7	14.7	3.5	0.7	1.1	b	b
1871	25.7	17.6	17.9	3.3	0.9	1.5	b	b
1872	34.9	17.2	17.0	3.3	1.0	1.1	b	b
1873	32.6	16.3	16.8	3.1	1.9	1.5	b	b
1874	27.9	16.3	17.1	1.8	2.4	2.8	1.3	b
1875	21.0	17.6	16.7	2.5	1.6	3.4	3.5	b
1876	18.8	14.3	11.5	3.3	1.8	3.7	2.8	b
1877	20.7	13.5	10.3	3.5	2.3	3.8	4.7	b
1878	21.2	13.3	11.5	3.9	3.1	3.7	2.2	b
1879	19.5	13.6	11.3	6.2	3.3	3.4	2.5	b
1880	18.5	13.0	15.7	8.6	2.7	3.8	1.1	b
1881	31.4	9.7	10.8	7.4	2.3	4.2	0.8	b
1882	31.8	10.4	9.7	8.2	4.1	3.7	2.1	b
1883	32.3	10.5	13.5	6.3	5.3	4.6	1.6	b
1884	34.7	10.8	12.2	5.1	3.2	7.1	2.4	b
1885	31.5	12.0	13.1	5.6	3.5	6.9	4.3	b
1886	25.3	14.9	14.9	8.3	6.4	8.6	5.3	b
1887	21.8	14.9	14.0	8.7	9.7	8.2	6.3	b
1888	20.1	15.1	13.4	10.0	9.4	8.4	6.1	b
1889	22.4	15.4	14.8	8.0	5.7	7.7	7.6	b
1890	20.3	12.5	11.6	6.5	11.4	12.3	7.8	b
1891	20.3	9.6	9.9	6.6	13.6	12.7	8.5	b
1892	20.9	6.0	9.0	7.3	10.8	13.5	14.3	b
1893	18.1	6.4	10.0	8.2	16.6	13.2	9.7	b
1894	18.9	6.2	10.6	6.4	15.1	13.5	13.8	b
1895	12.4	9.1	17.9	5.9	13.7	12.9	13.9	b
1896	9.3	5.7	11.7	6.2	19.8	19.0	15.0	0.6
1897	9.8	4.3	12.3	5.7	25.7	14.3	11.2	b
1898	7.5	4.3	11.0	5.4	25.6	17.4	13.0	1.0
1899	5.6	3.3	10.2	4.1	24.9	20.1	19.6	0.7
1900	4.1	2.2	8.0	4.2	22.3	25.6	20.2	0.8
1901	4.4	2.5	6.3	4.8	27.9	23.2	17.5	1.2
1902	4.4	2.1	4.5	4.8	27.5	26.5	16.5	1.2
1903	4.7	3.1	4.1	5.4	26.9	24.0	15.9	1.6
1904	5.7	4.8	4.4	3.4	23.8	21.8	17.9	1.4
1905	4.0	6.3	5.2	2.6	21.6	26.9	18.0	1.0
1906	3.5	4.6	3.3	2.2	25.6	24.8	20.2	1.8
1907	2.9	4.4	2.7	1.6	22.2	26.3	20.1	2.8
1908	4.1	6.0	3.9	1.6	16.4	21.5	20.0	2.7
1909	3.4	4.4	3.3	1.9	24.4	22.6	16.0	1.9
1910	3.0	4.5	2.9	2.3	20.7	24.8	17.9	2.5
1911	3.6	6.0	3.3	2.4	20.8	18.1	18.1	3.0
1912	3.3	4.8	3.1	1.5	18.7	21.3	19.4	2.6
1913	2.9	3.6	2.3	1.4	22.2	21.3	24.3	1.9
1914	2.9	2.9	2.0	1.2	23.3	22.8	21.0	2.9

[a]Computed from the data in Table 44 and data concerning total immigration in the sources there cited.
[b]Less than 0.5 per cent.

the proportion of total immigration rises throughout the period under consideration. The movement from each country exhibits some sharp deviations from its general trend which challenge attention and which will be given more consideration when discussing the several countries separately. The immigration from Italy is particularly erratic, but there are many other peculiar movements, the explanation of which should be helpful in ascertaining the causes of changes in migration.

The "Old" and the "New" Immigration.

In comparing the fluctuations in the immigration from selected countries, we have found, on the whole, a general family resemblance in the curves for the countries of northern and western Europe, or the sources of the so-called "old" immigration, and also, a general similarity among the curves for the countries of southern and eastern Europe, or the sources of the so-called "new" immigration. Let us note the similarities and differences in the cyclical fluctuations of these two groups, as represented in Chart 36.

CHART 36

RELATIVE VIOLENCE OF CYCLICAL FLUCTUATIONS IN THE "OLD" AND "NEW" IMMIGRATION: 1870-1914.

Percentage deviations from seven-year moving averages

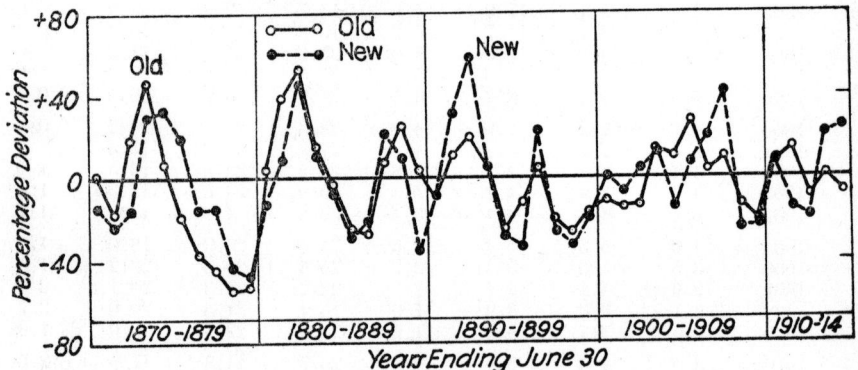

ªNumerical data in Table 46.

The immigration from the "old" sources and that from the "new" sources show substantially the same sequence of cyclical fluctuations in their annual totals from the seventies to the opening of the Great

War. But, in the later decades of the pre-war period, the new immigration is subject to the more violent fluctuations, increasing more in boom years and decreasing more in depression years than the old immigration. In addition to general differences in the degree of fluctuation, a few noticeable special differences in the direction

TABLE 46.—CYCLES IN THE "OLD" AND THE "NEW" IMMIGRATION: 1870-1914[a]

Percentage deviations from seven-year moving averages

YEAR ENDING JUNE 30	"OLD"[b]	"NEW"	YEAR ENDING JUNE 30	"OLD"	"NEW"
1870......	+ 1.0	—14.5	1895....	—12.5	—33.5
1871......	—16.8	—23.8	1896....	+ 4.5	+22.7
1872......	+18.8	—15.0	1897....	—20.2	—26.4
1873......	+46.6	+31.7	1898....	—26.9	—32.3
1874......	+ 7.0	+33.0	1899....	—16.6	—19.9
1875......	—19.4	+19.5	1900....	—11.6	0
1876......	—37.6	—15.3	1901....	—14.6	— 6.8
1877......	—44.5	—14.9	1902....	—14.2	+ 4.0
1878......	—54.6	—43.8	1903....	+13.3	+11.8
1879......	—53.5	—47.5	1904....	+10.1	—14.1
1880......	+ 4.3	—12.5	1905....	+27.4	+ 7.1
1881......	+39.1	+ 8.9	1906....	+ 3.9	+20.0
1882......	+52.8	+45.6	1907....	+ 9.9	+41.7
1883......	+15.6	+10.8	1908....	—13.3	—24.5
1884......	— 3.6	— 8.0	1909....	—22.6	—23.5
1885......	—24.9	—29.3	1910....	+ 8.7	+ 7.9
1886......	—27.2	—21.3	1911....	+14.5	—15.3
1887......	+ 7.9	+21.4	1912....	— 8.9[c]	—19.3[c]
1888......	+24.6	+ 9.5	1913....	+ 0.9[c]	+21.4[c]
1889......	+ 3.8	—35.1	1914....	— 7.7[c]	+24.0[c]
1890......	— 9.9	— 8.6			
1891......	+10.3	+31.4			
1892......	+19.5	+57.7			
1893......	+ 4.7	+ 5.6			
1894......	—24.1	—28.8			

[a]Computed from data in reports of the U. S. Immigration Commission, *Statistical Review of Immigration, 1820-1910*, and in the reports of the Commissioner General of Immigration, U. S. Bureau of Immigration, for the years subsequent to 1910.
[b]See footnotes to Table 4 for countries included under "Old" and "New."
[c]In computing moving averages for these years, the average immigration in 1911 to 1914 was substituted for the actual immigration in 1915, 1916, and 1917, respectively.

and extent of change appear in these two immigration series. Thus, in the fiscal year ending June 30, 1906, the "old" immigration declined while the "new" rose. In 1911 the "old" rose slightly, the "new" fell. In 1913, the "new" rose much more rapidly than the "old," and continued to rise in 1914 while the "old" declined.

A comparison with the cycles in the production of pig iron in the United States indicates that in the discrepancies of 1906 and 1911 the "new" immigration conforms more closely than the "old" to the fluctuations in pig iron production. However, such industrial expansion as is indicated by pig iron production in 1912 and 1913 is scarcely sufficient to offer an obviously adequate explanation of the marked increase in the immigration from southern and eastern Europe in the year ending June 30, 1913.

Both immigration series show a moderately high degree of agreement with the cyclical fluctuations in pig iron when immigration for twelve months ending June 30th is compared with production in the year ending the previous December.[1]

Emigration to Selected Countries (Chart 37)

In analyzing the fluctuations in emigration by country of intended future residence of the emigrant, we have again selected for comparison the aggregate of the countries of northern and western Europe, frequently designated as the "old" sources of immigration; the aggregate of the countries of eastern and southern Europe, known as the "new" sources; and lastly, a few of the constituents of these two groups: namely, Italy, Austria-Hungary, Russia, Greece, the United Kingdom, Scandinavia, and Germany.

Emigration declined to all the selected countries in the year ending June 30, 1909, and continued to decline in 1910 for Scandinavia and eastern and southern Europe except Greece. It rose to all these countries in 1911 and 1912, except to Germany; fell in 1913 to all but Greece; and rose in 1914 to all but Greece and Italy.

By the year ending June 30, 1919, or at least by 1920, emigration to each of the countries under consideration exhibited a recovery from the small volume of the war period; but, under the influence of the restrictions on immigration imposed in 1921, which have tended to discourage emigration as well as immigration, there has been in recent years a distinct downward trend in emigration from the United States.

It is evident that there is a substantial similarity in the direction of the year-to-year changes in the number of emigrants to these several European countries. The most striking exception to the general movement is the heavy exodus to Greece in 1913, when the

---

[1] The Pearsonian coefficient of correlation is $+.63 \pm .06$ for the "old" immigration and pig iron and $+.68 \pm .06$ for the "new."

citizens of that country were hurrying home to answer the call to the colors for the Balkan Wars.

There are, however, differences in degree of fluctuation. The decline in emigration in the prosperous years 1909 and 1910, from the high point reached in the depression year 1908, is most marked

CHART 37

FLUCTUATIONS IN NUMBER OF EMIGRANTS FROM THE UNITED STATES TO SELECTED EUROPEAN COUNTRIES: 1908-1924[a]

Ratio Scale

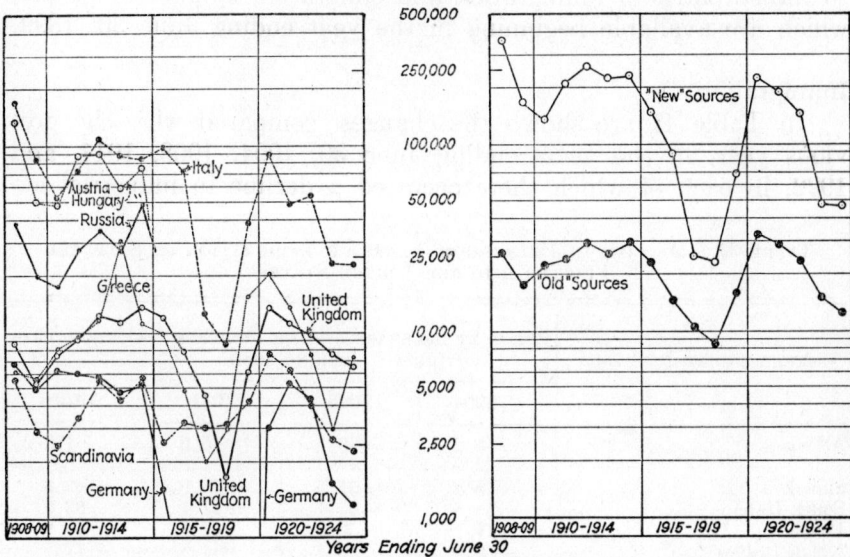

[a] The annual statistics of emigration for the several countries are given in the *Annual Report of the Commissioner General of Immigration*, 1924, pp. 119-121, U. S. Bureau of Immigration. For list of countries classified as "old" and "new" sources, respectively, see footnotes to Table 4.

for the countries of southern and eastern Europe. (See the right hand section of Chart 37). The movement to Scandinavia in 1909 and 1910 is more akin, however, to that of Italy, Austria-Hungary, and Russia than it is to the relatively small decline in Germany and the United Kingdom. Of the several emigration movements represented in Chart 37, the least susceptibility to employment conditions in the United States is evidenced by the emigration to Germany.

Comparison of Selected Groups or Races.

In the reports of the U. S. Immigration Commission in 1910, the interpretation was advanced that the response to industrial conditions, particularly in the way of exodus, is most obvious among the immigrants from southern and eastern Europe, inasmuch as a larger proportion of these are "simply transients whose interest in the country is measured by the opportunity afforded for labor."[2] We have found some support for this conclusion in preceding paragraphs dealing with immigration from separate countries and with the groups contributing the so-called "old" and "new" immigration. Additional significant contrasts are evident when attention is turned to the statistics of immigration and emigration by race or people, which are available beginning in the year ending June 30, 1899.

Immigration.

In Table 47 are shown the changes, compared with the previous year, in the years ending June 30, 1904, 1908, 1911, and 1922, in each of which there occurred a decline in industrial ac-

TABLE 47.—DECLINE IN DEPRESSION YEARS OF IMMIGRATION OF SELECTED PEOPLES INTO THE UNITED STATES[a]

YEAR ENDING JUNE 30	PER CENT DECREASE (—) OR INCREASE (+) FROM PRECEDING YEAR			
	1904	1908	1911	1922[b]
All races................	—5.2	—39.1	—15.6	—61.6
Slovak..................	—18.8	—61.5	—33.9	—82.9
South Italian............	—18.8	—54.4	—17.1	—82.0
Polish..................	—17.7	—50.7	—44.3	—69.9
North Italian............	— 2.0	—52.1	— 1.5	—77.8
German.................	+ 4.2	—21.4	— 6.9	+29.2
Irish...................	+ 4.8	— 5.9	+ 4.9	—56.0
Hebrew.................	+39.4	—30.7	+ 8.3	—55.0
English.................	+45.8	— 4.0	+ 7.0	—44.3

[a]Computed from statistics in *Annual Report of the Commissioner General of Immigration*, 1924, p. 114, U. S. Bureau of Immigration.
[b]Affected by quota law restrictions.

tivity accompanied by a decline in total immigration. Of the several leading races tabulated, the Polish, South Italian, and Slovak show the most consistent tendency to drop sharply in the given depression years. Of course, it is difficult to determine how

[2]United States Immigration Commission, *Abstract of Reports*, Vol. 1, p. 179.

much of the decline in 1922 is due to depression conditions and how much to the restrictive legislation which went into effect in May, 1921.

The data in Table 47 furnish a first approximation of the relative degree to which the immigration of various races is checked by business depression. For example, the depression of 1908 evidently had a relatively slight effect on English and Irish immigration, but reduced the Polish and Italian immigration to less than half that of the preceding year.

Whether these differences are merely peculiar to the particular depression years selected or are characteristic of general tendencies may be determined somewhat more completely by examination of Chart 38, which shows the movement of the immigration of selected

CHART 38

FLUCTUATIONS IN IMMIGRATION, BY RACE: 1899-1914.

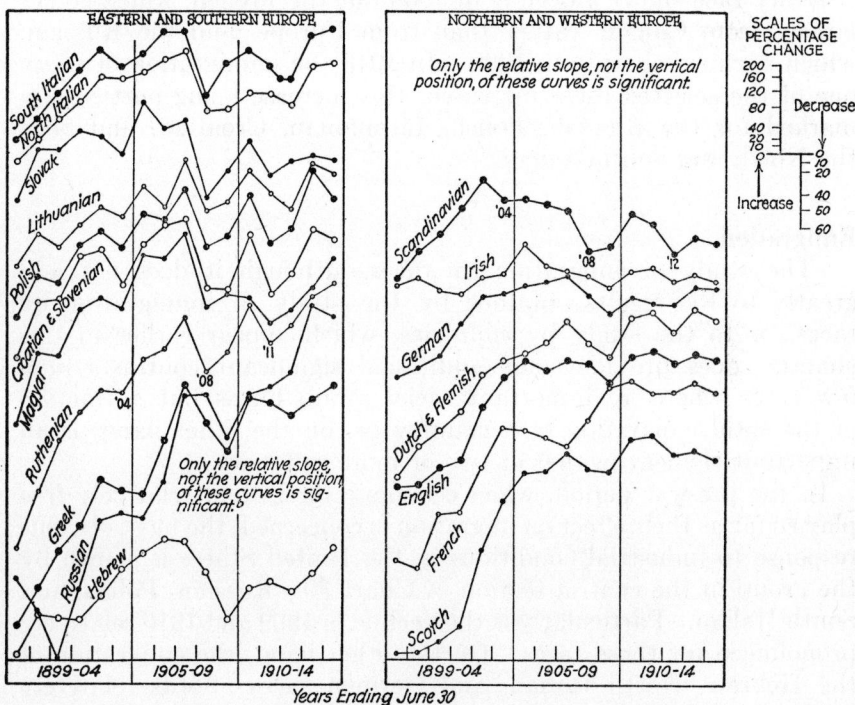

Years Ending June 30

.For the numerical data from which these curves were plotted, see the *Annual Report of the Commissioner General of Immigration*, 1924, pp. 113-114.

bFor a more complete discussion of the method of constructing the above chart, **see** footnote (b) to Chart 27, in Chapter VII.

races over the period from 1899 to 1914 (years ending June 30).

The left-hand section of Chart 38 portrays the fluctuations in the annual totals of immigration for the leading races of eastern and southern Europe; the right-hand section, for the races of northern and western Europe. The relative percentage decline of two series in any selected year may be approximated by comparing the vertical changes in the corresponding curves with the aid of the scales of percentage change to the right of the chart.

Of these two groups, the restraining effect of the depression conditions of 1904, 1908, and 1911, is more evident in the immigration of the races of eastern and southern Europe. There are exceptions, of course, to this generalization if attention is given to the separate races. For example, the immigration of North Italians and of Greeks declined but slightly in 1904 and 1911, and the immigration of Russians and Hebrews not at all.

Every race shows a decline in 1908 but the French, which comes largely from Canada rather than from Europe, and the Russian, which declined sharply in 1909. In 1913 the immigration of every one of the selected races increased, this increase being particularly marked for the Russian, Polish, Lithuanian, Croatian, and both the North and South Italian.

Emigration.

The study of emigration by races, although it does not add greatly to the results obtained by the study of immigration by races, or to the study by countries, which appear earlier in this chapter, does provide some additional significant contrasts in a few cases where an important racial group forms but a fraction of the total emigration of a country or, on the other hand, is an important element in that of two or more countries.

In the pre-war period, when economic forces had relatively free play so far as their effect on migration is concerned, the most obvious response to industrial conditions in the United States is shown by the group in the central section of Chart 39—Russian, Polish, and South Italian. Particularly is the decline in 1909 and 1910 relatively pronounced for these races. On the other hand, the emigration of the Hebrew, North Italian, and German races affords relatively little susceptibility to the ups and downs in industrial conditions in the United States.

CHART 39

EMIGRATION BY RACE

Fluctuations in the Number of Emigrants of Selected Races in the Pre-war Period: 1908-1914[a]

Ratio Scale

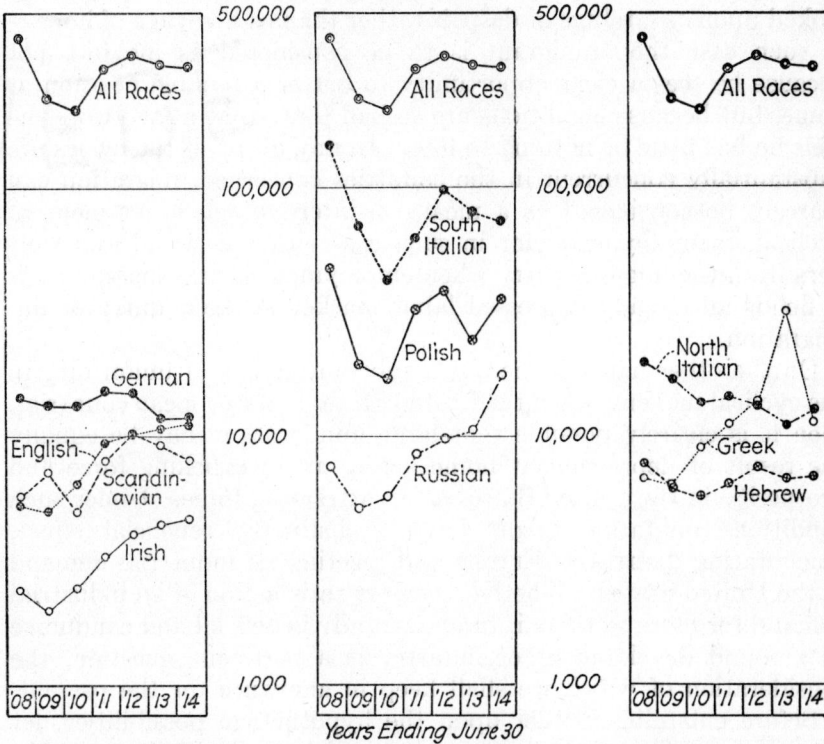

[a]For the numerical data from which the above chart was plotted, see the 1924 *Annual Report of the Commissioner General of Immigration*, p. 118.

THE INTERNATIONAL COMPARISON OF INDUSTRIAL CYCLES

Significance.

It is obviously pertinent to our problem to inquire into the extent to which business cycles are internationally concurrent. If, for example, the crest of prosperity is reached simultaneously in Germany and the United States, and if the high tide of immigration from Germany coincides closely with the peak of prosperity, then it would seem reasonable to assume, so far as the choice of a particular time of departure is concerned, that the immigrant is attracted by unusually promising opportunities, rather than driven by the bitter necessity of seeking an adequate livelihood elsewhere. Conversely, if a relatively large movement of immigrants coincides with depression conditions in both the country from which they come and the country to which they go, then migration must be looked upon as a refuge of despair rather than as a voyage of hope— in such case the immigrant is to be considered as moving, not because he sees a clear opportunity to better a tenable position at home, but because conditions are so bad there that at the worst he feels he has little or nothing to lose. In any event, if the cycles are substantially concurrent in the countries concerned, migration can scarcely be considered as a means of international adjustment of cyclical unemployment; for in such case either it withdraws workers from the home country when employment is at a maximum or it floods an already depressed labor market in the country of immigration.

On the other hand, if there is a substantial lack of uniformity in the cyclical movements in the United States and European countries, then it is entirely possible that large immigration may be equally the result of depression at home acting as an expelling force and prosperity in the United States as an attracting force. Under such conditions migration might have a distinctly beneficial effect, ameliorating distress in Europe and meeting an industrial demand in the United States. Whether the easy satisfaction of an industrial demand for more workers is fundamentally beneficial and conducive to a sound development of industry is a pertinent question, the consideration of which we shall keep in abeyance for the present.

Before enlarging further upon the hypothetical possibilities, let us endeavor to discover the degree to which cyclical movements in industry do synchronize in the several important countries.

Material Used in International Comparisons.

There have been several detailed comparative studies of cycles in the more important industrial countries, the most significant for our purposes being various studies on British economic conditions, consideration of which is deferred to the subsequent section of this chapter dealing with the United Kingdom, and also a monograph by Professor Alvin H. Hansen, based upon monthly data for the period from 1902 to 1908, and dealing with cycles in the United

States, Great Britain, and Germany.[3] Professor Hansen divides his series into three groups: the Investment, Industrial, and Banking Groups, respectively. Of these, the Industrial Group is most pertinent to a study of migration. For the United States the Industrial Group is constituted of wholesale commodity prices, pig iron production, railroad gross earnings, imports, and immigration; for Germany, of wholesale prices and pig iron production; and for Great Britain, of imports and exports.

After careful analysis of these three composites, Professor Hansen comes to the conclusion that "the cyclical movements are quite closely concurrent," that is, there is a general tendency for the periods of prosperity to coincide in these countries and likewise for the depression troughs to be reached about the same time.

Our own analysis of comparative economic conditions in this and other countries is based chiefly upon certain statistical indices of economic activities, to be described presently, and upon portions of descriptive annals of industrial and agricultural conditions prepared by Dr. Willard Thorp, of the research staff of the National Bureau of Economic Research.

Composite Indices of Economic Activity.

To facilitate the international comparison of business cycles, we have utilized composite indices of economic activity in the respective countries. For the United States we made use of a composite index prepared by Professor W. F. Ogburn and Dorothy S. Thomas, for the years from 1870 to 1920, using nine economic series: namely, wholesale prices (1870-1915), commercial failures (1870-1920), bituminous coal production (1870-1920), pig iron production (1870-1920), railroad freight ton mileage (1882-1920), bank clearings outside New York City (1881-1915), employment in Massachusetts (1889-1920), railroad mileage constructed (1870-1888), and imports (1870-1888).[4] In constructing this index a mathematical trend curve was fitted to each series, the percentage deviations therefrom computed, and the results expressed as cycles, in units of the typical or standard deviation. Then the cycles thus obtained for each separate series were averaged to obtain the composite index.

For the United Kingdom, Germany, and Italy, we have com-

[3]Alvin Harvey Hansen, *Cycles of Prosperity and Depression in the United States, Great Britain and Germany—A study of Monthly Data 1902-1908*, University of Wisconsin Studies in the Social Sciences and History, Number 5.

[4]"The Influence of the Business Cycle on Certain Social Conditions," *Quarterly Publication of the American Statistical Association*, September, 1922, p. 327.

puted composite indices of cyclical fluctuations in economic conditions by methods substantially similar to those used in the
computation of the index for the United States just described. In
choosing the constituent series for these "industrial composites," as
we shall designate them, we have selected series which are representative of important factors in the economic activities of the given
country, which show at least a fair degree of homogeneity in their
cyclical fluctuations, and lastly, which are available, with minor
exceptions, over the entire period from 1870 to 1913.

The five series used for the United Kingdom are: wholesale
prices, the value of exports, the tonnage of coal and of pig iron
produced, and the per cent of unemployment among trade union
members. For each series the cyclical fluctuations were computed
by finding the percentage deviations from a seven-year moving
average, smoothed to eliminate minor irregularities and to extend
the average at the ends of the period. The results were then expressed in multiples of the typical or standard deviation for the
respective series, and an unweighted arithmetic average of these
five series was computed to obtain the composite index. Inasmuch
as the price, export, and production series will ordinarily have
positive values when unemployment is low and negative values
when unemployment is high, the cycles of the unemployment series
were reversed in sign when combining them with the other series to
form the composite, so that, for example, in a period of large unemployment the sign of the unemployment index is negative.

The series used for the industrial composite for Germany are
wholesale prices, the value of exports, the production of anthracite
coal (*Steinkohlen*), and the production of pig iron. The methods
of computation were similar to those used in preparing the composite index for the United Kingdom.

The satisfactory data available for analyzing cyclical fluctuations
of the economic conditions in Italy are relatively scant. The only
series used in constructing the composite are the value of imports
and the value of exports, hence this index may appropriately be
designated as an index of Italian foreign trade. Inasmuch as the
great bulk of coal used in Italian industries is imported and a large
portion of some of the more important agricultural products, such
as wine and olive oil, are exported, the index of foreign trade is
probably a fairly good index of economic conditions in Italy, but it
is obviously not as reliable as the composite indices for the United
States, the United Kingdom, and Germany.

Certain limitations of the method used in constructing these composite indices will, of course, be recognized. For one thing, they may convey an exaggerated impression of the homogeneity of cyclical fluctuations in the given country. The averaging of several series obscures differences which may not be altogether unimportant in their effects on migration tendencies. Furthermore, the use of moving averages in estimating the trend, in some instances, such as toward the end of a depression period which is followed by a rapid recovery, results in extending the computed depression period beyond the time when in absolute terms the several economic phenomena are beginning to show signs of recovery. For example, in 1879, the production of pig iron in Germany was 2,227,000 tons, as compared with only 2,148,000 in 1878, but because this increase is less than the computed increment to the trend line from 1878 to 1879, the movement in the cycle curve from 1878 to 1879 appears as a decline for pig iron.

This tendency may account for occasional discrepancies between the evidence presented by the cycle curve and the descriptive accounts of variations in business conditions. Inasmuch as the cycle curves for migration and the industrial composites are computed by the same method, occasional minor discrepancies between interpretations which rest on the unadjusted statistics and those based upon the cycle curves do not necessarily affect the validity of comparisons between the cycle curves.

International Similarities in Business Cycles (Chart 40)

A comparison of the cycles of economic conditions in the United States, the United Kingdom, Germany, and Italy reveals that the fluctuations in the first three countries show marked similarities, although the agreement is by no means complete or invariable. In each of these three countries there was a boom in the early seventies followed by a decline in the middle part of the decade which continued well toward the end. Likewise, each experienced a boom in the early eighties, a decline near the middle of the decade, and a recovery in the late eighties or in the first years of the following decade, then a depression in the middle nineties, and a recovery again at the turn of the century. In each, a depression appears in 1904, a marked rise culminating in 1907, and a sharp decline in 1908, followed in a year or two by the beginning of a recovery which, during the remainder of the period prior to 1914, is not broken in any of the three countries by a reaction as severe as that of 1908.

CHART 40

INTERNATIONAL COMPARISONS OF CYCLES IN INDICES OF ECONOMIC
CONDITIONS: 1870-1913[a]

*Percentage deviations from seven-year smoothed moving averages, ex-
pressed as multiples of their standard deviations*

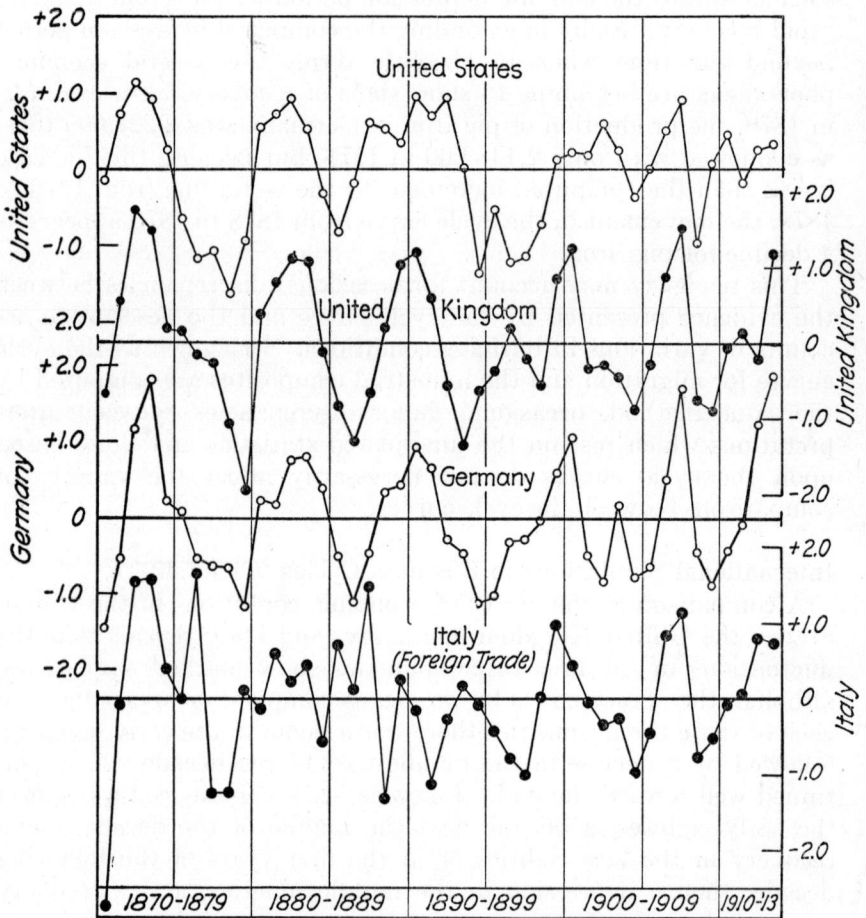

[a]Numerical data in Table 48, except for the United States index, which is plotted
from computations made by W. F. Ogburn and Dorothy S. Thomas, published in the
Journal of the American Statistical Association, September, 1922, p. 327.

TABLE 48—CYCLES IN ECONOMIC CONDITIONS AND IN IMMIGRATION TO THE UNITED STATES: 1870-1913[a]

Percentage deviations from smoothed seven-year moving averages, expressed in multiples of their standard deviations

YEAR	INDUSTRIAL COMPOSITES			EMIGRATION TO THE UNITED STATES		
	UNITED KINGDOM	GERMANY	ITALY	UNITED KINGDOM	GERMANY	ITALY
	A	B	C	D	E	F
1870	—0.67	—1.44	—2.72	+0.33	......	—0.69
1871	+0.55	—0.53	—0.07	+0.30	—0.24	—0.69
1872	+1.75	+1.18	+1.56	+0.91	+1.74	+2.40
1873	+1.48	+1.81	+1.58	+1.81	+1.32	+2.29
1874	+0.20	+0.22	+0.40	+0.16	—0.76	+0.74
1875	+0.17	+0.08	0	—0.91	—1.35	—1.06
1876	—0.17	—0.53	+1.66	—2.09	—1.59	—1.46
1877	—0.26	—0.63	—1.24	—2.67	—1.89	—1.46
1878	—1.06	—0.66	—1.22	—2.41	—1.89	—1.20
1879	—1.93	—1.16	+0.12	—0.94	—1.81	—0.69
1880	+0.39	+0.23	—0.12	+1.60	—0.03	—0.32
1881	+0.80	+0.18	+0.61	+1.19	+2.17	+0.53
1882	+1.11	+0.77	+0.23	+0.88	+1.55	+1.41
1883	+1.08	+0.81	+0.45	+0.87	+0.80	+0.86
1884	—0.11	+0.40	—0.56	—0.52	+0.33	—1.30
1885	—0.82	—0.50	+0.72	—1.13	—0.50	—1.40
1886	—1.29	—1.10	+0.14	—0.65	—1.05	—0.24
1887	—0.66	—0.47	+1.48	+0.97	—0.40	+0.71
1888	+0.20	+0.34	—1.30	+0.84	—0.27	+0.44
1889	+1.02	+0.44	+0.26	+0.03	—0.37	—1.01
1890	+1.20	+0.93	—0.14	—0.37	+0.04	+0.77
1891	+0.60	+0.68	—1.11	+0.09	+1.21	+0.85
1892	—0.56	—0.28	—0.26	+0.24	+1.63	+0.21
1893	—1.34	—0.48	+0.18	+0.63	+0.69	+0.56
1894	—0.63	—1.12	—0.08	—0.92	—1.02	—1.02
1895	—0.38	—1.02	—0.41	+0.65	—0.89	—0.86
1896	+0.20	—0.31	—0.78	—0.34	—0.72	—0.03
1897	—0.21	—0.28	—1.00	—0.83	—1.12	—0.66
1898	—0.56	—0.02	+0.02	—0.98	—1.09	—0.53
1899	+0.85	+0.60	+0.98	—0.21	—0.85	—0.56
1900	+1.25	+1.05	+0.44	+0.16	—0.79	—0.25
1901	—0.33	—0.49	—0.04	—0.17	—0.72	—0.13
1902	—0.29	—0.84	—0.34	—0.29	+0.35	+0.54
1903	—0.44	+0.17	—0.26	+0.08	+0.85	+0.78
1904	—0.88	—0.78	—0.98	+0.83	+0.01	—0.56
1905	—0.29	—0.64	—0.44	—0.34	+0.02	+0.95
1906	+0.87	+0.51	+0.84	+0.61	+0.48	+1.19
1907	+1.51	+1.71	+1.14	+1.71	+0.73	+0.89
1908	—0.76	—0.45	—0.77	—1.40	—0.68	—2.16
1909	—0.89	—0.88	—0.52	—0.79	—0.32	+0.01
1910	—0.06	—0.42	—0.08	+0.33	+0.25	—0.01
1911	+0.13	—0.08	+0.06	—0.06	—0.12	—0.88
1912	—0.21	+1.24	+0.80	—0.26	—0.74	—0.29
1913	+1.18	+1.88	+0.74	+0.24	+0.45	+1.16

[a] Sources:

A. *United Kingdom Industrial Composite.* Computed from: (1) wholesale prices of "total materials" (Statist); (2) the value of exports of British and Irish produce; (3) the production of coal; (4) the production of pig iron from British and foreign ores; and (5) the per cent unemployed in trade unions (signs reversed).

B. *Germany Industrial Composite.* Computed from: (1) wholesale prices, according to series published by Otto Schmitz, in *Bewegungen der Warenpreise;* (2) production of pig iron; (3) production of anthracite coal (Steinkohlen); and (4) the value of exports.

C. *Italy Industrial Composite.* Computed from the value (1) of imports and (2) of exports.

D. Great Britain, Commercial Labour and Statistical Department, *Emigration and Immigration—Copy of Statistical Tables relating to Emigration and Immigration from and into the United Kingdom,* 1892, and 1899 to 1909. These statistics pertain to the emigration of persons of British and Irish origin.

E. Kaiserliches Statistisches Amt, *Vierteljahreshefte zur Statistik des Deutschen Reichs.*

F. Computed from quarterly data of immigration from Italy to the United States, 1870 to June, 1888, and monthly data from July, 1888, to 1913 inclusive. (Table 49, footnote "a").

The index for Italy conforms reasonably well to the above described general tendencies, with the exception that the decline in the seventies is interrupted by a sharp recovery in 1876, and the movement of the Italian index through the eighties and the early nineties conflicts in some years with the direction of movement of the indices for the United States, Great Britain, and Germany, and is on the whole more erratic. Whether these differences are chiefly due to significant peculiarities in the economic conditions of Italy or are merely the result of the less adequate basis for the Italian index, may be open to question. Since the late nineties, the index for Italy also conforms approximately to the movements which have been mentioned as common to the other three.

The emphasis in the above paragraphs on similarities in the major swings of business conditions in the United States, Great Britain and Germany, should not be interpreted as implying that there are not many minor differences. To illustrate, in the eighties the low tide of activity is reached in the United States in 1885 but not until 1886 in Great Britain and Germany; in 1892 a rise is evidenced in the United States, while activity is declining in Germany and Great Britain; the decline of 1896 is peculiar to the United States; the reaction in 1901 is slighter in the United States than in the other two countries; in 1902, depression is deepening in Germany while a considerable improvement is shown in the United States; and in 1911, a mild depression is evidenced in the United States but not in Germany or Great Britain. More consideration will be given to these differences in subsequent paragraphs when making a comparison of economic conditions and emigration from each country separately considered. On the whole, however, the degree of similarity illustrated in Chart 40 indicates that inasmuch as the major swings in immigration to the United States coincide with the major cycles in industrial conditions in the United States, as has been pointed out in previous chapters, it follows that the upward swings in the cycles of emigration to the United States, must, in general, occur in periods of relative prosperity in the European countries of emigration. It remains to test this tentative conclusion by closer examination of the fluctuations in migration from the several important countries.

Selected Countries.

In the preceding pages we have noted the outstanding differences in the flow of migration from various countries to the United States and the extent to which there are similarities in the business cycles of leading industrial countries.   Let us now examine somewhat more closely the economic conditions in a few of the leading countries of emigration and the concurrent state of prosperity or depression in the United States, with the object of ascertaining, if possible, what influences are primarily responsible for cyclical fluctuations in migration.   The countries to which chief attention is given are the United Kingdom, Germany, and Italy.   Also the fluctuations in emigration to the United States from Russia, Sweden, and Austria-Hungary are briefly analyzed.

IMMIGRATION FROM THE UNITED KINGDOM

During the early decades of the nineteenth century the United Kingdom contributed the major part of the immigrant stream to the United States; and, with the enactment of the quota laws of 1921 and 1924, which allotted relatively large quotas to the northern European countries, British immigration has again been brought into a position of relatively large importance.[5]

Degree of Agreement between Business Cycles in the United States and the United Kingdom.

In several previous studies of business cycles, attention has been given to the extent to which business cycles move synchronously in Great Britain and the United States.   Professor Alvin H. Hansen, in his study of cycles in industrial conditions in the years 1902 to 1908, by months, reached the conclusion that the cyclical movements in the United States and Great Britain are quite closely concurrent.[6] Also, Professor Warren M. Persons and his associates, in a study of British economic conditions, demonstrated that, with certain note-worthy differences, there was a marked similarity in business cycles in the United States and Great Britain in the years 1903 to 1914, but that the British index, however, frequently lagged after that for the United States;[7] and Miss Dorothy S. Thomas, in a recent study, finds, for the same period covered by our analysis (1870 to

[5]In this chapter the term "British" is applied to the entire United Kingdom, in-cluding Great Britain and Ireland, and, unless so specified, references to "Great Britain" do not necessarily include Ireland.

[6]Alvin Harvey Hansen, *Cycles of Prosperity and Depression in the United States, Great Britain aud Germany—A Study of Monthly Data 1902-1908,* University of Wisconsin Studies in the Social Sciences and History, Number 5.

[7]*The Review of Economic Statistics, Supplement,* June, 1922, "An Index of British Economic Conditions, 1903-1914," by W. M. Persons, N. J. Silberling, and W. A. Berridge.

1913), a high degree of agreement between fluctuations in economic conditions in these two countries.[8]

The reader may form his own conclusions concerning the degree of this similarity by examining the composite indices for the United States and Great Britain in Chart 40 or 41. The general similarity is fairly obvious, but so also are certain differences. The British turn in 1879, and also in 1886, is a year later than the corresponding movement in the United States; a decline in 1888 and 1889 does not appear in the index for the United Kingdom as it does in the composite index for the United States; 1892 is a year of improvement in the United States but not in Great Britain; the index for the latter country recovered in 1894 but that for the United States continued to decline; the decline of 1896 in this country has no equivalent movement in Great Britain until 1897 and continues there in 1898; the boom in the early part of the century came in 1900 in Great Britain and in 1902 in the United States; and the depression of 1908 continued in 1909 in Great Britain, but the latter country did not experience a depression in 1911.

Peculiarities in the Immigration from the United Kingdom.

We have a graphic representation of the changes in the movement of immigration from England and Ireland in Chart 32, page 156, covering the years ending June 30, 1880 to 1914. In terms of the conditions shown by our industrial composite for the United Kingdom, in the boom years of the early eighties, immigration was high, particularly from England in 1882 and Ireland in 1883. With the industrial decline to 1885 and 1886, immigration likewise declined. The next peak in immigration appears in 1888, simultaneously with a period of business revival in Great Britain. The next ten years are marked by a decline in the number of immigrants from England and Ireland, varied only by a slight recovery in Irish immigration in 1891 and an accentuated decline for both countries in 1894, followed by a temporary recovery in 1895. If we allow for a few months lag, we find some movements which suggest that bad conditions in the United Kingdom diminish emigration, and some which indicate the contrary. The decline in 1894 follows the depression of 1893, the rise in 1895 follows the temporary revival in Great Britain in 1894, and the accentuated decline in the year ending June 30, 1909, accompanies depression conditions in Great Britain. But, on the other hand, the immigration boom, particularly

[8]Dorothy S. Thomas, *Social Aspects of the Business Cycle*, pp. 149-151.

from England, in 1903 to 1905, and in 1905 from Ireland also, accompanies a period of decline or depression in British industry.

At first inspection, all this appears somewhat confusing; for in some years an increase in immigration from these countries appears to coincide with good conditions; in others, with bad conditions.

As a second method of approach, we turn to Chart 34 on page 159. This chart shows the fluctuations in the ratio of immigration from the stated country to total immigration. The most striking movements in the English and Irish curves are the sharp decline in the year ending June 30, 1892, and the sharp increase in 1895 and again in 1904 and 1905. Evidently, if we consider only British conditions, we reach the conclusion that the hard times which existed there in the latter part of 1890, and in 1891 and 1892, materially checked emigration from the United Kingdom as compared with the movement from other countries; and that the marked increase in 1895 may be associated with the revival which occurred in Great Britain in 1894 and the spring of 1895. On the other hand, the rise in 1903, 1904, and 1905, which is relative as well as absolute, occurs in years which are marked by declining industrial activity in Great Britain.

It is evident from the above that even a comparison between conditions in Great Britain and fluctuations in the ratio between total immigration to the United States and that from England and Ireland does not lead us to a clear-cut conclusion concerning the relation between immigration and economic conditions in the home country.

We get a better indication of the causes of cyclical fluctuations in emigration from the United Kingdom if we compare this emigration movement with economic conditions in both the United States and Great Britain (Chart 41).

Emigration and Economic Conditions in the United States and the United Kingdom.

With the aid of Chart 41, we can make visual comparison of the relation between cycles in emigration from the United Kingdom to the United States and the concurrent economic conditions in these two countries. The emigration curves do not agree closely and consistently with economic conditions in either country; but there is a fair degree of agreement in major features. Good business conditions common to both countries are usually accompanied or closely followed by high emigration, and bad conditions by low

CHART 41

BUSINESS CONDITIONS AND EMIGRATION FROM THE UNITED
KINGDOM: 1870-1913[a]

Cycles in Emigration to the United States Compared with Business
Conditions in the United Kingdom (Fig. A) and the United
States (Fig. B)

*Deviations from seven-year smoothed moving averages, expressed as
multiples of their standard deviations*

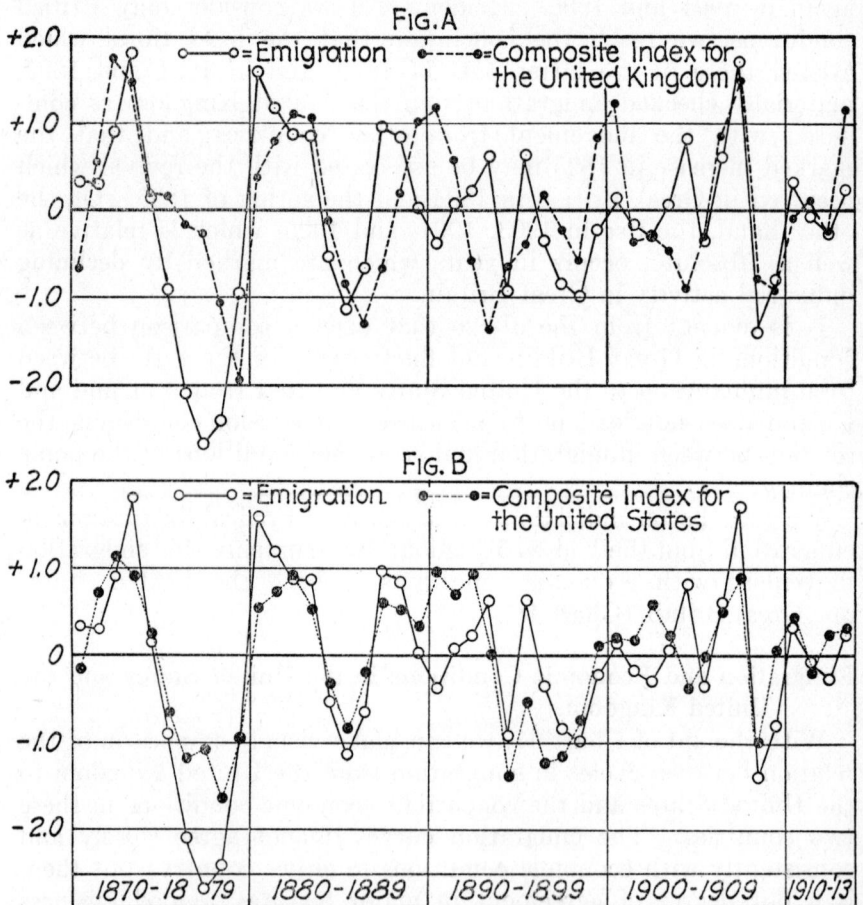

FIG. A

○—○ = Emigration   ●----● = Composite Index for
the United Kingdom

FIG. B

○—○ = Emigration   ●----● = Composite Index for
the United States

1870-18 79   1880-1889   1890-1899   1900-1909   1910-13

[a]For numerical data see Table 48 and footnote to Chart 40.

emigration; but where conditions in the two countries are not similar, the emigration movement appears to agree somewhat better with the index for the United States than with that for the United Kingdom.

These instances where the migration movement differs from one business cycle curve but agrees with the other are of special interest. The beginning of recovery in emigration in the late seventies and in 1886 agrees best with the concurrent changes in the index for the United States. Also, in the years 1888 and 1889, and in 1894 and 1896, the emigration curve and the United States composite, but not the British composite, decline. On the other hand, the decline in the emigration movement in 1901 and 1902 can be explained more plausibly by reference to economic conditions in Great Britain than to those in the United States, for 1902 is a boom year in the latter country. The emigration boom in 1904 coincides with depression in both countries. The recovery in emigration in 1909, despite the continuance of depression in the United Kingdom, evidences the effect of industrial recovery in the United States.

The tentative conclusion upon the basis of the evidence presented in Chart 41 is, that the general movements in economic conditions in the United States and the United Kingdom are similar, and that prosperity in the two countries ordinarily means higher emigration from the United Kingdom to the United States; depression, lower emigration. When, as not infrequently happens, the cyclical changes in the United Kingdom come somewhat tardily as compared with the similar movements in the United States, the movement in emigration usually agrees more closely with the ups and downs of industry in the latter country. The emigration decline of 1902 and the boom of 1904 are not, however, consistent with this explanation.

It may be suggested that by allowing a lag of one or two years we may find a good correspondence between depression in Great Britain and emigration therefrom. But upon examination of the curves for such possible relations, we find that with a one year lag attributed to emigration there is no consistent agreement, either direct or inverse, between British business conditions and emigration. With a two-year lag there is a moderate degree of inverse correlation, that is, a tendency for poor business conditions in Great Britain to be followed two years later by increased emigration to the United States, and for good conditions to be followed by decreased emigration. However, for the period as a whole, this agreement is not as close as that found between concurrent conditions of prosperity and high emigration, or depression and low emigration.[9] Furthermore, inasmuch as depression in the United Kingdom is ordinarily accompanied or preceded by depression in the United States, the assignment of such a two-year lag to the influence of British economic conditions upon British emigration would involve the rather implausible assumption that poor employment conditions in the United States stimulate emigration from the United Kingdom or that they act much more promptly upon British emigration than do conditions in the United Kingdom.

Quarterly Cycles of Employment in the United Kingdom and the United States.

The discussion in the preceding pages is based upon annual data. Quarterly statistics afford the basis for attention to some details which are not ascertainable from annual statistics. For some twenty-five years prior to the Great War, there are available quarterly or monthly statistics of immigration from Great Britain and Ireland to the United States, of unemployment among trade union members in the United Kingdom, and estimates of factory employment in the United States, the preparation of which is explained in Chapter III. For convenience in discussion, the signs of the unemployment series were reversed in plotting and the resulting curve in Chart 42 may be described as an "employment curve." Also, the curve for immigration to the United States from the United Kingdom will be designated herein as the "emigration curve."

[9]The Pearsonian coefficients of correlation between the cycles of emigration and industrial conditions afford some evidence in support of the conclusions reached by graphical analysis. They are: British emigration to the United States with British industrial composite, concurrent items, $+.421 \pm .08$; with emigration lagging one year, $+.06 \pm .10$; with emigration lagging two years, $-.26 \pm .08$; British emigration with the United States industrial composite, concurrent items, $+.56 \pm .07$; emigration lagging one year, $+.37 \pm .09$; two years, $+.03 \pm .10$.

Dorothy S. Thomas, in *Social Aspects of the Business Cycle*, pp. 148-151, finds that for the period from 1862-1913 the coeficient of correlation between her index of British business cycles and total emigration from the United Kingdom "reaches a maximum of $+.48$ with synchronous items. For the first half of the period, 1862-91, the correlation is $+.63$ for synchronous items; but for the second half, 1892-1913, the positive coefficients are not significant and a maximum negative correlation of $-.40$ occurs with a lag of two years." This suggests the possibility that, in the second half of the period, conditions in Great Britain, allowing for a lag of two years, are the major factors determining fluctuations in emigration from the United Kingdom. However, upon examination of the relation between emigration from the United Kingdom to the United States and business conditions in the United States, she finds that even "for the second half of the period, 1892-1913, the maximum $+.52$ was again for synchronous items," and hence slightly greater than the maximum correlation with British conditions($-.40$, with a lag of two years assigned to emigration). Thus, using somewhat different data and methods of computation from those used by us, she reaches substantially similar conclusions.

Through the first decade covered by this chart, the movement in emigration from the United Kingdom to the United States is frequently converse to the movement of employment in the United Kingdom. Thus from 1887 to 1889, inclusive, emigration is decreasing and employment increasing; in the next three years, em-

CHART 42

QUARTERLY CYCLES OF EMPLOYMENT CONDITIONS AND OF IMMIGRATION FROM THE UNITED KINGDOM TO THE UNITED STATES[a]

Unit = one standard deviation

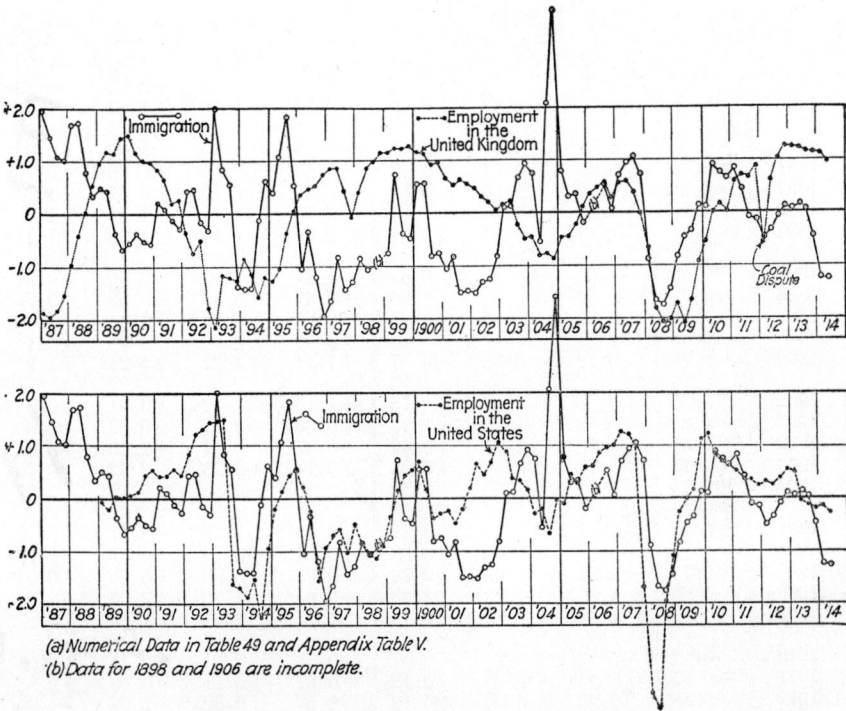

(a) Numerical Data in Table 49 and Appendix Table V.
(b) Data for 1898 and 1906 are incomplete.

ployment declines and emigration increases. This inverse relationship is somewhat less obvious in the next succeeding years, although in the second half of 1904 an exceptionally high peak in the emigration movement from the United Kingdom coincides with the low point in the employment cycle. The sharp decline in the depression of 1908 is quite similar in the two series, and, aside from a tendency in the upturn in 1909 for employment in the United Kingdom to lag after the corresponding change in immigration, the two movements agree fairly well in the recovery period. Except for a decline in one quarter of 1912, due largely to a coal strike, the employment

TABLE 49.—QUARTERLY CYCLES IN EMPLOYMENT CONDITIONS IN THE UNITED KINGDOM AND IN IMMIGRATION THEREFROM TO THE UNITED STATES: 1887-1914

Corrected for seasonal variation. Unit = one standard deviation.

YEAR	IMMIGRATION FROM THE UNITED KINGDOM TO THE UNITED STATES[a]				EMPLOYMENT IN THE UNITED KINGDOM[b]			
	1ST Q	2D Q	3D Q	4TH Q	1ST Q	2D Q	3D Q	4TH Q
1887	+1.98	+1.45	+1.09	+1.01	−1.88	−1.95	−1.84	−1.52
1888	+1.68	+1.71	+0.79	+0.32	−0.96	−0.41	+0.02	+0.52
1889	+0.50	+0.43	−0.37	−0.69	+0.94	+1.16	+1.14	+1.42
1890	−0.56	−0.37	−0.51	−0.57	+1.48	+1.15	+1.00	+0.96
1891	+0.21	+0.10	−0.11	−0.27	+0.83	+0.65	+0.20	+0.25
1892	+0.44	+0.46	−0.15	−0.31	−0.36	−0.75	−0.51	−1.77
1893	+1.99	+0.82	+0.56	−1.39	−2.16	−1.17	−1.21	−1.26
1894	−1.41	−1.41	−0.12	+0.61	−0.86	−1.14	−1.58	−1.21
1895	+0.40	+1.06	+1.83	+0.53	−1.28	−1.03	−0.36	+0.04
1896	−1.05	−0.34	−1.20	−1.96	+0.37	+0.46	+0.52	+0.74
1897	−1.66	−0.83	−1.43	−1.30	+0.84	+0.85	+0.44	−0.09
1898	−0.85	−1.07	°	°	+0.39	+0.84	+0.98	+1.14
1899	−0.76	+0.72	−0.38	−0.47	+1.14	+1.21	+1.21	+1.27
1900	+0.55	+0.56	−0.81	−0.75	+1.15	+1.12	+0.91	+0.96
1901	−1.05	−0.82	−1.50	−1.47	+0.65	+0.52	+0.62	+0.55
1902	−1.51	−1.30	−1.25	−0.82	+0.47	+0.31	+0.20	+0.05
1903	+0.10	+0.12	+0.67	+0.93	+0.17	+0.23	−0.22	−0.49
1904	+0.75	−0.55	+2.08	+3.82	−0.46	−0.80	−0.77	−0.87
1905	+0.79	+0.31	+0.37	−0.17	−0.46	−0.43	−0.21	+0.12
1906	°	°	+0.53	+0.08	+0.37	+0.49	+0.57	+0.29
1907	+0.71	+0.96	+1.06	+0.72	+0.55	+0.60	+0.39	−0.01
1908	−0.89	−1.66	−1.73	−1.43	−0.64	−1.80	−2.06	−2.01
1909	−0.82	−0.45	−0.32	+0.14	−1.72	−2.08	−1.64	−0.92
1910	+0.11	+0.90	+0.77	+0.67	−0.53	+0.01	+0.18	+0.04
1911	+0.85	+0.45	−0.08	−0.12	+0.61	+0.71	+0.68	+0.88
1912	−0.48	−0.33	−0.07	+0.12	−0.54	+0.62	+1.03	+1.25
1913	+0.08	+0.17	+0.06	−0.42	+1.24	+1.22	+1.16	+1.14
1914	−1.22	−1.24	......	......	+1.12	+0.97	......	......

[a]Deviations from 28-quarter moving average, computed from quarterly and monthly data given in U. S. Bureau of Statistics, *Tables Showing Arrivals of Alien Passengers and Immigrants, 1820 to 1888*; the *Monthly Summary of Commerce and Finance*, for July, 1888, to December, 1905; and the publications of the U. S. Bureau of Immigration for the remainder of the period.
[b]Deviations from mean for the period, computed from percentages of trade union members unemployed (signs reversed), Great Britain Commercial, Labour and Statistical Department, *Abstract of Labor Statistics*, 1887-1912; Trade Board, *Labor Gazette*, 1912 to 1914.
°Data incomplete.

movement does not reflect the slump in immigration in the latter part of 1911 and the early part of 1912.

Let us see whether some of these peculiarities may not be explained by reference to the curve for employment in factories in the United States, given in the lower section of Chart 42, together with the curve for immigration from the United Kingdom to the United States.

Upon examination of the facts concerning employment conditions in the United States, we find that, as a rule, those years when rising emigration is concurrent with declining employment in the United Kingdom are also years when the employment conditions in the United Kingdom and in the United States are not similar. Thus, from 1887 to 1889,[10] industrial activity in the United States slackened while British employment rose; in 1890 to 1892, inclusive, factory employment conditions in the United States improved while British employment declined; in 1896, employment in the United States declined but in Great Britain rose; in 1902, the United States movement is upward but in Great Britain it is downward; in 1908 and 1909 the upward turn comes more quickly in the United States, and the depression of 1911 is more clearly defined in the United States movement.

In each of the periods just mentioned emigration from the United Kingdom tended to increase when employment conditions were improving in the United States and becoming less favorable in the United Kingdom; and similarly, emigration declined when employment conditions became less favorable in the United States and more favorable in Great Britain.

On the other hand, in those periods when employment is improving in both countries, emigration is, as a rule, also increasing; when employment in both countries is declining, emigration also diminishes. For example, see 1906 to 1909. Neither employment conditions in the United States nor in Great Britain afford an obvious explanation for the sharp boom in emigration in 1904.

To summarize, the flow of emigration from the United Kingdom to the United States agrees to a large extent with the course of employment in the latter country, whether the concurrent movement in employment in Great Britain is similar or dissimilar to that in the United States.

British Emigration to Countries other than the United States.

During the period from 1870 to 1913 there was a substantial volume of emigration from the United Kingdom to countries other

[10]See Charts 32, 34, and 41.

than the United States. A complete analysis of cyclical fluctuations in British emigration would, consequently, involve a thorough study of business cycles in all the countries to which large numbers of British emigrants are attracted. This is a task we have not undertaken. However, even without an examination of economic conditions in the countries of destination, we can profitably compare the fluctuations in emigration to these "other countries" and to the United States. If these two streams of emigration fluctuate in close accord, it would be reasonable to conclude that the cyclical changes in employment opportunity in the United States and other host countries are essentially similar, or, as an alternative explanation, that conditions in the country of emigration are the dominating factor. On the other hand, if marked differences appear in the fluctuations of emigration to the United States and to "other countries" some weight is added to the other evidence tending to show that conditions in the home country of the emigrant are not the predominant influence in determining when his departure takes place.

In fact, the cycles in emigration from the United Kingdom to countries other than the United States show many dissimilarities to the cycles of emigration to the United States, indicating that these two movements are not clearly dominated by conditions in the United Kingdom or they would evidence more similarity. On the whole, the cycles of "other emigration" agree less closely with business conditions in the United Kingdom than do the cycles of emigration to the United States.[11]

In a few instances the relation between these two emigration movements is not readily explained by conditions in the United States. For example, in 1902 a boom in the United States was accompanied by declining emigration to the United States and increasing emigration to other countries; and in 1904 depression in the United States was accompanied by increasing British emigration thereto and declining emigration to other countries. As a rule, in those years in which the direction of change in the business cycle curve in the United States is dissimilar to that in Great Britain, the cyclical fluctuations in emigration to the United States agree, in direction of movement, with the business cycle in the United

[11]This conclusion is based upon the analysis of graphs of the cycles in emigration and business conditions, not reproduced here, supplemented with mathematical computation of the Pearsonian coefficients of correlation, which are $+.22 \pm .10$ for concurrent items in "other emigration" and British business conditions, and $+.42 \pm .08$ for emigration to the United States and British conditions.

States, while such agreement is evidenced less frequently by emigration to the "other countries." This adds some evidence, though not in itself sufficient to be conclusive, to indicate that the tendency for emigration to the United States in these years to agree with conditions in the United States, rather than in the home country, is not merely accidental but directly caused by the industrial conditions in the United States. For example, in 1896 economic activity in the United Kingdom increased, but slumped in the United States, and British emigration to the United States, but not to other countries, declined. A similar situation existed in 1911. Also, in 1909 conditions improved in the United States more rapidly than in Great Britain, and British emigration to the United States increased, though emigration to other countries declined.

IMMIGRATION FROM GERMANY

Immigration from Germany to the United States has experienced two great booms, one following the revolutionary disturbances in 1848 and culminating in 1854, when the recorded number of immigrants from Germany was 215,009; and a second wave culminating in 1882, with a total of 250,630, representing almost 32 per cent of the total immigration into the United States in that year. Subsequent to 1882 the general trend of immigration from Germany has been downward; though from 1900 to 1904 there was an increase, and thereafter up to the beginning of the war period the annual movement decreased only slightly. (See Chart 32).

Proportion of Total Immigration (Chart 34).

In the seventies and eighties, immigration from Germany constituted, in most years, from twenty to thirty per cent or more of the total immigration to the United States; but in each year from 1900 to 1914, with the exception of 1904, it represented less than five per cent. This ratio to the total immigration declined during the depression of the seventies, rose sharply in 1881 and remained at this new high level for five years, then began a long decline, broken only by temporary recovery movements, notably in 1903 and 1904, 1908, and 1911.

Business Cycles in Germany and the United States.

Particularly in the first two decades after 1870, the fluctuations in economic conditions in the United States and Germany, as indicated by the industrial composites previously described, show a substantial degree of similarity.[12] A tendency appears for the turns in the German curve to occur one year later than the corresponding changes in the United States composite. For example, the changes in direction which occurred in the United States composite in 1873, 1879, 1883, 1886, and 1909 are comparable with the changes in the German curve in 1874, 1880, 1884, 1887, and 1910, respectively. However, in the early nineties and again in the early part of the following decade, the decline toward depression becomes pronounced sooner in Germany than in the United States.

The German industrial composite exhibits some noteworthy differences from the United States composite. In 1892 economic activity diminished in Germany but increased in the United States; and in 1896, diminished in the United States but not in Germany. Conditions in Germany took a turn for the worse in 1901 and 1902 but improved in 1903; while industrial activity in the United States declined only slightly in 1901, improved in 1902 and declined in 1903. Again, in 1911 Germany experienced an industrial improvement while in the United States there was a mild depression, and the German boom in 1912 and 1913 was more pronounced than that in the United States. In both countries there was a decline in 1904, then a rise in 1907, and a decline in 1908.[13]

Emigration from Germany and Business Conditions.

In Chart 43 we have a comparison of the cycles of emigration from Germany, first (Fig. A) with business cycles in Germany, and, secondly, (Fig. B) with business cycles in the United States. Generally speaking, high emigration corresponds with the prosperity phase of the business cycle both in Germany and in the United States, and low emigration with depression in both countries.[14]

Where the movements are not concurrent, there is some evidence of a tendency for emigration to anticipate changes in conditions in Germany, as in the changes in emigration in 1873, 1882, and 1909; whereas changes in emigration are usually concurrent with cyclical

[12]See Chart 40, p. 174.

[13]The coefficient of correlation between the composites is $+.35 \pm .09$ if concurrent items are compared, or $+.31 \pm .09$ if a one-year lag is assigned to the industrial composite for Germany.

[14]The coefficients of correlation, for concurrent items, are $+.40 \pm .09$ for German industrial conditions and emigration from Germany to the United States, and $+.54 \pm .07$ for such emigration and industrial conditions in the United States. If a one-year lag is assigned to emigration, the coefficients are $+.17 \pm .10$ with German industrial conditions, and $+.52 \pm .08$ with conditions in the United States.

CHART 43

BUSINESS CONDITIONS AND EMIGRATION FROM GERMANY: 1870-1913

Cycles in Emigration to the United States Compared with Business
Conditions in Germany (Fig. A) and the United States (Fig. B)

*Percentage deviations from smoothed seven-year moving averages,
expressed as multiples of their standard deviations*

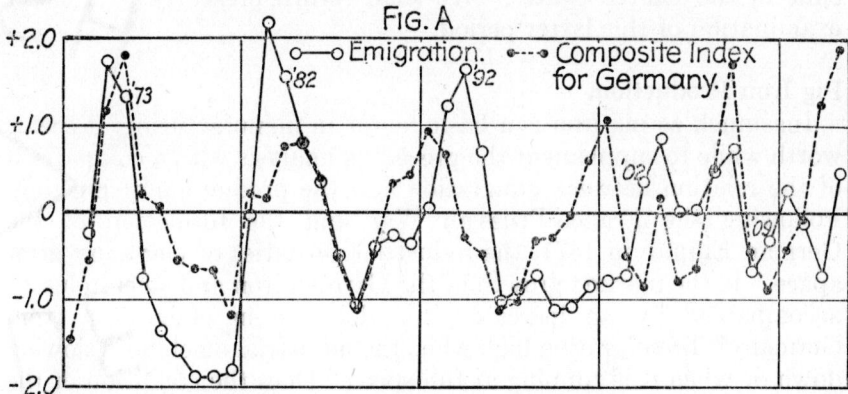

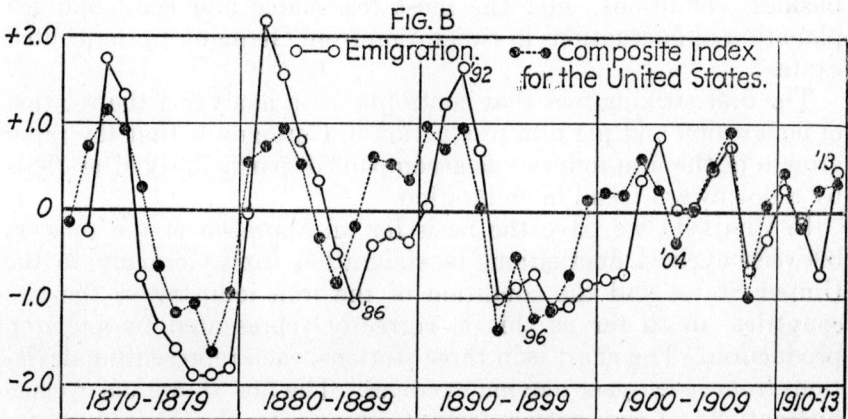

*For numerical data see Table 48 and footnote to Chart 40.

changes in the United States, or, as in 1886, 1904, and 1913, become
evident in the year following. When we examine the periods in
which the cyclical movements in the two countries are most conflicting, we find that in 1892 improving business conditions in the

United States and declining activity in Germany are accompanied by increasing emigration; that the decline in 1896, unique to the United States, is followed, somewhat tardily, by a decline in emigration in 1897; and that in 1902 German emigration is increasing and industrial conditions in the United States improving, while conditions in Germany are on the decline. On the contrary, in 1903, emigration increased despite the beginning of industrial decline in the United States. We shall return presently to a closer examination of this latter period.

Pig Iron Production.

Inasmuch as pig iron is a basic factor in manufacturing, it seems worth while to supplement the preceding analysis with a comparison of the relation between emigration and the production of pig iron. Following the Franco-Prussian War and the formation of the German Empire in 1871, the industrial activities of Germany grew apace. Is the marked growth of the German iron and steel industry accompanied by an increase or a decrease in emigration from Germany? Is emigration high when the industrial machine is slowing down or when it is running at full speed? Does the condition of the iron industry in the United States or in Germany, as an index of business conditions, offer the most reasonable and consistent explanation of fluctuations in emigration from Germany to the United States?

The first striking fact that confronts us in analyzing the relation of emigration and pig iron production in Germany is that the rapid growth of the iron industry is accompanied, particularly after 1881, by a downward trend in emigration.

In Chart 44 we have the basis for an appraisal of the relation between cyclical fluctuations in emigration from Germany to the United States and the condition of the iron industry in the two countries, in so far as this is correctly represented by pig iron production. The chart is in three sections, each representing deviations from seven-year moving averages. The first shows the cyclical fluctuations of emigration from Germany to the United States compared with pig iron production in the United States, with vertical scales in units of the respective standard deviations of the two series. The second section shows a similar comparison for emigration and pig iron production in Germany. The third compares the two pig iron curves in terms of percentage deviations from seven-year moving averages, and consequently does not iron out

CHART 44

CYCLES IN EMIGRATION FROM GERMANY TO THE UNITED STATES
AND IN PIG IRON PRODUCTION[a]

Units: Fig. A and Fig. B = one standard deviation; Fig. C = one per cent

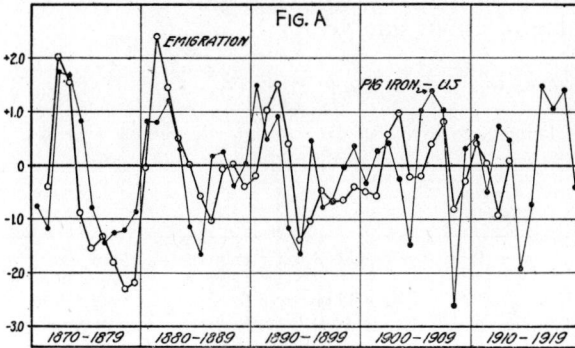

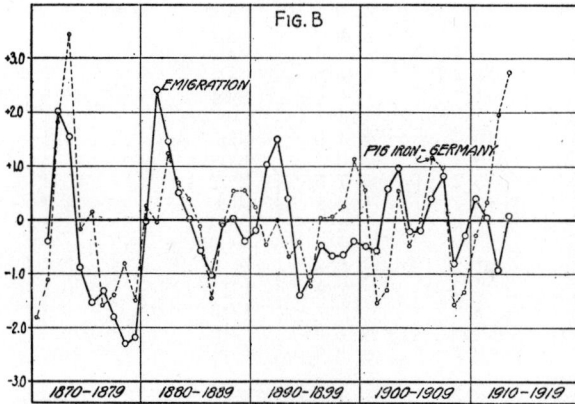

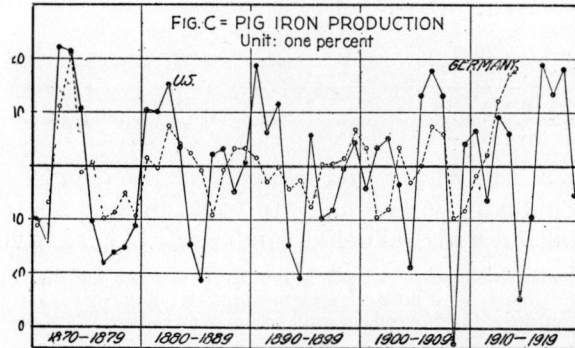

[a]Sources: pig iron curves in Fig. A, from Table 14; in Fig. B, computed from Table 50; in Fig. C, direct from Table 50. The emigration curve is identical with that in Chart 40, except that the moving averages from which the deviations are taken are not smoothed.

differences in the curves due to differences in their degree of fluctuation.

As illustrated by Fig. A of Chart 44 emigration from Germany to the United States shows a relatively high degree of correlation with pig iron production in the United States, but at frequent points indicates a lag of about one year.

TABLE 50.—CYCLES IN PIG IRON PRODUCTION IN GERMANY AND THE UNITED STATES: 1870-1914

Percentage deviations from seven-year moving averages

YEAR	UNITED STATES[a]	GERMANY[b]	YEAR	UNITED STATES	GERMANY
1870	− 9.9	−11.2	1895	+ 5.9	− 7.5
1871	−14.8	− 6.9	1896	− 9.8	+ 0.2
1872	+22.1	+11.1	1897	− 8.1	+ 0.4
1873	+21.3	+21.0	1898	− 0.4	+ 1.6
1874	+10.7	− 1.2	1899	+ 4.6	+ 6.9
1875	−10.2	+ 0.8	1900	− 4.0	+ 3.4
1876	−18.1	− 9.8	1901	+ 3.5	− 9.5
1877	−16.1	− 8.7	1902	+ 5.2	− 8.0
1878	−15.2	− 5.0	1903	− 3.2	+ 3.4
1879	−11.1	− 9.3	1904	−18.8	− 3.0
1880	+10.4	+ 1.6	1905	+13.1	0
1881	+10.1	− 0.3	1906	+17.8	+ 7.2
1882	+15.2	+ 7.5	1907	+13.1	+ 6.0
1883	+ 3.7	+ 4.2	1908	−33.1	− 9.7
1884	−14.6	+ 2.4	1909	+ 4.1	− 8.2
1885	−21.2	− 0.8	1910	+ 6.7	− 1.7
1886	+ 2.2	− 9.1	1911	− 6.3	+ 2.1
1887	+ 3.2	− 0.7	1912	+ 9.1	+12.1
1888	− 4.8	+ 3.3	1913	+ 6.1	+17.0
1889	+ 0.7	+ 3.3	1914	−24.3	−14.2
1890	+18.7	+ 1.6			
1891	+ 6.3	− 2.9			
1892	+11.5	− 0.1			
1893	−14.7	− 4.2			
1894	−20.9	− 2.6			

[a]Computed from data in Table 12-A.
[b]Computed from annual statistics published in *Volkswirtschaftliche Chronik-Abdruck aus den Jahrbüchern für Nationalökonomie und Statistik* and in *Stahl und Eisen*.

Likewise, in Fig. B, we find evidence of a tendency for activity in the iron industry in Germany to coincide with the fluctuations in emigration, but with less definite indication of a lag in emigration.[15]

[15]The Pearsonian coefficients of correlation are (1) emigration and pig iron in the United States, +.57 ±.07 if no lag is assigned, and +.44 ±.08 with a lag of one year ascribed to emigration; (2) emigration and pig iron in Germany, +.58 ±.07 with no lag, and +.14 ±.10 with lag of one year.

In fact in some instances, the emigration movement precedes the corresponding change in pig iron production. For example, emigration reached high points in 1872 and 1881, and a low level in 1894, while the corresponding points in the pig iron curves are in 1873, 1882, and 1895, respectively.

The suggestion conveyed by the analysis of these two sections of the chart is that cyclical fluctuations in industrial conditions in the United States and Germany are substantially similar but that in some instances the United States movement anticipates the German movement by about a year, and that coincident high industrial activity in the two countries is accompanied by large emigration from Germany and an industrial depression by small emigration. This apparent dominance of the "pull over the push" may find some explanation in the fact that the fluctuations in industrial conditions in the United States appear more violent than those in Germany. This is illustrated by the comparison of the two pig iron curves in the lower section of Chart 44, expressed as percentage deviations from seven-year moving averages. As a rule, the American curve rises higher in prosperity and falls further in depression, so that even when industrial expansion in the two countries coincides, the greater volume of the American fluctuation affords one logical explanation of its effectiveness in attracting an increase in immigration from Germany.

Employment in Germany and the United States (Chart 45)

A comparison of employment conditions in the United States and Germany, by quarters, from 1901 to 1908, affords an opportunity for further study of a period which is marked by substantial differences in the concurrent status of industry in these two countries. From 1901 to 1904, inclusive, the cyclical movement of quarterly employment in Germany was, on the whole, contrary to the corresponding movement in the United States, particularly in 1902, which was a year of low employment in Germany but a boom year in the United States. In 1905 to 1908, on the other hand, the two employment curves show better agreement, though the German labor market does not exhibit a recovery movement in the second half of 1908 such as occurred in the United States.

The cyclical movement in emigration from Germany appears in this period to be determined by, or at least to vary with, employment conditions in the United States. With the exception of minor irregularities and an occasional lag of from one to three

quarters, it rises with the curve for United States factory employment in 1901 and 1902, falls with it in the latter part of 1903 and
most of 1904, and exhibits a general upward tendency in common
with it after 1904 until checked by the depression of 1908.

CHART 45[a]

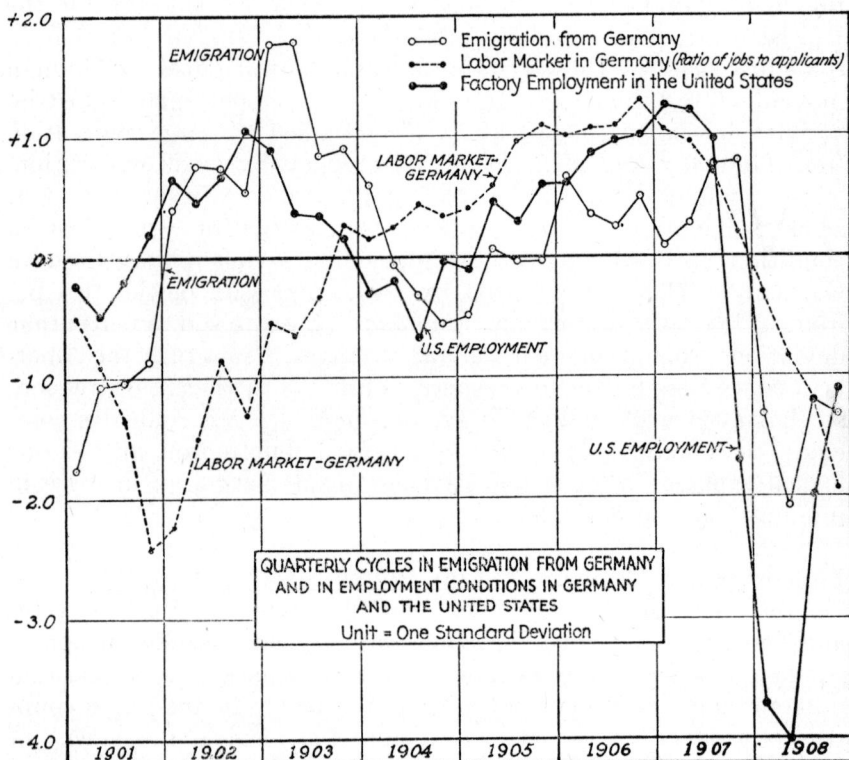

QUARTERLY CYCLES IN EMIGRATION FROM GERMANY
AND IN EMPLOYMENT CONDITIONS IN GERMANY
AND THE UNITED STATES
Unit = One Standard Deviation

[a]The numerical data for the German series are in Table 51; the quarterly cycles for
factory employment in the United States are averages of the monthly cycles in Appendix
Table V.

Emigration from Germany to Countries other than the United States.

The official recorded emigration from Germany to countries
other than the United States from 1870 to 1913 was relatively
small, exceeding ten thousand persons only in a few years, and
constituting as a rule less than twenty per cent of total emigration.[16]

[16]Kaiserliches Statistisches Amt, *Vierteljahreshefte zur Statistik des Deutschen Reichs*,
total emigration from principal ports of departure.

The cyclical movements of this "other emigration" evidence a fair degree of similarity to the cycles in emigration to the United States, particularly in the first two decades after 1870, but there are a number of instances in which the direction of the cyclical movements of these two streams of emigration are divergent, such as the changes, compared with the previous year, in 1889, 1892, 1893, 1906 to 1908, and 1910 to 1912.[17] The occurrence of such divergencies is also indicated by the fact that emigration to other countries varies, for example, from 23 per cent of the total in 1876 to only 7 per cent in 1882, and from 4 per cent in 1907 to 26 per cent in 1912 and 1913, this diversity indicating that there is a reasonable

TABLE 51.—QUARTERLY CYCLES IN EMIGRATION AND THE STATE OF THE
LABOR MARKET, GERMANY, 1901-1908

Deviations from the mean adjusted for seasonal variation.   Unit = one standard deviation

YEAR	EMIGRATION FROM GERMANY[a]				RATIO OF APPLICANTS TO JOBS (SIGNS REVERSED)[b]			
	1ST Q	2D Q	3d Q	4TH Q	1ST Q	2D Q	3D Q	4TH Q
1901	−1.76	−1.07	−1.03	−0.86	−0.51	−0.91	−1.35	−2.42
1902	+0.39	+0.76	+0.73	+0.54	−2.23	−1.50	−0.85	−1.31
1903	+1.77	+1.78	+0.84	+0.90	−0.54	−0.65	−0.33	+0.27
1904	+0.59	−0.07	−0.32	−0.56	+0.15	+0.24	+0.43	+0.33
1905	−0.48	+0.07	−0.04	−0.03	+0.40	+0.58	+0.95	+1.08
1906	+0.66	+0.34	+0.24	+0.49	+1.00	+1.07	+1.08	+1.29
1907	+0.08	+0.27	+0.76	+0.78	+1.05	+0.94	+0.68	+0.18
1908	−1.32	−2.08	−1.20	−1.32	−0.31	−0.83	−1.20	−1.93

[a]Computed from monthly statistics published by the Kaiserliches Statistisches Amt, *Vierteljahreshefte zur Statistik des Deutschen Reichs.*
[b]Computed from statistics of the number of applicants per 100 jobs in employment offices, in *Der Arbeitsmarkt*, J. Jastrow, editor, for the years prior to 1907; and in *Reichs-Arbeitsblatt*, Kaiserliches Statistisches Amt, for 1907 and subsequent years.

likelihood that cyclical fluctuations in emigration were not dominated primarily by economic conditions in Germany but that the conditions in the countries of destination were exercising a considerable influence upon such cyclical movements.

Influence of Crop Failures.

The suggestion occurs that agricultural rather than industrial conditions in Germany may explain emigration. We have not made a close statistical study of crop yields in Germany but have com-

[17]Based upon a comparison of the cyclical curves in Chart 43 with a similar curve for "other emigration," not here reproduced.

pared the general tenor of crop reports with the current volume of emigration, and also with the changes in emigration in the following year, inasmuch as the effect of crop failures, if any, would not, in many cases, be fully effective upon emigration until the succeeding year. We find no close or consistent relationship between harvests and emigration. Poor crop years are sometimes years of low, sometimes of high, emigration. They are sometimes followed by increased emigration, but almost equally often by decreased emigration. Similarly, years of excellent crops are sometimes accompanied or immediately followed by rising emigration, in other years by declining emigration.

To illustrate, poor crops in 1873 are followed, in the succeeding year, by a sharp cyclical drop in emigration,[18] in 1874 by a mild drop, in 1880 by a sharp rise, in 1881 by a drop, in 1886, 1889, and 1891, by a moderate rise. Likewise, in about fifty per cent of the cases in which good or excellent crops are reported, the cyclical change in emigration in the following year is a decrease; in the other fifty per cent, an increase.

IMMIGRATION FROM ITALY

The flow of immigration from Italy to the United States from 1870 to 1914 was characterized by a pronounced upward trend, both in actual numbers and in proportion to the total immigration to this country.[19] In fact, in recent decades Italy has become the largest single contributor to the stream of immigrants entering the United States. In the twenty-four years ending June 30, 1924, about three and one half million immigrants designated Italy as their country of origin or of last permanent residence. A large proportion of these, however, subsequently returned to their native land. The immigration movement from Italy has also been characterized by a strong cyclical movement, which fact suggests the special desirability of a comparison between it and cycles in economic activity in the United States and Italy.

Business Cycles in Italy and the United States (Chart 41)

We have previously noted, in comparing business cycles in the United States with those in important European countries, that the cycles in Italy, either because of the less adequate information

[18]See Chart 43.
[19]See Charts 33 and 35, in the early part of this chapter.

upon which the index for Italy was based, or because of peculiarities in the economic life of that country, evidence the least resemblance to the business cycles in the United States.

With which movement, then—cyclical fluctuations in Italy or cyclical fluctuations in the United States—are the fluctuations in immigration most nearly comparable? A preliminary answer to this question is given by the facts presented in Chart 46, which contains comparisons of the cycles in Italian immigration to the United States, first, in the upper section of the chart, with Italian foreign trade, and, secondly, in the lower section, with economic conditions in the United States.

The impression received from an examination of this chart is that the agreement between concurrent items is appreciably closer between Italian immigration and the United States industrial composite than it is between Italian foreign trade and Italian immigration. Nor does it appear obvious that a different conclusion would be reached if a lag were assigned to the influence of economic conditions upon immigration.[20]

In a few years, such as 1893, immigration increases with activity in Italy despite an industrial decline in the United States, but as a rule in those instances in which the index of Italian foreign trade shows marked differences from the United States industrial composite—as in 1876, 1888, and 1902—the course of immigration is apparently dominated by the course of economic activity in the United States. However, in some of the years in which changes in immigration from Italy are not closely similar in direction or degree of change with economic conditions in the United States—as in 1889 and 1896—some argument is afforded for the theory that activity in Italy decreases emigration, and vice versa, for in 1889 foreign trade boomed and emigration to the United States declined, and in 1896 foreign trade declined but immigration boomed. This absence of a clear and consistent relationship between foreign trade and emigration from Italy suggests the desirability of utilizing additional bases of comparison. Industrially, Italy is different in essential respects from the other leading emigrant countries which we have considered. The typical Italian immigrant comes largely

[20]These conclusions are further supported by the coefficients of correlation, which, with their "probable errors", are as follows: for concurrent items, only $+.34 \pm .09$ for foreign trade and immigration and $+.55 \pm .07$ for the United States composite and immigration; and, with a one year lag assigned to immigration, only $+.16 \pm .10$ for foreign trade and immigration and $+.35 \pm .09$ for the United States composite and immigration.

CHART 46

BUSINESS CONDITIONS AND IMMIGRATION FROM ITALY: 1870-1913.

Cycles in Immigration from Italy to the United States Compared
with Cycles in Foreign Trade in Italy (Fig. A) and with
Business Conditions in the United States (Fig. B)

Unit = one standard deviation

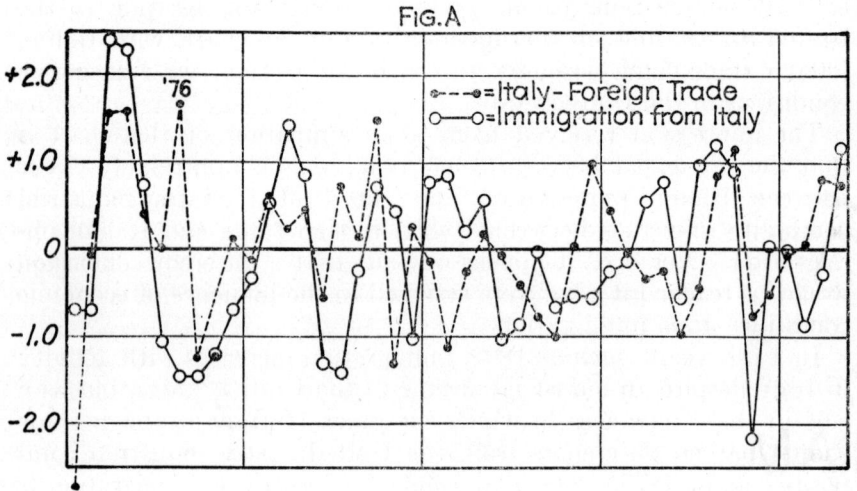

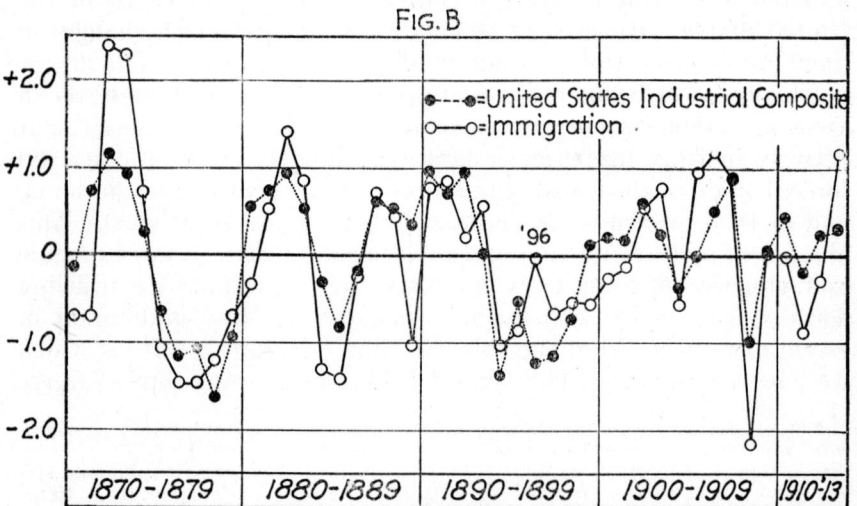

FIG. A

●----●=Italy-Foreign Trade
○——○=Immigration from Italy

FIG. B

●----●=United States Industrial Composite
○——○=Immigration

1870-1879 1880-1889 1890-1899 1900-1909 1910-13

.For numerical data see Table 48 and footnote to Chart 40.

from the agricultural classes, where he has occupied the status of a laborer.   Consequently, it is particularly pertinent to inquire as to the extent to which crop conditions in Italy account for fluctuations in emigration from that country.

Aggregate Value of Leading Crops in Italy (Chart 47)

As an aid to the determination of the relation between crop conditions and emigration, we have constructed an index of the aggregate annual value of leading crops in Italy.   Inasmuch as a large crop may bring low prices in some years, but in others, because of adverse conditions in other parts of the world, may be accompanied by good prices, it appeared probable that an index of the product of quantity and price would give the best evidence of the prosperity of the agricultural classes.   The crops used in this index are wheat, maize, wine, rice, and olive oil, for the years 1884 to 1913, inclusive.   The estimated values of the several crops, together with a brief footnote description of the method used, are given in Table 52.

Crop Values in Italy and Pig Iron Production in the United States.

In view of the fact that Italy is predominantly an agricultural country, whereas the Italian laborer in this country engages primarily in industrial operations, it is desirable to ascertain whether crops in Italy or industrial conditions in the United States exercise the greater influence upon the cyclical fluctuations of immigration from Italy.   For this purpose we have used the index of aggregate values of leading crops in Italy described in the above paragraph and the volume of pig iron production in the United States.   It does not appear probable that the effect, if any, of crop conditions in Italy would become apparent until after some months, hence the comparisons made are chiefly between immigration in the fiscal year ending June 30th, and crop values and pig iron production of the calendar year ending on the preceding December 31st.   This is tantamount to assuming an approximate lag of six months in the effect of crops or of industrial activity upon immigration.

The outstanding relations are evident upon examination of Chart 47.   The cyclical fluctuations in immigration from Italy, and those in pig iron production in the United States, in the years 1884 to 1914 inclusive, show a general, although not invariable, similarity in their general contour.   As a rule, a change in pig iron is accompanied, either in the same year or in the following year, by a

change in immigration, similar in direction at least. In the central
part of the period, the agreement with fluctuations in pig iron
appears to be best when the immigration ending June 30th is
compared with pig iron production for the twelve months ending
December 31st of the preceding year; but prior to 1889 and in

TABLE 52.—ESTIMATED VALUE OF LEADING CROPS IN ITALY: 1884-1913ᵃ

Unit: first column = one standard deviation; others, = one million lire

YEAR	TOTAL OF THE FIVE CROPS		WHEAT	MAIZE	WINE	RICE	OLIVE OIL
	CYCLES	VALUE					
1884	—0.96	2,256.4	823.5	351.1	684.0	126.2	271.6
1885	—0.33	2,421.0	771.8	309.7	946.9	124.0	268.6
1886	+1.81	2,958.8	791.8	319.0	1,376.2	134.5	337.3
1887	+0.02	2,494.2	837.3	286.1	1,036.0	116.0	218.8
1888	—0.64	2,396.7	731.4	276.5	985.4	80.6	322.8
1889	—1.46	2,130.5	770.0	322.7	739.7	131.8	166.3
1890	+1.10	2,758.1	917.2	294.8	1,119.4	93.5	333.2
1891	+2.19	2,931.2	1,071.9	294.2	1,183.7	110.1	271.3
1892	—0.39	2,188.7	859.9	283.7	781.4	104.4	159.3
1893	—0.24	2,254.7	872.3	283.5	739.8	67.9	291.2
1894	—1.68	1,778.8	700.2	211.7	593.8	72.8	200.3
1895	—0.66	1,991.7	732.8	277.2	630.4	77.8	273.5
1896	+0.51	2,322.3	981.7	294.0	829.4	53.7	163.5
1897	—1.43	1,903.5	677.1	250.8	708.8	91.8	175.0
1898	+0.48	2,637.2	1,111.5	333.4	856.4	92.9	243.0
1899	—0.44	2,474.1	1,054.5	348.2	877.5	99.9	94.0
1900	+0.14	2,788.7	1,030.6	368.3	1,044.3	142.4	203.1
1901	+1.51	3,397.5	1,292.3	433.3	1,192.9	133.4	345.6
1902	—0.73	2,709.9	1,020.9	324.4	1,036.0	133.8	194.8
1903	+0.82	3,302.2	1,338.3	406.4	1,053.0	152.4	352.1
1904	—0.41	2,998.3	1,220.3	413.5	1,022.0	152.2	190.3
1905	—0.19	3,024.0	1,254.4	444.2	790.8	135.4	399.2
1906	—0.86	2,919.8	1,330.4	424.8	893.5	145.8	125.3
1907	+1.24	3,637.6	1,382.1	404.2	1,347.6	164.9	338.8
1908	—0.85	3,048.4	1,339.0	438.2	1,035.0	150.8	85.4
1909	+0.43	3,694.1	1,596.9	479.2	1,050.1	141.8	426.1
1910	—1.67	3,018.0	1,191.1	484.5	966.7	135.0	240.7
1911	+1.17	4,262.3	1,455.1	470.0	1,791.5	153.3	392.4
1912	+0.43	4,078.6	1,409.0	520.1	1,853.2	147.2	149.1
1913	+0.91	4,323.1	1,705.0	516.2	1,671.7	179.3	250.9

ᵃThe "cycles" are deviations from a seven-year moving average of the estimated total value of the five crops. The values of the separate crops were computed by multiplying annual production by the average export prices of the given commodity in the year in question, except that for wheat the average prices in the markets of the Kingdom were used. Sources: Minister of Agriculture (Italy), *Annuario Statistico Italiano*, 1884 to 1914; and *Year Book of the International Institute of Agriculture—Statistical Bureau 1909-1921*.

CHART 47

IMMIGRATION FROM ITALY COMPARED WITH PIG IRON PRODUCTION
IN THE UNITED STATES AND CROP VALUES IN ITALY:
1884-1913ᵃ

Unit= one standard deviation

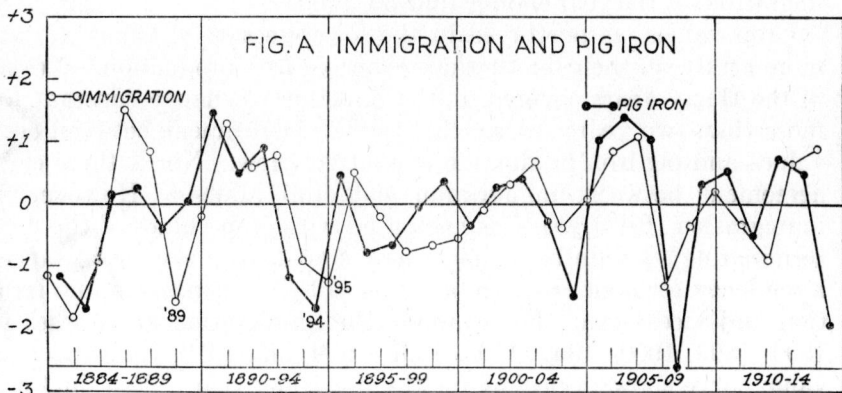

FIG. A IMMIGRATION AND PIG IRON

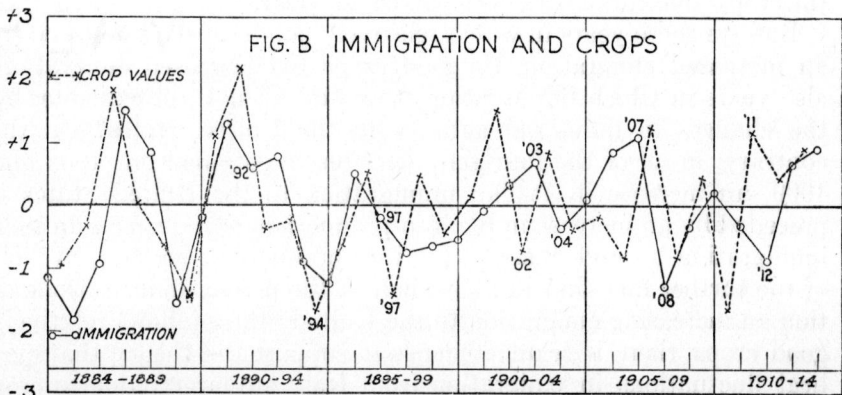

FIG. B IMMIGRATION AND CROPS

ᵃCycles in immigration from Italy into the United States are computed frcm data
given in Table 44; the cycles in United States pig iron production, Table 14; crop values
in Italy, Table 52.   The pig iron and crop data are for calendar years; the immigration
data, for years ending June 30th.

several years beginning in 1904, the best agreement is reached
when immigration for the year ending June 30th is compared with
pig iron production for the year ending the following December
31st. This apparent tendency for immigration to anticipate changes

in pig iron production may be explainable largely by the fact that the bulk of the immigrants credited to any fiscal year actually arrive in the second half of the year, that is, between January and June, inclusive, so that, for example, the effect of the industrial boom indicated by pig iron production in 1909 would, if there is little or no lag in its effect on immigration, be evident in the immigration for the year ending June 30, 1909.

Crop values, as portrayed in the lower section of Chart 47, are more erratic in their fluctuations than pig iron production. Never, in the thirty years covered, is the direction of change constant for more than two years. Also, the degree of agreement between crop values and pig iron production is relatively low. Nor is there close agreement between immigration and crop values.[21] However, if immigration (fiscal years) is compared with crop values of the year terminating six months earlier, there is evident in several instances a tendency for poor crops to be followed by an increase in immigration and vice versa. For example the immigration curve rises in 1890, 1893, 1900, 1903, 1905, 1907, 1909, and 1913, while the crop value curve shows a decline for the preceding year. Also, in 1892, 1897, 1904, 1908, and 1912, the immigration curve declines while the crop value curve rises in the preceding year.

But are these years in which relatively poor crops are followed by an increased emigration, or good crops by decreased emigration, also years in which immigration from Italy is not well explained by the changes in industrial activity in the United States? On the contrary, in all of the fourteen years just mentioned but 1905 and 1909, an increase in Italian immigration to the United States is preceded by an increase in pig iron production, or a decrease in such immigration by a decrease in pig iron production; so that, in view of the further fact that in about half of the period under consideration an increasing emigration to the United States follows relatively good crops, there is scant evidence to support the theory that cyclical fluctuations in emigration from Italy are largely due to crop conditions in the preceding year.[22]

[21]The coefficient of correlation between crop values and pig iron production, when concurrent items are compared, is $+.32$ with a "probable error" of $+.11$; and between crop values in calendar years and Italian immigration to the United States in the respective years ending six months later is $+.31 \pm .11$.

[22]The relationship between the three series under discussion may also be expressed in customary mathematical terminology, that is, by stating the coefficients of correlation, which are $+.50 \pm .09$ for pig iron production and immigration from Italy in the fiscal year ending six months later; and only $+.31 \pm .11$ for the corresponding comparison between Italian crop values and immigration from Italy.

The general conclusion would appear to be that immigration from Italy to the United States exhibits a better agreement with pig iron production in the United States than it does with crop values in Italy. It remains to test this assumption by other methods of approach.

Fluctuations in Immigration Peculiar to Italy.

In addition to the above comparison between the statistical evidences of fluctuations in crop values, pig iron production, and immigration from Italy, an examination was made of the unique movements in immigration from Italy; for it appears plausible that further knowledge of the influences which account for fluctuations in Italian migration may be obtained by examining the circumstances surrounding marked changes in the ratio of immigration from Italy to total immigration.

We have had occasion to note the fluctuations in this ratio (See Chart 35 and Table 45), and also the fluctuations in the actual numbers from Italy (Chart 33 and Table 44). These two sets of fluctuations are frequently similar. In eleven years in the two decades ending in 1914, an increase in actual numbers of immigrants from Italy results in an increase in the fraction of total immigration which arrived from that country, indicating that there has not been an equivalent change in the other elements in the immigrant stream. However, there are also several instances, such as 1902 and 1903, where a substantial change in the number of immigrants brings no equivalent change in the ratio to total immigration.

Comparisons with Crop Conditions.

A comparison of the marked changes in the ratio of immigrants arriving from Italy to total immigration with descriptive statements of crop conditions[23] prevailing in the preceding calendar year reveals a slight tendency for a relative increase in this ratio to be preceded by somewhat poorer crops than the years in which there is a relative decline in immigration. In the five years ending June 30, 1892, 1904, 1907, 1908, and 1910, this ratio declined one tenth or more from the ratio of the preceding year. In the years ending the preceding December crops are reported as excellent in one, good in two, and fair in two. On the other hand, in seven years (1891, 1893, 1896, 1897, 1906, 1909, and 1913) in which the ratio increased

[23]Based, not on our index of aggregate values of leading crops, but on descriptive statements of crop conditions compiled by Dr. W. L. Thorp.

one-tenth or more, good crops are reported for only two of the preceding years, fair for three, and poor for two. However, in three instances (1894, 1897, and 1910) in which poor crops or agricultural depression are recorded, there is no substantial increase in the immigration ratio for the following fiscal year. So again, we reach the conclusion that while there may be a slight tendency for poor crops to stimulate unusual emigration from Italy, and vice versa, it cannot be said to be a pronounced tendency.

Comparisons with Pig Iron Production in the United States.

Taking into account the general upward trend in the fraction of total immigration represented by the number of immigrants from Italy, the movements in this ratio which particularly challenge explanation are the declines or low points in 1875, 1880 and 1881, 1884 and 1885, 1889, 1892, 1894 and 1895, 1900, 1904 and 1905, 1908, and 1912 (Chart 35, p. 160).

It will be noted that in most of these instances, a relatively low immigration from Italy—low relative to total immigration—coincides with or immediately follows more or less marked periods of industrial depression, or at least of slackening activity, in the United States. This frequent coincidence between industrial depression and relatively low immigration from Italy suggests that Italian immigration is unusually sensitive to industrial conditions in the United States.

Emigration to Countries other than the United States.

Emigration from Italy was large long before the movement of Italian emigrants to the United States reached a substantial volume. In each year prior to the eighties, emigration to the United States was less than ten per cent of the total emigration to transoceanic countries, Europe, and the Mediterranean countries.[24] In the eighties and nineties, it only occasionally amounted to over twenty per cent of the total. But from 1900 to 1914, the proportion going to the United States ranged from 23 to 45 per cent. As a rule, this ratio was relatively high, as compared with the immediately preceding and succeeding years, in prosperous years in the United States, such as 1903 and 1906, and relatively low in the periods marked by depression tendencies, namely, 1901, 1904, 1908, and 1911. This fact adds some additional weight to the evidence supporting the

[24]Based upon the statistics of emigration published by the Director General of Statistics, Italy.

conclusion that cyclical fluctuations in migratory currents to the United States are determined largely by conditions in this country; for if conditions in Italy were the dominant factor, we should expect the ratio of total emigration going to the United States to show less sensitiveness to economic conditions in the United States.

OTHER COUNTRIES OF EMIGRATION

For the remaining sources of emigration to the United States, we have not attempted to make statistical comparisons of the kind made for the United Kingdom, Germany, and Italy; but for some of them we have endeavored to trace the effect of exceptionally good or exceptionally poor business or crop conditions upon the concurrent or immediately subsequent volume of emigration. Also, when substantial changes appear in the proportion of total immigration made up by immigrants from the stated country, we have sought to ascertain whether special conditions existed in the country of emigration to which the change might reasonably be attributed. This survey is intended to be suggestive rather than exhaustive. The data concerning immigration which are utilized in these comparisons appear largely in Tables 44 and 45 and the accompanying charts (32, 33, 34, 35) in the early part of this chapter; and the statements concerning conditions in the selected countries are based chiefly upon Professor Wesley C. Mitchell's treatise on *Business Cycles*, and upon the recently published "Business Annals" prepared by Dr. Willard L. Thorp, of the Staff of the National Bureau of Economic Research.

Sweden.

Immigration to the United States from Sweden reached its maximum with a total of almost sixty-five thousand in the year ending June 30, 1882, but since 1893 the annual inflow of immigrants from that country has exceeded thirty thousand only in the two years ending June 30, 1902, and 1903, respectively. The waves of the cyclical movement in Swedish emigration to the United States since 1870 have coincided substantially with the alternations of prosperity and depression in the United States, that is, with a slump following 1873, another in the middle eighties, a minor decline in the years ending June 30, 1889 and 1890, a marked decline in the nineties beginning with the depression of 1893-1894, and further slumps in the years ending June 30, 1904, 1908, and 1912.

On the other hand, an examination of the major features of agricultural and industrial conditions in Sweden does not afford an equally consistent explanation of the cyclical fluctuations in Swedish emigration to the United States. For example, excellent crops in 1892 and 1906 were followed in the respective fiscal years ending six months later, by a decline in emigration to the United States; but in 1890 and 1900, by an increase. Likewise, poor crops in 1902 were followed by increasing emigration, but poor harvests in 1904 by decreasing emigration.

Also, when we turn to the general business or industrial conditions in Sweden, no obvious consistent relation appears between cyclical changes in emigration to the United States and the concurrent prevalence of good or bad times in Swedish industry. For example, the years 1892, 1893, and 1894 were characterized in Sweden by depression in business, and were followed by declining emigration to the United States; also, in 1895 conditions underwent a substantial improvement, and emigration to the United States in the year ending June 30, 1896, increased decidedly. In these years, it would appear that bad conditions in Sweden diminished emigration, while good conditions stimulated it. On the other hand, the prosperous years of 1896, 1897, and 1898 were followed by low emigration, and the poor harvests and industrial depression of 1902 in Sweden were followed by increased emigration to the United States, which reached a peak, for this century, of approximately forty-six thousand in the year ending June 30, 1903.

In brief, while conditions in Sweden have probably exerted some influence upon fluctuations in emigration to the United States in the period since 1870, that influence has usually been consistent with, or at least less effective, than the attracting and repelling power, respectively, of good and bad conditions in the United States.

Russia.

Immigration to the United States from Russia was relatively small prior to the eighties, not reaching ten thousand in any one year. It increased sharply in the year ending June 30, 1882— rising from about 5,000 in the previous year to almost 17,000. Either the prosperous conditions in the United States in the early eighties or the beginning of outrages against the Jews in Russia in April, 1881, offer a plausible explanation for this spurt. Likewise, after further persecution of the Jews in 1883 and 1884, immigration from Russia, which had slumped somewhat following the spurt of

1882, again rose to about 17,000 in the years ending June 30, 1885 and 1886, and then, with the improvement of conditions in the United States, rose rapidly to a peak of 81,511 in 1892. In these years good conditions in America acted as an attracting force and bad conditions in Russia as an expelling force, for in July, 1890, there was a revival of the attacks against the Jews and in 1891 the expulsion of the Jews from Russia was ordered by Imperial edict. Also, 1891 and 1892 were depression years in Russia with crop failures and famine conditions.

In 1893 conditions improved in Russia, but depression set in in the United States, accompanied by a decline in immigration from Russia.

The poor harvests of 1896 and 1897, contrary to the tendencies just noted in the previous occurrences of that kind, are followed, in the years ending June 30, 1897 and 1898, respectively, by a decided decrease in emigration to the United States, both absolutely and relatively to immigration from other countries.

From this point, immigration from Russia rapidly increased, both in good years and in bad years, until it reached a high point of about 263,000 in the year ending December 31, 1906. It is not obvious whether this 1906 boom was due to the coincident industrial activity in the United States or to the depression and disturbed conditions which prevailed in Russia in 1905 and 1906 and for some years prior thereto. It is noteworthy, however, that this rapid rise in the years prior to 1908 is shared by other emigrant countries, so that for several years after 1899, there is no marked change in the proportion between immigration from Russia and that from other countries (see Chart 35).

The Russian movement yielded to the general slump in immigration in 1908 and continued to decline in 1909, and again in 1911, then exhibited a spectacular increase to a total of about 291,000 in the twelve months ending June 30, 1913, and about 345,000 in the year ending December 31, 1913.

Though Russia had experienced a depression tendency toward the close of 1911, together with crop failures and some famine conditions, 1912 was a period of industrial activity, which continued into 1913, and crops were excellent in both 1912 and 1913; hence we do not find in Russian economic conditions an obvious explanation for the unprecedented increase in emigration. Nor, as we have noted in previous chapters, does the industrial boom in the United States in 1912 appear exceptional enough to account for the intensity of the immediately subsequent increase in immigration, particularly from Russia, Italy, and Austria. On the whole, the evidence is less clear for Russia than it is for the other European countries studied that economic conditions in the United States have dominated the fluctuations in migration.

Austria-Hungary.

The fraction of total immigration to the United States originating in Austria-Hungary rose rapidly from less than five per cent in the seventies to 25.6 per cent in the year ending June 30, 1900, and from then to the opening of the war remained relatively steady, never reaching 27 per cent and falling below 20 per cent only in 1911. The large influence of industrial activity in the United States upon immigration from Austria-Hungary is indicated by the fact that from 1900 to 1914 each decline in pig iron production in the United States—that is, in 1901, 1904, 1908, and 1911 (Chart 35)—is accompanied by a concurrent decline in the ratio of immigration from Austria-Hungary to the total immigration. Sharp increases in this ratio in the years ending June 30, 1874, 1884, 1890, and 1896 challenge attention. Some significance in this connection may be attached to the fact that in Austria at least, which at that time was contributing the major portion of the immigration from Austria-Hungary, the respective calendar years terminating six months prior to the four years of relatively large immigration just mentioned were years of poor crops or, as in 1895, of agricultural depression despite good crops. However, too much importance should not be attached to such fragmentary data. A closer examination of the conditions of economic activity in Austria-Hungary would doubtless reveal further interesting relationships, but we have not thought it necessary to subject the heterogeneous conditions of the Dual Empire to close study, in view of the fact that probably clearer conclusions can be drawn from the data concerning the more homogeneous countries to which major attention has been given in this chapter.

CHAPTER SUMMARY

The above study of the international aspects of cyclical fluctuations in the current of migration, particularly of the immigration movement into the United States, reveals that this movement is on the whole dominated by conditions in the United States. The "pull" is stronger than the "push."

In those relatively infrequent periods when prosperity in the United States is coincident with depression in the country of emigration, the tendency for emigration to the United States to be high would presumably have the effect of ameliorating unemployment in the home country.

On the other hand, when, as frequently is the case, periods of prosperity or of depression are common to the United States and the leading countries of emigration, the effect is less fortunate. When prosperity is being experienced, emigration is relatively high; when depression reigns, it is relatively low. In earlier chapters we have seen that despite the sensitiveness of the flow of immigration to industrial conditions in the United States, the net effect of cyclical fluctuations in immigration is to aggravate, on the whole, the unemployment problem in the United States. It would appear that, in those periods when cyclical conditions in the two countries are similar, the effect on cyclical unemployment in the countries of emigration must be even less favorable than in the United States, for in such periods the emigrant tends to leave when industrial conditions are good and to remain at home when they are bad.

CHAPTER IX

SEASONAL FLUCTUATIONS

An analysis of seasonal changes in immigration and emigration is desirable for two purposes, first to make possible the correction of the crude data for typical seasonal variation so that the cyclical element may be more readily analyzed; and secondly, as a basis for comparison with the seasonal fluctuations in employment.

CORRECTION FOR NORMAL SEASONAL VARIATION

Necessity.

With few exceptions, immigration and emigration both exhibit pronounced seasonal fluctuations. Furthermore, when statistics of the total movement are separated into their constituents, the several elements are found to exhibit different typical seasonal movements. To illustrate, the typical seasonal for the "no occupation" group is essentially different from that for the groups for which the designated occupations are "laborer" or "farm laborer." In all groups, however, the seasonal is sufficiently pronounced to make direct analysis of the original data difficult. To facilitate study of the susceptibility of the migratory currents to cyclical fluctuations in employment, it is necessary, as we have noted in previous chapters, to determine the typical seasonal movement and by abstracting this typical seasonal fluctuation from the original data, to leave a residue which represents the best available estimate of the influence of the remaining elements—trend, cycle, and accidental factors.

In most instances, it has been found desirable to eliminate also the influence of the trend, leaving "cycles" which represent the influence of cyclical and "accidental" factors alone.

Period.

An examination of graphs of the various immigrant and emigrant series reveals the fact that prior to the middle of 1914 most of them evidence a reasonably consistent seasonal movement, but that in subsequent years, the war, the abnormal situation in transport immediately following the war, and the influence of the quota act, have distorted the seasonal movement from any close resemblance to that exhibited prior to the war. Consequently, it has seemed expedient to base the computation of the normal seasonal, in most instances, upon the pre-war years, despite the fact that for many series data are available for only five pre-war years (beginning Jan. 1, 1909).

Method.

For the longer series, such as male immigrants, beginning in 1893, the typical seasonal has been obtained by adding and averaging like months (e. g. all the Januarys) and adjusting the results for any upward or downward bias ascribable to a trend in the data. The adjusted results were then translated into percentages of their mean, giving *twelve seasonal indices* or type numbers.

In some cases, particularly for shorter series where the seasonal indices were to be used in isolating the cyclical movement, they have been computed by somewhat more refined methods, principally by the link-relative method developed by Professor Warren M. Persons or by finding the typical percentage deviation from a trend-cycle curve obtained by computing a twelve-month moving average and adjusting this average to make it represent our best estimate of the course of the cycle and trend.

Quota-Period Seasonals.

With the exception of certain classes of arrivals who are not counted against the quotas, the immigration law of 1921 limited the number of aliens of any nationality who might be admitted in any one year to three per cent of the foreign-born persons of such nationality resident in the United States as shown by the Census of 1910, and permitted a maximum of twenty per cent of the annual quota for any nationality to be admitted in any one month. The new quotas begin to be available on July 1st of each year, hence this law has tended to concentrate arrivals in July and the four following months. It was, therefore, necessary to make a special computation of the typical seasonal variation for the period since the quota law went into effect. This computation was based upon immigration data for the period from July, 1921, to June, 1924, inclusive. Such a short period, of course, does not give a clearly adequate basis for estimating the typical seasonal movement under the 1921 restrictive law; but the use of the indices so computed yields a cycle curve which appears to be a reasonable estimate of the post-war cycle in immigration (see Chart 24 in Chapter VI).[1]

PRE-WAR SEASONAL TENDENCIES IN ARRIVALS

In the following pages, we first examine the pre-war seasonal movements in arrivals, in departures, and in the net result of arrivals less departures. We then turn to an examination of the available evidence concerning seasonal fluctuations of employment in those industries in which immigrants engage in large numbers, in order to lay the basis for determining to what extent seasonal fluctuations in migration synchronize well with seasonal variations in employment opportunities.

In most cases seasonal changes are described in terms of *typical seasonal fluctuations*, by which is meant that part of the total observed fluctuations which are, on the average, ascribable to seasonal influences as distinguished from the longtime trend and cyclical influences; but in one or two instances (see Chart 55) attention is directed to the *crude seasonal distributions*, which are the average distributions of the data over the months of the year without any adjustment for the fact that the distribution may be in part due to a growth factor.

Principal Similarities.

The major features of the seasonal movements of the various groups of immigrants can be quickly noted by scanning Charts 48 and 49, and the tables upon which they are based.

For most classes of incoming aliens, the volume is small in January and February, with an incoming rush in March, April, and May, a falling off in midsummer, and a moderate recovery in September and October, followed by a decline in November and December.

Male and Female Immigration.

Inasmuch as the movement of male immigration has been the primary series used in our analysis of the cyclical aspects of industry, it is pertinent to inquire as to what differences exist between the seasonal fluctuations of the male immigrant group and those of other immigrant groups.

[1]The Immigration Act of 1924 again modified the seasonal movement in immigration by its provision that not more than *ten* per cent of any annual quota may be admitted in any month except in cases where such quota is less than 300 for the entire year.

Chart 48
Seasonal Fluctuations in Alien Arrivals[a]
Note the similarity from year to year in the shape of the curves.

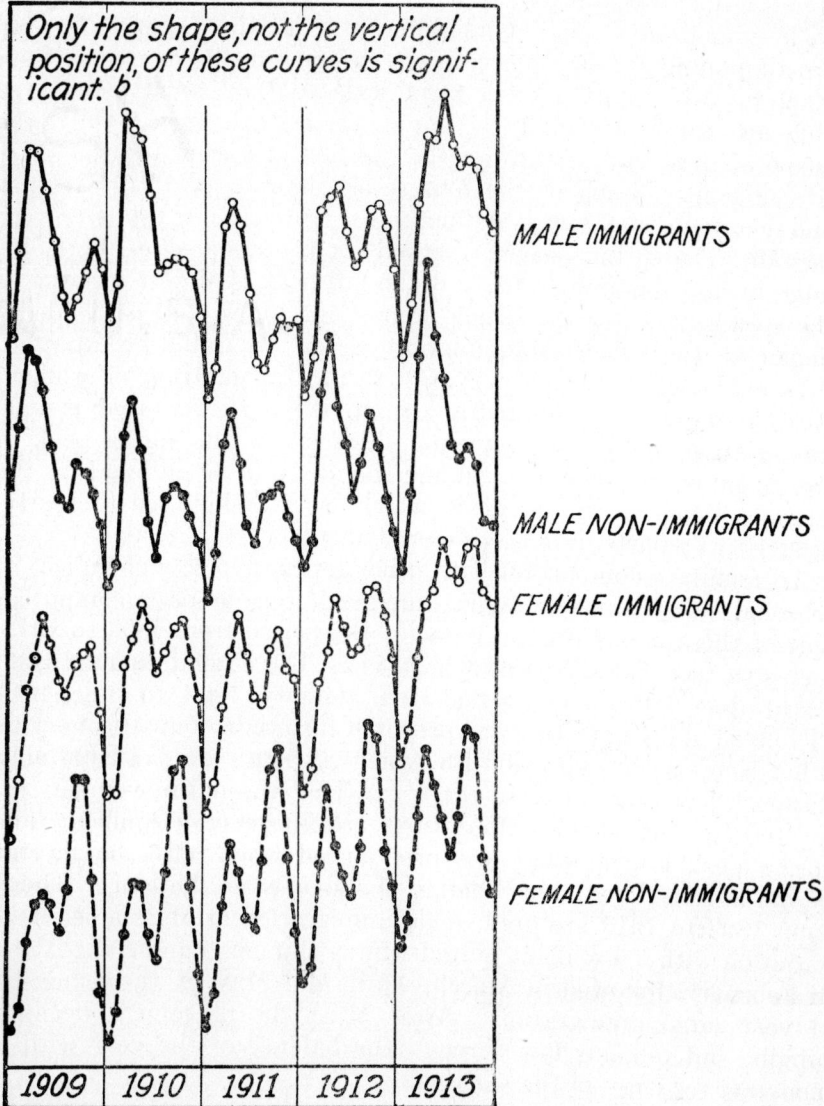

Only the shape, not the vertical position, of these curves is significant.[b]

MALE IMMIGRANTS

MALE NON-IMMIGRANTS

FEMALE IMMIGRANTS

FEMALE NON-IMMIGRANTS

1909 1910 1911 1912 1913

[a]The numerical data for male immigrants are in Appendix Table II. The other curves are plotted from monthly data published by the U. S. Bureau of Immigration and Naturalization in its monthly *Immigration Bulletin.*

[b]For a more complete discussion of the method of constructing the above chart, see footnote (b) to Chart 27, in Chapter VII.

The differences in the seasonal tendencies of male and female immigration are indicated in Chart 48. The four curves represent male immigrants, male nonimmigrants, female immigrants, and female nonimmigrants, respectively, for each of the five years from 1909 to 1913, plotted on a ratio scale so that equal percentage changes are represented by equal vertical changes. Only the shape of these curves and not the position of a curve on the chart is significant. Each of the four series shows a decidedly regular and characteristic seasonal fluctuation throughout this five-year period. The spring peak is marked for the male series, both immigrant and nonimmigrant; but the fall peak is almost as large as the spring peak for the female immigrant series, and is decidedly higher for the female nonimmigrant series. As would be expected, it is evident from these curves that the immigration of women, particularly of the nonimmigrant group, is less affected than is male immigration by the inducements which create the spring peak in the incoming movement, including the desire to be on hand for the summer boom in employment which, as we shall see presently, occurs particularly in outdoor employment.

To facilitate comparison with other series, two sets of indices of seasonal fluctuations in male immigration have been computed. One of these is based upon data for the period from 1893 to 1913, inclusive (see Table 58 and Chart 54). The second computation, based upon data for the period from January, 1909, to June, 1914 (Table 53 and Chart 49), was prepared for use in comparisons with other elements in migration for which statistics are available only during a few years prior to the war. The seasonal movements indicated by these two computations are, in general, similar. The spring peak is somewhat less pronounced when only the shorter period is considered; but whether the shorter or the longer period from 1893 to 1913 are used, male immigration exhibits a seasonal variation with a low point in mid-winter (January) and a slight rise in February, followed in March, April, and May by three months of very large immigration. After May, the movement declines rapidly and remains low through the balance of the year with a moderate recovery in the early fall.

Various noteworthy differences among the seasonal movements of the several classes of arrivals are illustrated in Chart 49.

Citizens and Aliens.

The three curves in Fig. A, of Chart 49, represent, respectively, returning citizens of the United States, alien immigrants, and alien nonimmigrants. The seasonal distribution of arriving citizens is dominated by the summer tourist travel, with the bulk of arrivals in August, September, and October, in direct contrast with the alien groups, which reach their peak in April, or about five months earlier than the peak in the number of citizen arrivals.

CHART 49

PRE-WAR SEASONAL FLUCTUATIONS IN ARRIVALS[a]

Average of twelve months = 100

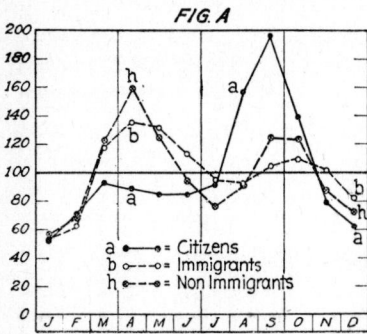

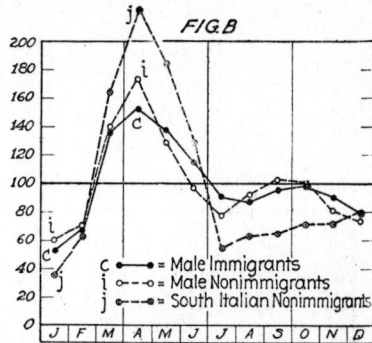

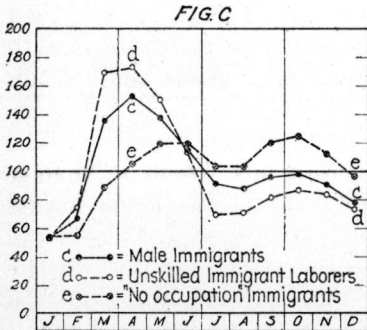

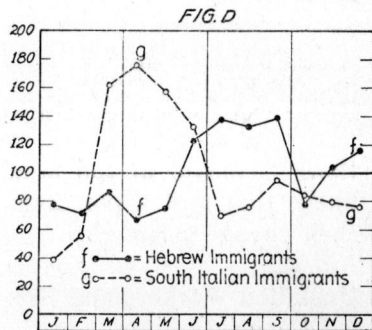

[a]Numerical data in Table 53, in columns lettered to correspond with the numbering of the curves in the above chart.

Immigrants and Nonimmigrants.

It is noteworthy that the seasonal movement of nonimmigrants bears a much closer resemblance to the immigrant seasonal than it does to the citizen seasonal. Whether both sexes are considered (Fig. A of Chart 49) or males only (Fig. B), we find that nonimmigrants show an even greater peak in April than the immigrants. This is notably true for the South Italian nonimmigrant group. On the other hand, we found, in examining Chart 48, that the seasonal movement of female nonimmigrants exhibits less tendency to peak in the spring. Thus it would appear that, while the alien nonimmigrant is on the whole guided in his choice of sailing months by much the same considerations that influence the alien intending to establish permanent residence in the United States, yet the tendency toward the spring concentration is most marked among

TABLE 53—INDICES OF PRE-WAR SEASONAL FLUCTUATIONS IN ARRIVALS*

Monthly average—100

MONTH	CIT-IZENS	IMMIGRANT ALIENS						NON-IMMIGRANT ALIENS		
		TOTAL	MALE	UN-SKILLED	No OCCUPA-TION	HE-BREWS	SOUTH ITALIAN	TOTAL	MALE	SOUTH ITALIAN
	a	b	c	d	e	f	g	h	i	j
Jan...	51.8	52.8	52.7	52.9	53.4	77.0	38.7	56.6	60.4	35.3
Feb...	71.4	62.8	66.9	74.3	55.0	70.9	55.7	68.5	70.6	62.2
Mar...	93.0	117.4	135.8	169.3	88.0	85.4	161.9	122.1	140.6	164.3
Apr...	88.7	135.5	152.4	173.5	105.3	66.1	175.9	159.1	173.6	222.0
May..	84.7	131.9	137.7	150.2	119.3	74.5	156.9	124.2	128.9	184.3
June..	84.7	113.6	114.9	113.8	119.3	122.6	132.3	94.6	97.2	128.4
July ..	91.5	95.0	90.8	69.4	103.1	137.1	69.9	76.5	77.9	54.7
Aug...	157.3	93.1	87.3	70.8	103.5	132.3	75.6	90.9	92.5	63.4
Sept...	196.3	104.9	95.8	81.1	120.0	138.3	94.4	124.4	103.0	64.3
Oct...	139.2	109.8	97.9	86.6	124.8	77.0	83.5	123.2	100.4	70.8
Nov...	79.2	100.8	90.1	83.9	112.1	103.4	79.4	87.3	81.0	71.9
Dec...	62.3	82.5	78.1	73.8	96.2	115.4	75.9	72.6	73.8	78.8

*Computed from U. S. Bureau of Immigration and Naturalization, *Immigration Statement and Inward Passenger Movement*, monthly issues July, 1907, to February, 1909; and *Immigration Bulletin*, monthly issues, March, 1909, to June, 1914. The periods covered by the data are as follows: Series a, b, and h, July, 1907, to June, 1914; series i, July, 1908, to June, 1914; series d, January, 1909, to December, 1913; and series c, e, f, g, and j, January, 1909, to June, 1914.

those elements in the nonimmigrant group for whom it is most likely that the opportunity for employment is the incentive for their voyage to America.

Unskilled Workers and Non-Workers (Fig. C, Chart 49).

Of special interest are the contrasts between the seasonal movements of those who represent additions to the unskilled element in the wage earning group in this country, and those immigrants who are listed as having "no occupation." In preparing Fig. C, in Chart 49, we assumed that those incoming immigrants listed as "laborers" and "farm laborers" might be grouped as "unskilled workers," and have compared the seasonal fluctuations of this group with those of the immigrant aliens in the "no occupation" group. While there is a close similarity in the direction of changes from month to month, with the exception that the spring peak of the "no occupation" curve is two months later than the peak for unskilled workers, the spring rush is distinctly more pronounced among the latter group. This suggests that employment considerations are among the factors explaining the relatively large immigration of the working classes in March, April, and May.

It will be observed from Fig. C that the seasonal curve for male immigrants is, in general, similar in shape to that for unskilled workers but exhibits a somewhat less pronounced variation.

Selected Races.

That immigrants of different races vary materially in their choice of months in which to immigrate is indicated in Fig. D of Chart 49. The South Italians, who participate in large numbers in summer construction activities, arrive chiefly in March, April, and May; whereas the incoming movement of Hebrews peaks in June to September.

PRE-WAR SEASONAL TENDENCIES IN DEPARTURES

(See Chart 50)

When we turn to the pre-war seasonal variations in departures, we find differences akin to those discovered in arrivals. The citizen element peaks in July; while the alien departures, notably of emigrants, are numerous at the close of the year. (Fig. A of Chart 50). As between male emigrants and male nonemigrants, the early winter boom is more pronounced in the emigrant group. That this outward rush at the close of the year is associated with employment conditions is suggested by the comparisons in Fig. C, Chart 50. The departures of those emigrants who indicate that they have no occupation reach a peak in June, July, and August; but the unskilled workers emigrate in largest numbers during the months of November and December. In Fig. D, we have the seasonal movements of male emigrants and of South Italians. The South Italians, both of the emigrant and of the nonemigrant groups, show a November and December movement which is more pronounced than that for male emigrants of all races combined. This outward rush of the South Italians in the early winter is probably due in part to their aversion to the relatively rigorous winter in the United States.

CHART 50

PRE-WAR SEASONAL FLUCTUATIONS IN DEPARTURES.

Average of twelve months = 100

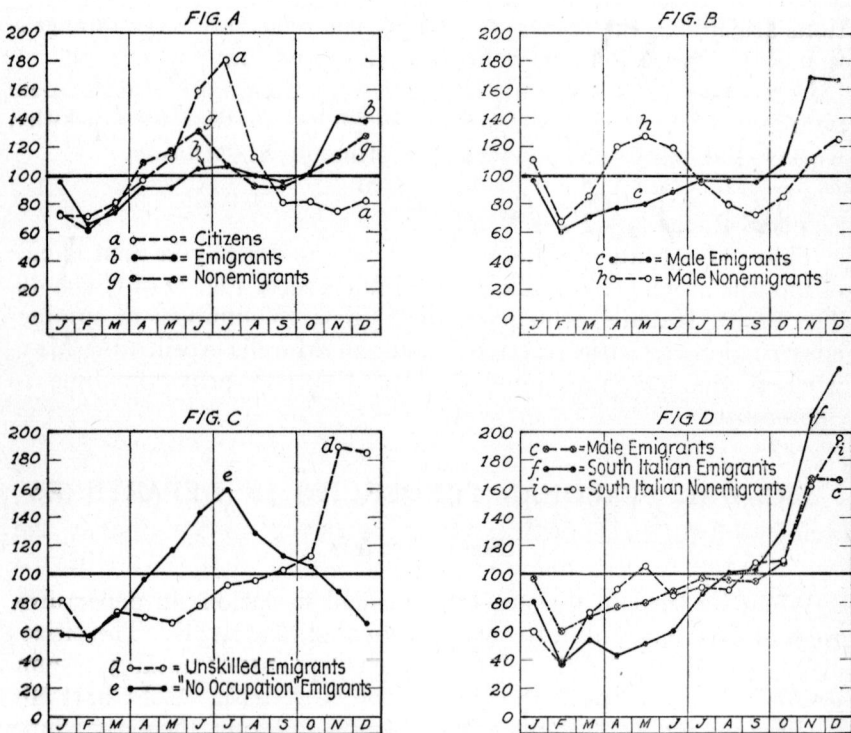

FIG. A

a o---o = Citizens
b •---• = Emigrants
g •--• = Nonemigrants

FIG. B

c •---• = Male Emigrants
h o---o = Male Nonemigrants

FIG. C

d o---o = Unskilled Emigrants
e •---• = "No Occupation" Emigrants

FIG. D

c •---• = Male Emigrants
f •---• = South Italian Emigrants
i o---o = South Italian Nonemigrants

•Numerical data in Table 54, in columns lettered to correspond with the numbering of the curves in the above chart.

PRE-WAR SEASONAL TENDENCIES IN NET MIGRATION

(See Chart 51)

The best evidence of the seasonal variation in the net migration of aliens covers the seven pre-war years from July, 1907, to June, 1914. When the number of departing aliens, both emigrants and nonemigrants, is subtracted from the number of arriving aliens, both immigrants and nonimmigrants, we find that in the seven years under consideration the seasonal distribution of the net movement is as given in the first two columns of Table 55.

TABLE 54.—INDICES OF PRE-WAR SEASONAL FLUCTUATIONS IN DEPARTURES*
Monthly average = 100

Month	Citizens	Emigrant Aliens					Non-Emigrant Aliens		
		Total	Male	Un-skilled	No occupation	South Italian	Total	Male	South Italian
	a	b	c	d	e	f	g	h	i
Jan.	71.3	94.9	96.2	81.7	57.1	80.0	72.9	110.7	59.4
Feb.	70.8	65.3	60.0	54.2	56.2	36.9	61.0	67.5	36.9
Mar.	.80.1	73.8	70.2	72.9	70.3	53.4	77.4	85.3	72.1
Apr.	96.3	90.2	76.8	69.4	96.5	43.4	108.8	120.0	89.0
May	111.4	90.7	79.7	65.8	116.6	50.7	117.6	127.3	105.5
June	159.1	105.0	87.9	77.6	142.8	59.5	130.7	119.6	84.5
July	180.5	106.2	96.4	92.0	159.9	86.5	105.8	96.3	90.5
Aug.	113.3	99.6	95.8	95.6	128.9	100.3	92.5	79.9	88.8
Sept.	80.3	95.2	95.0	102.7	113.0	102.6	91.1	72.2	108.0
Oct.	81.1	101.2	108.0	113.0	106.1	130.0	101.6	85.2	108.4
Nov.	74.3	140.6	167.5	189.4	87.2	211.6	113.8	110.9	161.5
Dec.	81.7	137.4	166.1	185.2	65.2	244.5	127.3	125.3	195.3

*Computed from statistics in the 1907 to 1914 issues of the monthly bulletin of the U. S. Bureau of Immigration and Naturalization. The periods covered by the data are as follows: Series b and g, July, 1907 to June, 1914; series d, e, f, and i, January, 1909 to June, 1914; and series a, c, and h, January, 1910 to June, 1914.

Similar data for male aliens have been used for the period from January, 1910, to December, 1913, inclusive, in arriving at the figures in the last two columns of Table 55. In Chart 51, we have a graphic presentation of the average distribution by months, first

CHART 51

PRE-WAR SEASONAL DISTRIBUTION OF NET IMMIGRATION.

Unit = one person

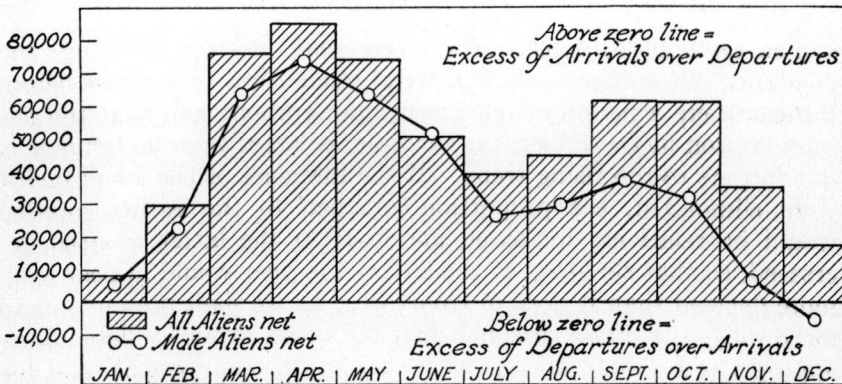

ᴀNumerical data in Table 55.

for aliens of both sexes combined, as shown by the cross-hatched bars, and, secondly, for male aliens only, as shown by the circles.

For both males and all aliens, the net movement is small in January, increases in February, reaches high tide in March, April, and May, ebbs somewhat in midsummer, recovers to a secondary peak in September and October, and then slumps rapidly in November and December.

TABLE 55.—PRE-WAR SEASONAL DISTRIBUTION OF THE NET MOVEMENT OF MIGRANTS[a]

(Thousands of persons)

MONTH	NET ALIEN MOVEMENT (ARRIVALS LESS DEPARTURES), BOTH SEXES. JULY, 1907, TO JUNE, 1914.		NET MOVEMENT OF MALE ALIENS (ARRIVALS LESS DEPARTURES). JAN. 1, 1910, to DEC. 31, 1913.	
	TOTAL IN 7 YEARS	AVERAGE FOR GIVEN MONTH	TOTAL IN 4 YEARS	AVERAGE FOR GIVEN MONTH
January	57.5	8.2	22.1	5.5
February	207.5	29.6	91.1	22.8
March	530.1	75.7	253.6	63.4
April	593.5	84.8	294.4	73.6
May	517.2	73.9	252.7	63.2
June	354.5	50.6	205.1	51.3
July	271.6	38.8	105.0	26.2
August	312.4	44.6	117.7	29.4
September	429.2	61.3	147.9	37.0
October	428.7	61.2	126.9	31.7
November	243.6	34.8	26.6	6.7
December	124.0	17.7	[d]21.1	[d]5.3

[a]Computed from statistics in the 1907 to 1914 issues of the monthly bulletin of the U. S. Bureau of Immigration and Naturalization.
[d]Excess of departures over arrivals.

The data under consideration represent, strictly speaking, the combined effect of seasonal and trend tendencies. The years before the war were a period of increasing immigration; and that the net immigration in December, for example, is larger than in January is due in part to the rising trend. If the influence of the trend factor were eliminated, the proportion assigned to the earlier months would be relatively increased and that in the latter months decreased, so that the drop at the end of the year would appear even more decided than it does in Chart 51. As we shall presently note more fully, the crude seasonal distribution as given in Table 55 is appropriate for comparisons with changes in employment, and for this reason, and also because of technical difficulties in the way of

satisfactorily determining the trend, we have made no attempt to
adjust for the growth factor in presenting the statistics of seasonal
fluctuations in net migration.

We have noted the characteristic features of the seasonal movement in the main migratory currents to and from the United States
before restrictive legislation intervened to modify the seasonal distribution; let us now note the corresponding seasonal movements
in the major occupations in which immigrants engage.

SEASONAL TENDENCIES IN SELECTED INDUSTRIES

The great bulk of newly arrived immigrants, as we have previously
noted, are engaged in manufacturing, coal mining, construction,
and railway maintenance; hence it becomes desirable to examine
the seasonal fluctuations in employment in these industries, in order
that we may determine whether the seasonal variations we have
observed in migration synchronize closely with changes in employment.

The data available for measuring seasonal variation in these
several industries are so fragmentary and diverse in nature, that
we feel impelled to give first some explanation of the nature and
limitations of the evidence from which our indices are constructed.
We then proceed to a comparison of these seasonal employment
indices with the corresponding indices for migration.

The evidence considered in arriving at our estimates for the
several industries is shown in Charts 52 and 53; and the numerical
indices are given in the accompanying tables. The final estimates
for comparison with fluctuations in migration appear in Charts 54
and 55. In comparing these charts, the reader should note that
the scales used in plotting have been varied so as to magnify the
fluctuations for some series, such as factory employment, so that
the changes will stand out more clearly.

Factory Employment (Chart 52, Fig. A).

In the process of testing for typical seasonal variation in factory
employment, we computed two indices, both of which appear in
Chart 52, Fig. A. The first, Curve (a), is based upon our estimates
of factory employment in Massachusetts, New Jersey, and New
York. The second, Curve (b), is based upon the Census of Manufactures statistics of factory employment in the United States in
the census years 1904, 1909, 1914, 1919, and 1921, and upon the

index of factory employment published by the U. S. Bureau of
Labor Statistics, for the years 1915 to 1924. To obtain the final
estimate, which appears as Curve (c) in Chart 54, Fig. A, an average
of the two indices was taken.

CHART 52

EVIDENCE OF SEASONAL VARIATION IN EMPLOYMENT IN SELECTED
INDUSTRIES[a]

Average of twelve months = 100

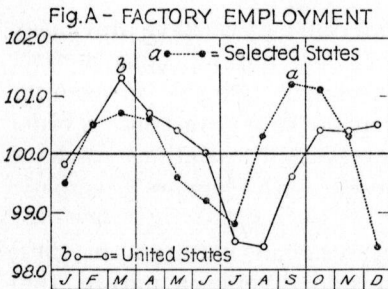

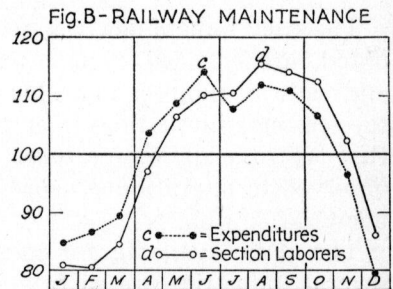

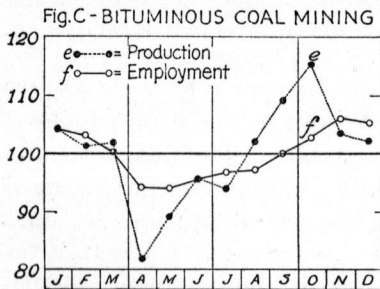

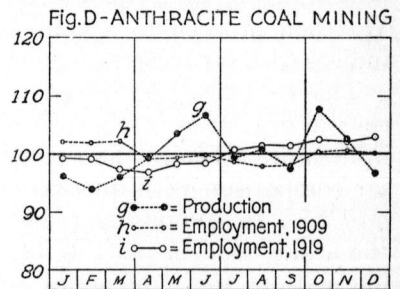

Fig.A – FACTORY EMPLOYMENT

a •----• = Selected States
b o----o = United States

Fig.B – RAILWAY MAINTENANCE

c •----• = Expenditures
d o----o = Section Laborers

Fig.C – BITUMINOUS COAL MINING

e •----• = Production
f o----o = Employment

Fig.D – ANTHRACITE COAL MINING

g •----• = Production
h •----• = Employment, 1909
i o----o = Employment, 1919

[a] For fuller statement of the nature and sources of the data used in constructing
curves "a" to "g", see Table 56. Curves "h" and "i" represent the average number of
men employed in anthracite mines in the census years 1909 and 1919. *Thirteenth
Census of the United States*, Vol. XI, p. 196; *Fourteenth Census*, XI, p. 278.

As indicated by this estimate, factory employment exhibits a
spring boom, a midsummer slump, a fall boom, and another slump
in midwinter.

Railway Maintenance (Chart 52, Fig. B).

Many foreign-born workers are engaged as section hands in the
maintenance of railway tracks and roadbeds. As a measure of

seasonal fluctuation in this occupation, we have the indirect evidence afforded by the amounts expended each month from 1910 to 1921 in the maintenance of way and structures, and also the number of track and roadway section laborers employed at the middle of the month, from July, 1921, to December, 1924, on Class I steam roads in the United States. A seasonal index of these

TABLE 56—INDICES OF SEASONAL VARIATION IN ACTIVITY IN SELECTED INDUSTRIES[a]

Monthly average=100

Month	FACTORY EMPLOYMENT			RAILWAY MAINTENANCE		COAL MINING		
						BITUMINOUS		ANTHRACITE PRODUCTION
	SELECTED STATES	UNITED STATES	COMPOSITE	EXPENDITURES	EMPLOYMENT	PRODUCTION	EMPLOYMENT	
	A	B	C	D	E	F	G	H
Jan....	99.5	99.8	99.6	84.8	81.0	104.2	104.2	96.1
Feb....	100.5	100.5	100.5	86.7	80.6	101.3	103.1	93.9
Mar....	100.7	101.3	101.0	89.4	84.7	101.9	100.3	96.0
Apr....	100.6	100.7	100.6	103.6	97.0	81.8	94.2	99.2
May...	99.6	100.4	100.0	108.7	106.4	89.1	94.0	103.5
June...	99.2	100.0	99.6	114.1	110.0	95.6	95.7	106.6
July...	98.8	98.5	98.6	107.7	110.4	94.0	96.7	99.4
Aug....	100.3	98.4	99.4	111.8	115.4	102.1	97.3	100.9
Sept...	101.2	99.6	100.4	110.9	114.0	109.1	100.0	97.5
Oct....	101.1	100.4	100.8	106.5	112.3	115.3	102.8	107.7
Nov....	100.3	100.4	100.4	96.3	102.2	103.5	106.0	102.5
Dec....	98.4	100.5	99.4	79.5	86.0	102.2	105.2	96.7

[a]=Computed from data, briefly described below, in such a way as to eliminate so far as practicable the influence of trend, cyclical variations and, in the case of the production and expenditure series, the effect of the varying length of months.

A=Employment in Massachusetts, New Jersey, and New York factories, 1904 to 1914. See Table IV, appendix.

B=Employment in factories in the United States, as given in the U. S. Census of Manufactures for 1904, 1909, 1914, 1919, and 1921; and in statistics of factory employment for 1915 to 1924, issued by the U. S. Bureau of Labor Statistics.

C=An average of Series A and B.

D=Expenditures for maintenance of way and structures, with adjustment for varying length of month, 1910 to 1921. Interstate Commerce Commission, *Thirty-Fifth Annual Report on the Statistics of Railways in the United States.*

E=Track and roadway section laborers at middle of month, July, 1921, to December, 1924. Interstate Commerce Commission, *Wage Statistics Class I Steam Roads in the United States,* monthly issues.

F=Tonnage of bituminous coal produced, 1913 to 1922, adjusted for varying length of months. U. S. Geological Survey, *Mineral Resources of the United States,* 1921, Pt. II, p. 464, and weekly reports of coal production in 1922.

G=Employment in bituminous coal mines, as given in the *Fourteenth Census of the United States, Mines and Quarries,* for 1909 and 1919; and in the U. S. Bureau of Labor Statistics, *Monthly Labor Review,* for April, 1920, to March, 1922.

H=Tonnage of anthracite coal produced, 1913 to 1921, adjusted for varying length of months, U. S. Geological Survey, *Mineral Resources of the United States,* 1921, Pt. II, p.465.

maintenance expenditures, with an adjustment for the varying length of the months, is shown as Curve (c) in Chart 52, Fig. B; and an index constructed from the aforementioned employment data appears as Curve (d). Although this index of employment is based upon a very short period, it is sufficiently well supported by the collateral evidence of the index of expenditures to lead us to accept it as a reasonably accurate approximation.

Railway maintenance is distinctly a warm-weather occupation, being low in the first quarter of the year, then rising rapidly to a high level in June and the following four months, then sharply declining in November and December.

Bituminous Coal (Chart 52, Fig. C.)

For monthly employment in bituminous coal mining, we have only the fragmentary evidence in the U. S. Census of Mines and Quarries for 1909 and 1919 and in the data issued by the Bureau of Labor Statistics for the two years from April, 1920, to March, 1922. An index based on these fragments appears in Curve (f) of Chart 52, Fig. C. The second curve on this chart represents seasonal fluctuations in the tonnage of bituminous coal produced, in the years 1913 to 1922, adjusted for the varying length of the months in the year. Bituminous coal mining is characterized by a large amount of intermittent employment, which is probably not fully reflected in the employment statistics. For this reason, and because of the fragmentary nature of the direct statistics of employment, we have used the index of variations in production as a measure of seasonal fluctuations in bituminous coal mining employment.

The resulting seasonal curve is almost the reverse of that computed for railway maintenance. The period of greatest inactivity occurs in the second quarter, notably in April, followed by an increase in the late summer and early fall and a decline again at the close of the year.

Anthracite Coal Mining (Chart 52, Fig. D)

The direct evidence of employment by months in anthracite coal mining is even scantier than for bituminous coal; and, accordingly, for an index of seasonal variation in this industry, we have utilized a curve based upon production in the years 1913 to 1921 (see Curve "g", Fig. D). This index exhibits only a mild fluctuation with peaks in June and October. Employment by months in the census years 1909 and 1919 (Curves "h" and "i") shows an even milder fluctuation.

Construction (Chart 53)

Seasonal fluctuations in the construction industry are of particular importance to the immigrant. It is a well-known fact that a large proportion of the unskilled work in outdoor construction is

CHART 53

SEASONAL FLUCTUATIONS IN CONSTRUCTION.

Average of twelve months = 100

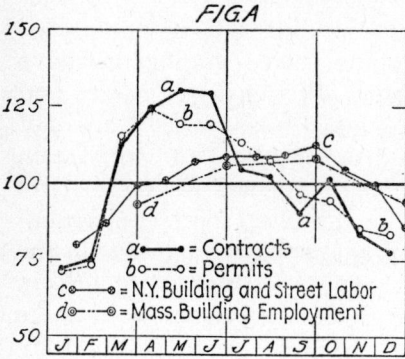

FIG. A

a•——• = Contracts
b o----o = Permits
c o——• = N.Y. Building and Street Labor
d •----• = Mass. Building Employment

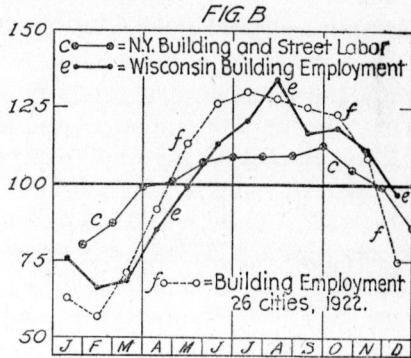

FIG. B

c •——• = N.Y. Building and Street Labor
e •——• = Wisconsin Building Employment

f o----o = Building Employment
26 cities, 1922.

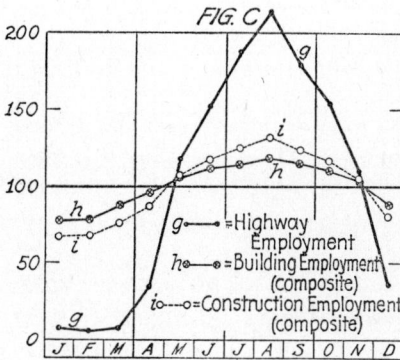

FIG. C

g •——• = Highway Employment
h •——• = Building Employment (composite)
i o----o = Construction Employment (composite)

.Sources:

Curve a = seasonal indices of the value of contracts awarded in 27 northeastern states, January, 1910, to June, 1922, computed by Mr. J. B. Hubbard, *Review of Economic Statistics*, January, 1924, p. 35.

Curve b = the value of permits in 66 selected cities, 1910-1922, ibid.

Curve d = unemployment inverted, computed from percentages of trade union building workers unemployed at the end of each quarter. The seasonal indices are: Mar. 31, 92.8; June 30, 105.6; Sept. 30, 107.9; Dec. 31, 93.6.

For data from which curves c, e, f, g, h and i, were constructed, see Table 57 and footnotes.

carried on by foreign-born laborers, including, probably, a large proportion of those temporary immigrants known as "birds of passage" and also other newly arrived aliens. The general seasonal character of the construction industry is a matter of common knowledge, but for quantitative measures of seasonal changes in the numbers employed in construction, we have been forced to rely upon estimates pieced together from fragmentary data obtained from various sources. The constituents used in this computation, together with the final estimate, are shown in Chart 53. The upper section of this Chart (Fig. A) affords an opportunity to compare

TABLE 57.—INDICES OF SEASONAL FLUCTUATIONS IN CONSTRUCTION EMPLOYMENT[a]

Average of the twelve months = 100

MONTH	BUILDING AND STREET LABOR IN NEW YORK STATE	BUILDING EMPLOYMENT IN WISCON-SIN	COMPOSITE INDICES		
			BUILDING	HIGHWAY CONSTRUC-TION	HIGHWAY AND BUILD-ING CON-STRUCTION
	A	B	C	D	E
Jan	79.7	75.2	76.6	7.3	66.7
Feb	86.6	65.9	77.4	5.6	67.1
Mar	99.1	68.0	86.9	6.6	75.4
Apr	100.5	84.7	94.8	33.8	86.1
May	106.7	99.5	105.1	116.9	106.8
June	108.2	112.5	111.3	151.4	117.0
July	108.6	120.1	114.1	187.8	124.6
Aug	109.0	133.5	118.2	213.2	131.8
Sept	112.2	116.2	114.6	178.3	123.7
Oct	104.1	117.8	110.0	153.8	116.3
Nov	99.6	110.6	103.7	109.8	104.6
Dec	85.4	96.2	87.5	35.7	80.1

[a]Computed from the following data:
Series A. Employment in New York building and street labor, 1902-1914 computed from percentage of trade union members unemployed at the end of each month. New York State Bureau of Labor Statistics, *Annual Report and Bulletins.*
Series B. Percentage change in the number of employees engaged in the construction of buildings, January, 1922, to December, 1924, *Wisconsin Labor Market*, monthly issues.
Series C. Weighted average of Series A, Series B, and employment in 1922 as reported by contractors in 26 cities, read from curve in *Seasonal Operations in the Construction Industries—Report of a Committee of the President's Conference on Unemployment*, p. 51.
Series D. Computed from statistics of the number of common laborers employed on Federal Aid projects in the fourteen states of the New England, Middle Atlantic and East North Central districts in 1922, 1923, and 1924, made available by the courtesy of Mr. J. G. McKay, Chief, Division of Highway Economics and Transport, U. S. Bureau of Public Roads; and from percentage changes in the number of employees engaged in the construction of highways in Wisconsin from January, 1922, to December, 1924, as reported in the *Wisconsin Labor Market.*
Series E. An average of Series C and D, with weights of (6) assigned to building and (1) to highways.

seasonal indices for the value of contracts awarded (Curve "a"), and the value of building permits (Curve "b"), with estimates of employment in building, computed from statistics of unemployment among trade union members in New York building and street labor, by months, and in Massachusetts building trades by quarters (Curves "c" and "d", respectively).

It is evident that the peak in building employment does not coincide with the peak of contracts awarded or of permits granted, but occurs some three or four months later. Consequently, though they have a wider geographical scope and extend over a longer period of years than the available direct statistics of employment or unemployment, it does not appear desirable to utilize the contract or permit figures as indices of seasonal variation in employment.

In Fig. B, the curve for New York building and street labor is repeated, and curves are added to indicate the seasonal variation in Wisconsin building construction during the three years from 1922 to 1924, inclusive, and also employment as reported by contractors in twenty-six cities of the United States in 1922. (See footnotes to Table 57 for sources.) To obtain a composite estimate of seasonal fluctuations in building employment, weights of six, three, and one were assigned to the New York, Wisconsin, and 1922 series, respectively, and the result is plotted as Curve "h" in Fig. C of Chart 53.

Our index of seasonal variation in employment on highway construction (Curve "g", Fig. C, Chart 53) is also admittedly only an estimate based upon fragmentary data. The statistics used cover the years 1922, 1923, and 1924, and include (1) the number of common laborers, by months, on highway projects receiving Federal aid in the fourteen states included in the New England, Middle Atlantic, and East North Central sections, and (2) employment on highways in Wisconsin. In computing the index of highway construction these two series were weighted by the relative population of the states represented.

Finally, a composite index of employment in construction (Curve "i" in Fig. C, Chart 53) was computed by combining the building and highway indices, assigning a weight of six to the building and one to the highway series. Obviously, this index of construction employment must be taken as a rough approximation. It indicates small activity in the first quarter of the year; increasing employment in the second quarter; maximum activity in the third quarter; and then a decline in October, November, and December.

In some of the subsequent comparisons, the index for railway maintenance and the index for construction have been weighted by the estimated numbers employed in these occupations in 1909 and combined into an index of "Selected outdoor industries" (Curve "f" of Fig. C, Chart 54).

Using the same method of weighting, the indices for all the industries under consideration—that is, factory employment, bituminous and anthracite coal mining, railway maintenance, and construction, have been combined into an index of seasonal fluctuations in "all selected industries" (Curve "g" of Fig. D, Chart 54).

Limitations.

Before proceeding further, it may be well to summarize the limitations of these indices of seasonal variation. In the first place, the object in mind has been to obtain evidence of seasonal fluctuations which may be applied to the years immediately preceding the Great War, since the indices of seasonal variation in migration are computed chiefly from data for these years. It has been necessary, however, to utilize some employment data applying to more recent years. Furthermore, these evidences of employment conditions have in some instances been fragmentary and indirect. While care has been taken to make the indices as representative of the actual conditions as possible, and we have no reason to believe that they are inaccurate in material respects, yet the existence of a considerable margin of possible error must be recognized.

A further source of possible misinterpretation of the significance of seasonal fluctuations in employment lies in the inadequacy of the available information concerning the extent of dovetailing of employment in various industries. When industries are separately considered, the aggregate account of seasonal fluctuation may be magnified by the failure to take into account that workers may shift from one industry to the other when periods of activity do not coincide. On the other hand, the consolidation of data for several industries may create the impression of a more uniform seasonal distribution of employment than actually exists for most workers. It is obvious from the data which we have been examining that factory employment is declining in midsummer while activity in the outdoor industries is increasing; but, unless idle factory workers shift readily to outdoor industries, a consolidation of the data for all the important industries may convey an exaggerated impression of the degree of seasonal regularity in employment. While such an index is useful for present purposes, it is not an adequate measure of the variation in employment for individual workers or groups of workers.

We have analyzed separately the seasonal fluctuations, first in migration, then in employment. We may now turn to a direct comparison of the degree of similarity in these seasonal movements.

COMPARISON OF SEASONAL TENDENCIES IN IMMIGRATION, EMIGRATION, AND EMPLOYMENT

The most significant of the several indices of seasonal changes in migration and employment which we have been discussing in the preceding pages are brought together in Chart 54. In each of the

CHART 54

SEASONAL FLUCTUATIONS IN EMPLOYMENT AND PRE-WAR MIGRATION*

Scales: No. 1 = Immigration and Emigration
No. 2 = Employment
Average of twelve months = 100

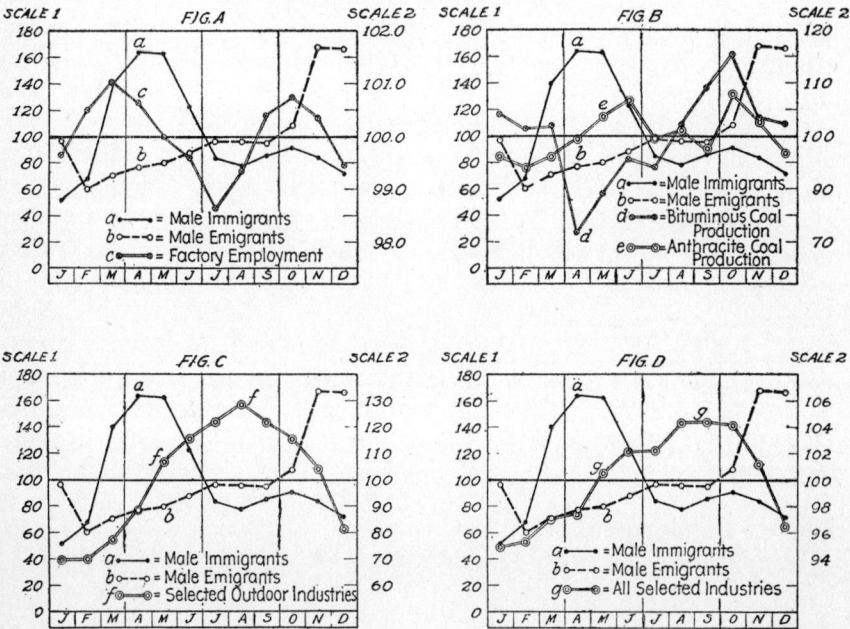

SCALE 1 — FIG. A — SCALE 2

a•——• = Male Immigrants
b o—-o = Male Emigrants
c •——• = Factory Employment

SCALE 1 — FIG. B — SCALE 2

a•——• = Male Immigrants
b o—-o = Male Emigrants
d •——• = Bituminous Coal Production
e o—-o = Anthracite Coal Production

SCALE 1 — FIG. C — SCALE 2

a•——• = Male Immigrants
b o—-o = Male Emigrants
f •——• = Selected Outdoor Industries

SCALE 1 — FIG. D — SCALE 2

a•——• = Male Immigrants
b o—-o = Male Emigrants
g •——• = All Selected Industries

*Numerical data for Curve "a" are in Table 58, column A; Curve "b", Table 58-A; Curve "c", Table 56-C; Curve "d", Table 56-F; Curve "b", Table 56-H; Curve "f", Table 58-C; and Curve "g", Table 58-D.

four sections of this chart the curves for male immigration and for male emigration are repeated, and for comparison therewith there is given, in Fig. A, the index for factory employment; in Fig. B, the index for bituminous coal and also for anthracite coal, both based on production; in Fig. C, the index for selected outdoor industries; and in Fig. D, the index for all selected industries. To avoid a possible misinterpretation of the relative violence of the seasonal fluctuations in the several industries, it should be noted that for each of the sections in Chart 54, Scale 2, for employment, has a different scale unit.

TABLE 58.—INDICES OF SEASONAL FLUCTUATIONS IN MIGRATION AND EMPLOYMENT[a]

Monthly average = 100

MONTH	MIGRATION		EMPLOYMENT	
	MALE IMMIGRATION	MALE EMIGRATION	SELECTED OUTDOOR INDUSTRIES	ALL SELECTED INDUSTRIES
	A	B	C	D
Jan...	51.7	96.2	69.4	94.9
Feb...	67.8	60.0	69.7	95.3
Mar...	139.7	70.2	77.2	97.0
Apr...	163.4	76.8	88.2	97.4
May..	162.6	79.7	106.7	100.5
June..	122.3	87.9	115.6	102.1
July...	83.9	96.4	121.9	102.2
Aug...	77.4	95.8	128.7	104.3
Sept...	85.2	95.0	121.8	104.4
Oct. ..	90.1	108.0	115.5	104.1
Nov...	83.6	167.5	104.1	101.2
Dec...	71.7	166.1	81.2	96.5

[a]The bases of the respective indices are:
A. Male immigrants, January, 1893, to December, 1913. (See Table II, in Appendix).
B. Male emigrants, January, 1910, to June, 1914.
C. A composite of indices for railway maintenance and construction (see Tables 56 and 57), weighted according to numbers employed in 1909.
D. A composite of the indices for factory employment, bituminous and anthracite coal mining, railway maintenance and construction (see Tables 56 and 57), weighted according to numbers employed in 1909.

Factory Employment (Fig. A, Chart 54).

Immigration agrees only moderately well with the seasonal fluctuations in factory employment. The peak in factory employment is reached earlier in the year, hence the bulk of the immigrants arrive after the maximum demand has passed. Both series exhibit a summer decline, a fall recovery, and a slump late in the year. For most of the year emigration is increasing while factory employment is decreasing, and vice versa. Emigration declines in February, due partly to the length of the month, while factory employment is increasing, and increases from March to July while factory employment is diminishing; also the high level in November and December corresponds with declining factory activity.

Coal Mining (Fig. B, Chart 54).

The low point in bituminous coal mining comes in the second quarter of the year, at the period when immigration is greatest, and the peak does not occur until some six months later; hence the spring rush of immigrants is premature if their destination is the bituminous coal mines.

The fluctuations in immigration are somewhat better timed for anthracite coal mining, as the peak of activity in this industry is reached after, rather than before, the high tide of arrivals. In both types of mining, a decline occurs in November and December, coincident with increasing emigration and declining immigration.

Selected Outdoor Industries (Fig. C, Chart 54).

The seasonal fluctuations in immigration are well timed for employment in the outdoor industries. The number of immigrants is small in the stagnant months of December, January, and February, increases with the spring rise in outdoor work, and reaches a peak early enough to make it possible for the bulk of newly arrived immigrants to participate in outdoor work throughout the extent of the summer boom. Then, as outdoor employment declines rapidly in the closing months of the year, the tide of emigration swells rapidly and the volume of immigration recedes.

All Selected Industries (Fig. D, Chart 54).

In general, the composite seasonal movement of employment in all the selected industries exhibits the same features as the index for outdoor industries, hence the comments just made for the outdoor industries can be applied to the combined seasonal fluctuations in employment in the entire group of industries under consideration. The heaviest immigration is when employment is increasing and somewhat in advance of the maximum in employment activity, and the decline in immigration and the increase in emigration at the close of the year coincides with the falling off of employment.

THE NET VOLUME OF ARRIVALS LESS DEPARTURES AND THE MONTH-TO-MONTH CHANGES IN THE NUMBER EMPLOYED

So far in this chapter we have been comparing the seasonal changes in employment and pre-war migration with reference to the time of year at which increases or decreases take place. There has been nothing in these comparisons to indicate how the volume of immigration or of emigration compares in number of persons with the corresponding change in the number of persons employed To the extent that migrants are members of the working class, the number of arrivals less the number of departures represents a net addition to the number of workers seeking employment. Unless this net addition is accompanied by an increase in the number of persons employed, the necessary result is an increase in the total number of unemployed persons in the United States. If, in a given month, the immigration of workers exceeds the emigration of workers by 50,000, and the increase in the number of employed in the United States is only 30,000, it is obvious that there has been a net increase of 20,000 in the number of the unemployed.

Fully satisfactory data for making comparisons of seasonal net migration and changes in employment are not available, but we have made the best approximation we could, in the following manner. In the first place, for the several industries which have been selected, for reasons previously indicated, as particularly significant when studying employment opportunities for immigrants, we have computed an estimate of the typical number of persons employed in each month of the year in the pre-war period. Statistics for the year 1909 were used in determining the average number of workers to be assigned to each industry. This computation yields an estimate of the typical month-to-month change in the number employed in factories, bituminous and anthracite coal mining, railway track maintenance, and construction work, when the cyclical tendencies have been as far as practicable eliminated, leaving the joint effect of the trend and seasonal factors. Inasmuch as the typical net migration, by months, represents a corresponding increase or decrease in population, it is appropriate to compare therewith the typical change in employment which results from the combined influence of the growth and seasonal elements.

The results of the employment estimates appear in Table 59 and Chart 55.

For the net migration to be used in comparison with the typical month-to-month change in employment, we have selected the excess of arriving over the number of departing male aliens. This group includes those male aliens who are officially classified as temporary migrants—that is, as nonimmigrants or nonemigrants. Many of these come for employment purposes, and hence it ap-

SEASONAL FLUCTUATIONS 233

CHART 55

THE PRE-WAR NET MIGRATION OF ALIEN MALES AND THE TYPICAL
MONTH-TO-MONTH CHANGE IN THE NUMBER EMPLOYED[a]

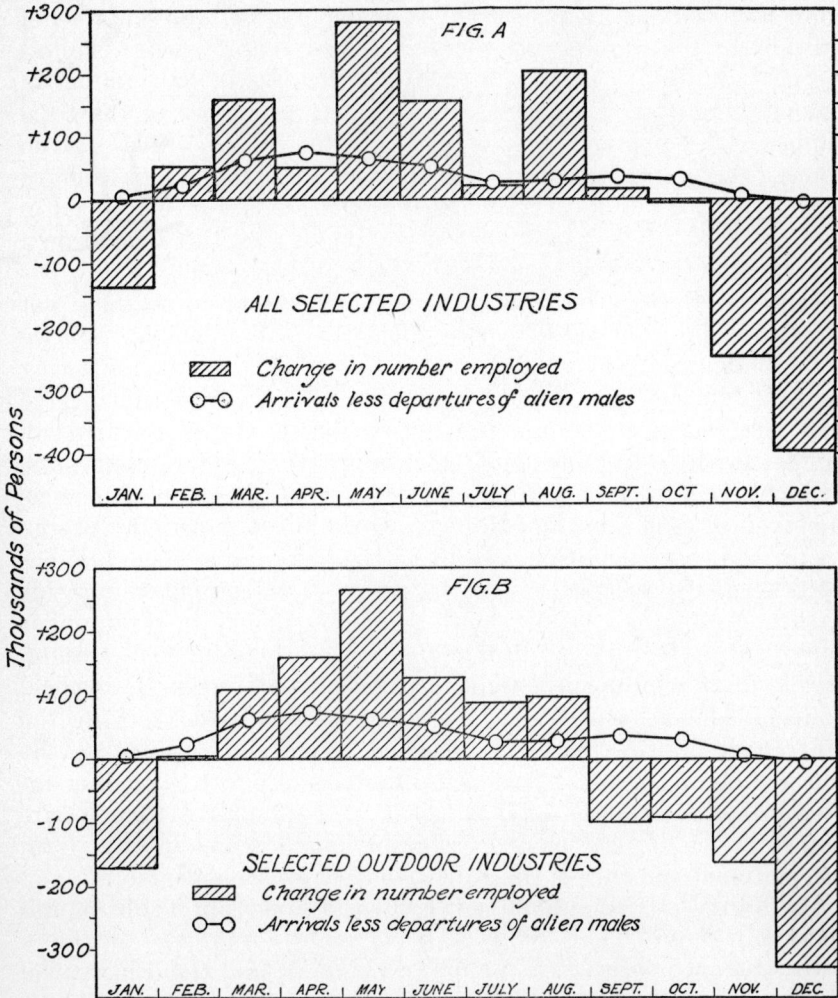

peared advisable to include them, as well as those officially listed as
immigrants, in calculating the volume of net migration.

In Chart 55, Fig. A, this net migration series is compared with
the month-to-month change in all the selected industries. A bar

above the zero line indicates the estimated increase in the number employed as compared with the preceding month; a bar below the zero line, an estimated decrease from the preceding month. The curve represents the typical pre-war net migration of males in the given month.

TABLE 59.—ESTIMATE OF THE SEASONAL DISTRIBUTION OF EMPLOYMENT IN SELECTED INDUSTRIES IN THE PRE-WAR PERIOD[a]

(Adjusted for cyclical variations but not for trend)

Thousands of persons

Month	NUMBER EMPLOYED IN GIVEN MONTH		INCREASE (+) OR DECREASE (−) FROM PRECEDING MONTH[d]	
	ALL SELECTED INDUSTRIES[b]	SELECTED OUTDOOR INDUSTRIES[c]	ALL SELECTED INDUSTRIES	SELECTED OUTDOOR INDUSTRIES
	A	B	C	D
Jan...	8,213.0	992.0	−136.6	−169.6
Feb...	8,266.9	996.6	+ 53.9	+ 4.6
Mar...	8,426.6	1,105.1	+159.7	+108.5
Apr...	8,477.4	1,263.9	+ 50.8	+158.8
May..	8,758.2	1,531.3	+280.8	+267.4
June..	8,912.3	1,661.3	+154.1	+130.0
July ..	8,932.7	1,752.5	+ 20.4	+ 91.2
Aug...	9,134.6	1,851.8	+201.9	+ 99.3
Sept...	9,150.4	1,755.4	+ 15.8	− 96.4
Oct...	9,146.0	1,666.2	− 4.4	− 89.2
Nov...	8,899.1	1,503.4	−246.9	−162.8
Dec...	8,504.0	1,173.7	−395.1	−329.7

[a]These figures represent an estimate of the joint effects of seasonal and trend factors. The indices of seasonal variation given in the preceding tables were applied to the numbers employed in the respective industries in 1909, as recorded in the Census or estimated from other sources, and then the results were adjusted by adding the estimated effect of trend movements as indicated by data for the years 1907 to 1914.
[b]Includes factory employment, bituminous and anthracite coal mining, railway maintenance, and construction.
[c]Construction and railway maintenance.
[d]Computed from Columns A and B, with allowance for trend in computing the December to January change.

Assuming that our estimates present a true picture of the typical changes in employment and in net male migration prior to the quota restrictions, we observe from Chart 55, Fig. A, and the tables upon which it is based, that in January there is a small net excess of alien male arrivals over departures, to the extent of about 5,500 persons, while employment in the selected industries decreases about 137,000. In the following eight months an excess of arriving over departing alien males is, in each case, accompanied by an increase in the number employed. In all these months but April, July, and September, the increase in employment exceeds the net volume of male arrivals. In October and November a decrease in employment is accompanied by a small net immigration, and in December a heavy decrease in employment is accompanied by a small excess of departing over arriving male aliens.

In other words, decreasing employment in January and November is aggravated by a small net excess of arrivals, and in October by net arrivals to the number of about 32,000. Also, in April, July, and September, the increase in employment is not sufficient to absorb the new arrivals.

Only in December, and then only to a small extent, is the slack created by a decrease in employment taken up in part by a net outgo of male aliens.

It is true that in five months—February, March, May, June, and August—the number of workers employed is increasing faster than the net inflow of male aliens, and if there chances to be a shortage of resident workers in these months, immigration may be looked upon as alleviating this shortage. On the other hand, if in these months the increase in employment is in fact not adequate to relieve an existing unemployment situation, then the net inflow of alien workers merely acts to check the decrease in unemployment.

In summarizing the above comparison of the typical net movement of alien males with the month-to-month change in employment ascribed to the growth and seasonal factors, it should be noted that the evidence presented should at best be taken as suggestive rather than conclusive. The data upon which the estimates are based are too fragmentary, and the margin of error involved in the computations too large, to justify treating the computed relations as more than rough approximations. Here, as in the greater part of this chapter, we are dealing with pre-war, and hence pre-restriction, conditions.

With the above qualifications in mind, we may summarize the evidence presented in Chart 55 and the accompanying tables as indicating that the seasonal distribution of male immigration and emigration is such as to aggravate unemployment in six months of the year and to alleviate it slightly in one. In the other five months, being those in which net male immigration is less than the increase in employment, its effect is to alleviate the effects of a shortage of resident workers, if such a shortage exists.

In Fig. B of Chart 55, a comparison similar to that just made for "all selected" industries is presented for "selected outdoor" industries. Not all of net male migration, of course, goes into these industries, but large numbers of the recent immigrants are employed therein, particularly in pick and shovel work.

Using the same method of interpretation applied to "all selected" industries, and assuming, for purposes of comparison, that the entire volume of net migration is absorbed in these outdoor industries, it would appear that in December a small excess in departures probably lessens slightly a tendency toward increasing unemployment; in six months—March to August, inclusive—the increase in employment is greater than the net number of male arrivals and hence male migration in these months is either alleviating a shortage of labor, or if such shortage does not exist, is merely slowing up the decrease in unemployment which would otherwise arise from increasing activity in these outdoor industries. In February the number of net arrivals is greater than the increase in employment; and in four months—January, September, October, and November— employment is decreasing while arrivals exceed departures, though in January and November the excess of arrivals is not enough to be of appreciable significance.

On the whole, the evidence favors the conclusion that in the months from March to August, inclusive, the seasonal distribution of net male arrivals is well adjusted to the changes in employment due to activities in construction and railway maintenance; that in January, November, and December the net movement is too small to be of great significance; and that in February, September, and October the new arrivals must look largely to other industries for employment.

SEASONAL FLUCTUATIONS IN IMMIGRATION UNDER THE QUOTA ACTS

The preceding discussion has referred, in the main, to the relation between the seasonal movements in migration and employment prior to the Great War. The quota acts of 1921 and 1924 caused material modifications in the seasonal distribution of immigration. The act of 1921 permitted up to twenty per cent of the annual quota to enter in any one month. As the immigration year begins July 1st, the effect of this provision was to concentrate the heaviest immigration in the months from July to November, inclusive. In the first year of the operation of the act, beginning July 1, 1921,

54.9 per cent of the total number of male immigrants arrived in these five months, July to November; in the next year 41.9 per cent; and in the third year, ending June 30, 1924, 63.0 per cent. In other words, the effect of this law was to encourage a large fraction of the total number of immigrants to enter just prior to the mid-winter slump in employment (see Chart 54).

The revision of the quota act in 1924, which limited to ten per cent of its annual quota the number admissible from a given country in one month, again changed the seasonal distribution. This ten-per cent provision tends to distribute immigration somewhat evenly throughout the year, especially from July to April, inclusive; but the distribution is still without regard to seasonal fluctuations in employment. Under this law approximately as many or more immigrants will be admitted in the months of November and December, when employment is declining, as in April and May when the demand for workers is increasing.

CHAPTER SUMMARY

Pre-war immigration and emigration each evidence a characteristic seasonal variation. Immigration, particularly of those classes which are most likely to furnish recruits to the ranks of the workers, has, in the pre-restriction period, a marked peak of activity in March, April, and May. Emigration on the other hand, is at a maximum in the closing months of the year. Consequently net migration shows a large excess of arrivals in the second quarter of the year, a secondary peak in the early fall, and a marked decline in November and December. In fact, a net outgo of alien males occurs in December.

Upon comparison with the seasonal fluctuations in those industries which are the primary employers of immigrant labor, we find that there are considerable differences in the degree to which the seasonal variation in migration and in employment is synchronous. The agreement is poor for bituminous coal mining, fair for anthracite coal mining and factory employment, and still better for the selected outdoor industries, namely construction and railway maintenance.

A comparison by months between net male arrivals and estimates of the typical month-to-month changes in the number of persons employed in the selected industries does not yield unequivocal evidence as to whether migration aggravates or lessens seasonal unemployment. It appears that, on the average, in three of the four months in which employment decreases, there is an excess of arriving over departing male aliens, resulting, presumably, in an aggravation of seasonal unemployment; that in three more months the increase in employment is not adequate to absorb the net arrivals; and lastly, that in the remaining five months of the year the excess of arrivals, which is numerically less than the increase in employment, may or may not be a helpful factor, according to whether or not the number of unemployed but employable resident workers is adequate to meet the increasing demand for labor. Obviously, any conclusions concerning the net effect of unrestricted migration upon the amount of seasonal unemployment must necessarily be stated with reservations because of the incomplete nature of the data available for the estimates and the involved nature of the computations to which these data must be subjected.

On the other hand, it is more apparent that the seasonal distribution of immigration under the quota act of 1921 was not well timed with respect to the normal seasonal fluctuations in employment, and that the same criticism, though possibly to a lesser extent, is applicable to the quota provisions as revised in 1924.

CHAPTER X

SUMMARY

The problem under discussion in the foregoing chapters is the relation of seasonal and cyclical fluctuations in employment to seasonal and cyclical fluctuations in migration, with particular reference to immigration into, and emigration from, the United States. The major issues may conveniently be recapitulated in two questions—namely:

(1) To what extent are fluctuations in migration attributable to fluctuations in employment?
(2) To what extent, in turn, are fluctuations in migration an ameliorating influence, and to what extent an aggravating factor, in employment and unemployment fluctuations?

Similarities in Fluctuations of Employment and Migration.

With reference to the first of the above questions, the facts presented in the preceding chapters show clearly that there are both strong cyclical and seasonal movements in immigration and emigration and abundant evidence that when immigration is not restricted the character of the cyclical variations, at least, is closely similar to the cyclical variations in employment opportunity in the United States. A fairly close similarity is also found in the seasonal movements. The seasonal peak in immigration is in the spring, well-timed for the summer increase in those outdoor activities in which many new immigrants ordinarily find employment; and the maximum emigration is reached in the late fall and early winter when jobs are becoming relatively scarce. Similarly, a period of depression in the United States is ordinarily accompanied or closely followed by a decline in immigration and an increase in emigration; and a period of prosperity, by an increase in immigration and a decline in emigration. This statement is not, of course, to be interpreted as signifying an invariable rule. For this and the other tendencies noted below, there have been various exceptions and qualifications mentioned in the more detailed analysis in the separate chapters which it is impracticable to repeat here in detail but to which some weight must be given in interpreting the significance of the tendencies here set forth. However, the various irregularities and exceptions which have been noted are by no means adequate to impair seriously the validity of the general conclusion that there is a close relation between cyclical and seasonal fluctuations in employment and the corresponding fluctuations in migration.

That this correspondence is more than a mere coincidence is suggested by the fact that, particularly for the cyclical fluctuations, there are a priori reasons for expecting that migration would be sensitive to employment conditions, and also by the further fact that when the migratory currents are separated into their several elements, it is found that it is just those elements which one would expect to be swayed in their choice of the particular time of arrival and departure by variations in the prospect of employment which do show, in fact, the closest correlation with employment conditions. The movements of those immigrants who have no gainful occupation are decidedly less responsive than the movements of the working element to cyclical and seasonal variations in employment.

Significant Differences in Cycles of Employment and Migration.

A close scrutiny of the cyclical movements of employment and migration reveals the fact that despite the general similarity in the appearance of the curves representing these series, there are also noteworthy differences. First, there are irregular fluctuations in immigration which cannot be readily explained merely by reference to the course of industrial activity. The relatively slight amount of immigration during the industrial activity of the war period affords an obvious example.

In the second place, even where the fluctuations of the several series are obviously interrelated, there are differences in the time at which the changes occur, in their relative violence, and in the number of persons directly affected. A recognition of these differences is essential to a clear understanding of the problem.

Frequently the turns in the migration movement lag behind the corresponding change in employment, indicating that the passage of some time is required before the full effect of a change in employment is felt upon migration. The extent of this lag varies in different cycles, and is also frequently found to vary on the downturn and the upturn of the same cycle.

In a few instances the effect of a change in employment conditions is not seen for almost a year afterward, but in other instances the fluctuations in employment and migration appear to be substantially concurrent. The more common lag in the migration fluctuations is from one to five months.

Relative Violence of Cyclical Fluctuations.

On the whole, the changes in migration are more erratic and more violent than those in industry. The seasonal variation in migration is more marked and the amplitude of the cyclical movements is, as a rule, greater than that of the corresponding fluctuations in employment. This comparison, however, refers to deviations in terms of percentages, and not to the number of persons affected by fluctuations in employment and migration respectively. An industrial depression usually brings a sharp decrease in immigration; but, owing to the larger total number of persons involved, a decline in employment which in percentage terms appears relatively less than the concurrent decline in immigration, may affect a much larger number of persons. However, as explained more fully in Chapters V and VI, numerical comparisons between migration and employment are most appropriate when cumulative migration is compared with changes in the number employed.

Effect of Migration upon the Cycle in Employment.

The demonstrated sensitiveness of immigration and emigration to employment conditions may lead to an exaggerated estimation of the efficacy of migration as a safety-valve for an overcrowded labor market in depression periods. We have seen that depression retards immigration and accelerates emigration, but the weight of evidence is, not only that these compensating movements are often not numerically adequate to decrease the number of workers in this country in a period of depression, but that, on the contrary, even in periods of low employment net immigration is sometimes steadily adding to the supply of workers. While immigration falls off materially when employment is slack, it never ceases entirely, and a considerable number of new workers arrive even during a depression period. True, there is at the same time an exodus, a movement which occasionally has exceeded immigration in volume, but, judging from the few depression periods for which complete statistics are available, there is, when the entire duration of the period of dull employment is considered, always a net immigration. (See Directors' footnote "a", p. 120).

Furthermore, there is no complete clearing house system for employment; and even if the outgoing stream equals the incoming in volume, the time lost in adjusting the new immigrant to a job aggravates the unemployment situation.

The International Aspect.

Particularly if the needs of two or more countries—the country or countries of emigration and the country or countries of immigration—are taken into consideration, it becomes evident that migration as it occurs is not, and scarcely can be, a consistently beneficial factor in its relation to cyclical unemployment. We have seen that to a large extent low employment occurs concurrently in the country of emigration and the country of immigration. In such periods it becomes virtually impossible for migration to ameliorate employment conditions in the one country without aggravating them in the other. If the emigrant leaves when industry is slack in his old home, he arrives in his new home when unemployment is likewise prevalent; and if he arrives when employment conditions are good, he ordinarily leaves his former home when the opportunities for employment are at their best.

Possible Indirect Effect Upon the Severity of Business Cycles.
Our analysis would be incomplete if we failed to mention the not inconsiderable probability that the inflow of large numbers of new workers into the United States in times of prosperity has been a factor in increasing the intensity of boom periods and consequently the severity of the subsequent depression. Our analysis is not of a nature to prove directly the relation just suggested; it merely indicates the existence in periods of prosperity of a large volume of new additions to the labor supply, which would make possible an intensified expansion of industry and, by tending to keep wages down, render less effective one of the possible checks to such expansion—namely, rising costs of production.

A further probable effect of migration which is suggested but not directly demonstrated by the data under examination is the aggravation of the turnover in industry, whether immigration is balanced by emigration or not; for it is constantly necessary to fit the new arrivals into jobs vacated by the departing aliens or by native workers crowded into other occupations, aside, of course, from those instances where the new arrivals take up work for which no labor force has previously been organized.

Summary.

In brief, whatever may be the basic causes of migration, there is a close relation between the cyclical oscillations of employment and those of immigration and emigration, and a moderately close resemblance in the respective seasonal fluctuations, with considerable reason to believe that this similarity, particularly in the cyclical oscillations, is due to a sensitiveness of migration to employment conditions.

With reference to the extent to which migration is responsible for seasonal unemployment, the facts presented in the preceding chapter lead us to be cautious in stating the general tendency. Prior to the Great War, the distribution of net migration was moderately well adjusted to seasonal changes in employment in those industries in which the newly arrived immigrants most frequently engaged. Hence, unless the availability of immigrant labor accounts in part for the development of seasonal tendencies in production—a point which cannot be proved, or at least has not been proved, by our method of analysis—it is not clear that unrestricted immigration materially aggravated the seasonal variations in unemployment.

However, after the introduction of the quota principle of restriction, with provisions which tend to modify the seasonal movement in immigration, it would appear that although the flow of immigrants is reduced in volume its distribution by months is now less likely than formerly to be well adjusted to the seasonal variations in employment.

As to cyclical fluctuations in unemployment, it would appear that, directly at least, migration is probably not a primary cause of such variations in unemployment; and that in some instances it is an ameliorative influence, in that in limited portions of depression periods it is withdrawing more workers than it is contributing. More frequently, however, it is a contributory factor to the evils of unemployment. This conclusion is based in part upon the fact that the timing of migration changes to cyclical changes in employment is imperfect; and secondly, upon the fact that the peaks and troughs of industrial activity frequently coincide in the countries of immigration and of emigration, in which case migration cannot be well adjusted to conditions in both countries. Also, although a decline in employment is usually followed by a decline in immigration, the incoming stream does not dry up entirely, and in those portions of depression periods in which there is a net immigration—

a not uncommon phenomenon—migration is feeding into industry more men than it is taking out. Lastly, the very fact of a known source of additional labor available through increased immigration in boom periods probably has lessened the pressure for regularization of industry.

APPENDIX

TABLE I.—MALE IMMIGRANTS, BY QUARTERS: 1868-1892[a]

(Thousands of Immigrants)

YEAR ENDING DEC. 31	TOTAL FOR YEAR[b]	QUARTER ENDING			
		MARCH 31	JUNE 30	SEPTEMBER 30	DECEMBER 31
1868	173.9	21.0	65.6	53.4	33.9
1869	235.2	23.8	103.7	63.9	43.8
1870	214.8	26.8	101.1	57.2	29.7
1871	204.7	17.2	86.4	56.8	44.4
1872	258.3	30.9	108.1	68.6	50.7
1873	256.7	32.0	124.5	60.6	39.6
1874	159.9	19.5	69.5	43.6	27.3
1875	121.9	19.8	49.2	33.3	19.6
1876	103.0	18.5	40.4	27.3	16.8
1877	84.3	13.2	34.7	21.6	14.7
1878	94.6	13.6	36.4	25.5	19.2
1879	159.0	15.1	52.1	42.4	49.4
1880	365.8	45.8	150.0	95.4	74.5
1881	442.2	50.4	190.4	104.1	97.3
1882	458.2	79.7	217.6	94.8	66.1
1883	341.7	46.9	156.0	73.8	65.0
1884	272.4	46.7	123.1	59.7	43.0
1885	199.6	28.8	94.9	43.7	32.3
1886	240.1	29.9	94.9	60.6	54.8
1887	322.0	46.6	144.7	72.3	58.4
1888	326.6	51.3	163.3	64.8	47.1
1889	258.3	37.5	113.6	56.6	50.5
1890	308.6	47.1	127.6	69.3	64.6
1891	369.4	63.5	156.7	80.9	68.4
1892	343.5	70.2	166.3	69.5	37.4

[a]Compiled from U. S. Bureau of Foreign and Domestic Commerce, *Monthly Summary of Commerce and Finance*, June, 1903, p. 4362, which gives quarterly data from July, 1857 to June, 1903, inclusive.
[b]Computed from full quarterly data before they were reduced to thousands.

APPENDIX

TABLE II—MALE IMMIGRANTS, BY MONTHS: 1892-1924[a]

(Thousands of Immigrants)

YEAR	TOTAL	JAN.	FEB.	MAR.	APR.	MAY	JUNE	JULY	AUG.	SEPT.	OCT.	NOV.	DEC.
1892	.....[b]	....	....	....	....	....	....	28.5	25.5	15.1	8.5	15.1	13.0
1893	308.2[c]	8.8	8.2	28.7	51.8	65.2	43.6	29.4	23.3	16.9	14.4	10.6	7.3
1894	141.1[c]	5.9	6.3	13.1	24.4	19.7	12.8	9.6	8.9	11.5	12.5	8.2	8.3
1895	186.1[c]	5.5	6.3	11.6	26.3	28.9	19.6	15.4	14.5	17.3	16.1	13.6	10.8
1896	188.8[c]	7.1	11.2	25.8	34.0	37.9	16.4	12.4	9.9	9.7	9.8	8.2	6.5
1897	129.8	4.8	5.8	14.1	21.0	21.3	11.8	8.3	7.3	9.6	10.1	8.1	7.8
1898	156.7	6.1	7.9	18.1	23.0	19.8	9.6	11.8	9.4	13.2	13.9	13.0	10.9
1899	231.5	7.2	9.9	21.9	28.2	34.7	23.3	14.8	15.1	16.3	21.6	21.3	17.1
1900	314.0	11.9	17.4	38.3	45.8	48.3	36.2	24.1	19.7	18.0	20.9	16.7	16.6
1901	362.5	13.2	20.5	35.0	51.0	59.2	36.1	22.1	20.4	26.4	24.7	28.2	25.7
1902	527.3	17.1	28.9	64.8	75.1	80.1	52.9	33.3	28.8	34.8	40.5	36.7	34.3
1903	660.3	23.5	37.6	75.5	100.3	99.8	68.1	43.9	41.0	46.8	51.2	43.9	28.7
1904	539.9	19.5	24.3	62.1	69.3	69.6	48.7	37.0	36.6	39.2	42.5	46.6	44.4
1905	745.3[c]	42.5	52.5	101.8	107.0	95.4	79.3	49.2	38.9	46.2	52.4	38.8	41.2
1906	857.3[c]	36.0	52.5	104.9	114.7	108.8	81.7	53.9	52.6	60.6	66.0	65.1	60.4
1907	961.8	40.6	51.2	113.7	116.9	137.8	111.2	65.2	63.2	64.4	72.5	80.4	44.8
1908	241.9	17.9	14.6	21.2	25.0	20.4	17.3	14.8	15.2	19.4	22.2	22.5	31.3
1909	665.7	33.3	52.7	90.0	89.0	73.7	55.8	41.6	37.1	41.1	47.4	55.7	48.1
1910	748.1	36.9	44.5	110.2	104.6	96.7	72.1	47.2	49.9	51.4	50.1	47.3	37.3
1911	488.2	24.1	28.7	60.5	69.9	60.8	42.9	29.3	28.4	33.6	37.5	35.7	36.8
1912	674.6	24.9	30.1	66.9	71.2	75.8	59.8	49.9	53.2	66.1	68.1	60.0	48.6
1913	936.0	30.8	40.4	69.2	99.7	97.4	124.8	94.7	84.6	87.0	82.9	65.6	59.0
1914	439.5	28.5	30.8	67.1	87.9	69.8	40.9	32.9	21.5	17.1	16.6	14.8	11.6
1915	153.4	9.1	7.9	11.5	14.5	15.7	13.7	13.0	13.4	14.1	14.6	14.4	11.3
1916	213.1	10.9	15.7	18.1	19.7	19.1	17.8	13.8	17.4	21.7	20.6	20.3	18.1
1917	90.3	15.6	11.2	9.9	12.7	6.6	6.7	5.5	5.6	4.8	4.5	3.4	3.8
1918	65.8	3.4	4.1	3.9	5.4	8.8	8.7	4.4	4.2	5.4	6.6	4.6	6.4
1919	137.7	5.9	6.8	8.7	10.5	9.0	10.7	11.0	11.7	13.9	16.3	14.1	19.0
1920	414.1	17.3	18.3	24.7	30.2	32.4	38.7	37.0	38.7	43.1	46.6	41.7	45.5
1921	290.2	37.2	32.9	35.1	32.4	36.2	23.1	17.0	18.1	16.6	14.9	15.8	11.0
1922	203.9	8.2	5.7	7.9	9.5	12.1	13.1	23.0	23.8	26.8	28.8	26.5	18.4
1923	460.4	16.6	18.9	29.5	33.9	33.6	27.6	53.5	54.5	53.4	50.8	54.3	33.9
1924	203.8	20.8	18.0	22.7	22.6	18.6	20.2	6.6	13.1	15.1	14.4	16.2	15.4

[a]The monthly data for July 1892 to June 1905, inclusive are compiled from the U. S. Bureau of Statics, *Monthly Summary of Commerce and Finance*; for the remainder of the period they are from the publications or records of the U. S. Bureau of Immigration.

[b]Monthly statistics of immigration by sex are not available prior to July, 1892.

[c]In 1893, 1894, 1895, 1896, 1905, and 1906, the totals of the monthly figures for male immigrants, when added to similar statistics of female immigrants also compiled by the U. S. Bureau of Statistics, give totals differing somewhat from the official totals published by the U. S. Bureau of Immigration.

TABLE III.—CYCLES IN MALE IMMIGRATION BY MONTHS, OR QUARTERS, 1890-1914[a]

Three-month moving averages of percentage deviations from trend, corrected for seasonal variation, and expressed in terms of their standard deviation (30.24 per cent)

YEAR	JAN.	FEB.	MAR.	APR.	MAY	JUNE	JULY	AUG.	SEPT.	OCT.	NOV.	DEC.
1890	.....	—0.3[b]	.....	.....	—0.3	.....	.....	+0.2	.....	.....	+0.4	.....
1891	.....	+0.7	.....	.....	+0.8	.....	.....	+1.1	.....	.....	+1.0	.....
1892	.....	+1.3	.....	.....	+1.6	.....	.....	+0.9	—0.3	—1.0	—1.0	—0.6
1893	—0.9	—0.8	—0.1	+1.3	+2.1	+2.3	+1.9	+1.1	+0.2	—0.7	—1.2	—1.5
1894	—1.6	—1.7	—1.5	—1.3	—1.2	—1.4	—1.4	—1.2	—1.0	—1.1	—1.2	—1.3
1895	—1.4	—1.5	—1.2	—0.7	—0.1	+0.1	+0.2	+0.5	+0.5	+0.4	+0.1	—0.1
1896	0	+0.2	+0.7	+1.2	+0.8	+0.4	—0.3	—0.5	—0.8	—1.0	—1.2	—1.3
1897	—1.4	—1.3	—1.1	—0.8	—0.8	—1.0	—1.3	—1.2	—1.1	—1.1	—1.2	—1.1
1898	—1.1	—1.0	—0.9	—0.9	—1.2	—1.2	—1.2	—0.8	—0 8	—0.7	—0.7	—0.8
1899	—0.9	—1.0	—0.8	—0.5	—0.4	—0.4	—0.5	—0.6	—0.3	—0.1	+0.1	0
1900	—0.1	0	+0.1	+0.2	+0.2	+0.2	0	—0.3	—0.6	—0.8	—0.8	—0.7
1901	—0.4	—0.4	—0.2	—0.1	0	—0.2	—0.5	—0.6	—0.6	—0.4	—0.3	—0.2
1902	0	+0.3	+0.6	+0.7	+0.6	+0.4	0	—0.1	0	+0.1	+0.3	+0.2
1903	+0.4	+0.5	+0.9	+0.9	+0.9	+0.7	+0.5	+0.4	+0.4	+0.4	0	—0.4
1904	—0.9	—0.8	—0.8	—0.6	—0.8	—0.7	—0.7	—0.6	—0.5	—0.3	0	+0.8
1905	+1.2	+1.4	+1.0	+0.7	+0.5	+0.4	+0.3	0	0	—0.1	0	+0.2
1906	+0.8	+1.1	+1.1	+0.9	+0.7	+0.6	+0.6	+0.7	+0.8	+1.1	+1.3	+1.4
1907	+1.3	+1.2	+1.1	+1.2	+1.4	+1.6	+1.5	+1.2	+1.3	+1.6	+1.3	+0.5
1908	—1.0	—1.9	—2.3	—2.5	—2.5	—2.5	—2.3	—2.1	—2.0	—1.8	—1.4	—0.6
1909	+0.4	+0.8	+0.6	—0.1	—0.5	—0.5	—0.5	—0.4	—0.4	+0.1	+0.4	+0.8
1910	+0.7	+0.9	+0.7	+0.5	+0.2	0	+0.2	+0.2	+0.2	+0.1	—0.1	—0.3
1911	—0.6	—0.8	—0.9	—1.0	—1.1	—1.2	—1.2	—1.2	—1.0	—0.9	—0.7	—0.5
1912	—0.5	—0.6	—0.7	—0.7	—0.7	—0.3	+0.1	+0.6	+0.9	+1.0	+0.8	+0.5
1913	+0.3	—0.1	—0.1	—0.1	+0.9	+1.9	+2.9	+2.9	+2.5	+1.9	+1.5	+0.8
1914	+0.2	—0.5	—0.6	—0.6	—0.9	—1.1	—1.4	—1.7	—2.1	—2.2	—2.3	—2.3

[a]Computed from data in Table II. Trend eliminated by computing percentage deviations from an eighty-four month moving average smoothed with the aid of French curves.
[b]The data for 1890, 1891, and the first half of 1892 apply to quarters centered in February, May, August, and November, respectively.

Table IV—Index of Factory Employment in Selected States, by Months, 1889-1923[a]

Massachusetts (1889-1923); New Jersey (1895-1919); New York (1904-1923)

1914 monthly average = 100

Year	Average	Jan.	Feb.	Mar.	Apr.	May	June	July	Aug.	Sept.	Oct.	Nov.	Dec.
1889	56.2	56.0	56.4	56.4	56.2	56.2	56.2	55.7	56.0	56.2	56.7	56.4	56.0
1890	57.3	56.1	57.0	57.5	57.4	57.4	57.4	56.5	57.0	57.7	58.4	58.0	57.7
1891	58.1	58.0	58.1	58.3	58.6	58.7	58.1	57.5	57.5	58.1	58.3	58.1	58.0
1892	60.4	58.8	59.6	60.3	61.3	61.1	60.3	59.6	59.7	60.7	61.4	61.3	60.7
1893	57.4	61.0	61.4	62.3	62.7	62.6	60.7	57.5	51.9	48.6	53.1	53.1	53.5
1894	53.6	52.5	53.4	53.5	54.5	54.9	53.8	51.9	50.8	51.2	55.1	56.0	55.4
1895	58.9	57.4	57.5	58.7	59.2	59.3	58.9	57.9	58.7	59.5	60.0	60.2	59.8
1896	57.5	59.2	59.7	59.7	59.6	59.2	57.5	54.8	53.3	54.9	56.7	57.0	57.8
1897	59.0	57.8	58.6	59.3	60.1	60.0	58.7	56.6	56.2	59.9	60.8	60.3	60.0
1898	60.5	59.6	59.9	61.1	61.2	60.3	60.2	58.9	59.4	60.4	61.7	61.6	61.7
1899	66.7	63.1	64.2	65.6	66.6	67.0	67.0	65.8	66.7	68.3	68.6	68.9	68.8
1900	69.2	69.9	70.4	71.0	70.4	70.2	69.0	66.5	67.3	68.4	69.2	69.1	69.3
1901	71.4	69.9	70.4	71.4	70.4	71.2	70.6	69.6	70.6	72.1	73.5	73.8	73.5
1902	77.2	75.7	76.1	76.9	76.9	76.9	76.1	75.5	76.2	77.9	79.6	79.6	79.0
1903	79.0	79.3	79.8	80.7	79.3	78.9	79.4	77.7	77.6	78.8	79.8	78.9	78.3
1904	79.1	77.0	78.2	79.6	79.9	78.9	77.8	76.5	77.5	80.4	82.1	81.2	79.6
1905	84.0	80.6	81.8	82.4	84.1	84.2	83.8	83.8	84.6	84.3	85.5	86.0	86.4
1906	88.7	86.9	86.6	87.4	87.6	88.0	89.1	89.3	89.6	89.7	90.1	91.0	89.6
1907	89.7	91.8	91.8	92.9	92.3	91.9	92.6	92.8	92.8	91.3	84.7	83.3	77.9
1908	79.4	75.5	74.2	74.2	72.6	73.1	74.8	80.7	84.4	82.6	85.8	86.8	87.5
1909	94.0	89.5	91.1	92.7	92.6	92.3	92.2	91.7	93.4	96.7	98.5	98.5	98.2
1910	98.9	99.9	100.2	99.2	98.8	98.6	98.1	98.1	98.8	99.0	99.0	99.3	97.8
1911	99.1	98.1	99.4	99.8	99.6	97.7	98.3	98.7	99.4	100.1	100.8	99.7	97.3
1912	101.2	99.0	100.9	101.3	101.2	100.2	99.2	98.9	102.4	103.6	104.0	102.8	101.2
1913	101.8	103.4	104.2	102.6	101.8	100.6	100.6	100.3	101.5	102.8	102.8	101.9	99.7
1914	100.0	101.0	102.3	103.5	102.8	101.5	100.3	98.2	97.8	99.5	100.0	97.4	95.7
1915	102.3	95.9	97.6	98.4	99.1	100.2	101.1	100.8	101.3	104.8	106.9	110.0	111.6
1916	117.5	112.5	114.8	115.8	118.0	116.8	116.8	116.2	116.7	119.2	120.7	122.8	124.1
1917	122.5	123.4	123.8	125.2	123.1	121.9	121.1	119.9	118.8	120.8	122.7	124.1	124.0
1918	125.0	123.6	125.1	126.6	126.1	126.3	126.5	127.7	125.7	125.4	121.4	123.3	121.8
1919	120.2	116.8	115.0	115.4	116.0	116.4	117.8	120.5	122.9	124.0	124.1	125.8	128.3
1920	120.1	128.2	126.9	129.0	127.7	125.6	123.7	122.1	119.2	117.4	115.1	107.5	98.8
1921	97.9	92.6	96.2	98.3	98.3	97.3	97.0	96.5	97.8	100.3	101.2	100.4	98.8
1922	103.2	97.3	99.9	100.6	98.8	99.4	100.3	100.3	103.2	106.1	109.2	111.3	112.6
1923	112.3	113.0	113.5	115.8	114.6	114.0	112.4	111.6	110.8	110.8	112.0	110.7	108.5

[a]Computed from estimates given in Tables 15, 16, and 17. For methods of arriving at these estimates, see Chapter III.

TABLE V—CYCLES OF FACTORY EMPLOYMENT IN SELECTED STATES, BY MONTHS:
1889-1914•

Percentage deviations from trend, corrected for typical seasonal variation and
expressed in multiples of the standard deviation, which = 4.55 per cent

YEAR	JAN.	FEB.	MAR.	APR.	MAY	JUNE	JULY	AUG.	SEPT.	OCT.	NOV.	DEC.
1889	0	0	—0.11	—0.29	—0.24	—0.07	—0.18	+0.26	+0.04	+0.04	+0.02	0
1890	—0.07	+0.13	+0.18	+0.07	+0.11	+0.24	+0.33	+0.53	+0.51	+0.55	+0.53	+0.55
1891	+0.51	+0.40	+0.35	+0.42	+0.46	+0.40	+0.62	+0.57	+0.51	+0.40	+0.44	+0.51
1892	+0.70	+0.86	+0.97	+1.30	+1.25	+1.12	+1.25	+1.30	+1.38	+1.43	+1.52	+1.41
1893	+1.43	+1.38	+1.60	+1.69	+1.67	+1.12	+0.33	—1.80	—3.38	—1.87	—1.74	—1.47
1894	—1.98	—1.78	—1.85	—1.58	—1.38	—1.63	—1.93	—2.35	—2.48	—1.21	—0.77	—0.86
1895	—0.22	—0.37	—0.02	+0.09	+0.18	+0.15	+0.22	+0.53	+0.51	+0.48	+0.66	+0.59
1896	+0.26	+0.26	+0.15	+0.02	—0.13	—0.66	—1.25	—1.85	—1.60	—1.19	—0.97	—0.62
1897	—0.79	—0.70	—0.62	—0.44	—0.51	—0.84	—1.21	—1.43	—0.44	—0.40	—0.51	—0.55
1898	—0.88	—0.99	—0.75	—0.84	—1.19	—1.10	—1.19	—1.12	—1.12	—0.97	—0.92	—0.84
1899	—0.53	—0.42	—0.11	+0.04	+0.15	+0.26	+0.20	+0.44	+0.62	+0.42	+0.57	+0.57
1900	+0.75	+0.66	+0.66	+0.33	+0.24	—0.07	—0.51	—0.33	—0.33	—0.35	—0.33	—0.22
1901	—0.24	—0.29	—0.15	—0.59	—0.40	—0.46	—0.40	—0.15	—0.07	+0.11	+0.24	+0.22
1902	+0.70	+0.57	+0.64	+0.51	+0.51	+0.35	+0.55	+0.66	+0.81	+1.05	+1.12	+0.99
1903	+0.90	+0.84	+0.90	+0.37	+0.24	+0.51	+0.40	+0.31	+0.31	+0.31	+0.13	+0.04
1904	—0.42	—0.40	—0.09	—0.04	—0.15	—0.44	—0.77	—0.88	—0.35	+0.09	—0.07	—0.13
1905	—0.15	—0.11	—0.07	+0.35	+0.55	+0.46	+0.51	+0.33	0	+0.26	+0.51	+0.99
1906	+0.81	+0.46	+0.57	+0.59	+0.84	+1.16	+1.23	+0.95	+0.70	+0.77	+1.12	+1.12
1907	+1.38	+1.10	+1.27	+1.10	+1.16	+1.38	+1.43	+1.05	+0.44	—1.23	—1.45	—2.42
1908	—3.30	—3.87	—3.96	—4.35	—4.07	—3.60	—2.11	—1.58	—2.26	—1.54	—1.16	—0.64
1909	—0.44	—0.33	—0.04	—0.09	+0.02	+0.04	—0.04	—0.02	+0.53	+0.92	+1.05	+1.36
1910	+1.45	+1.23	+0.92	+0.79	+0.92	+0.84	+0.90	+0.70	+0.48	+0.46	+0.66	+0.70
1911	+0.48	+0.51	+0.53	+0.46	+0.20	+0.40	+0.53	+0.31	+0.22	+0.37	+0.24	+0.11
1912	+0.20	+0.35	+0.35	+0.31	+0.29	+0.11	+0.09	+0.51	+0.53	+0.59	+0.48	+0.51
1913	+0.70	+0.64	+0.20	0	—0.07	—0.02	—0.04	—0.13	—0.09	—0.11	—0.15	—0.22
1914	—0.24	—0.20	0	—0.18	—0.26	—0.44	—0.81	—1.25	—1.14	—1.03	—1.43	—1.38

•Based upon index in Table IV, reduced to deviations from a curvilinear trend based upon preliminary
mathematical approximations smoothed with the aid of a French curve. Seasonal variation adjusted for
by method described in "The Measurement of Seasonal Variation," by Helen D. Falkner, in the *Journal of
the American Statistical Association*, June, 1924, pp. 167-179. Two sets of seasonal indices were computed,
one for 1889 to 1903, the other for 1904 to 1914.

APPENDIX

TABLE VI—CYCLES IN PIG IRON PRODUCTION, BY MONTHS, 1890-1914[a]

Percentage of trend, corrected for seasonal variation

YEAR	JAN.	FEB.	MAR.	APR.	MAY	JUNE	JULY	AUG.	SEPT.	OCT.	NOV.	DEC.
1890	117.5	121.5	121.5	120.9	122.4	121.3	119.3	118.7	120.1	118.1	116.0	112.0
1891	101.0	92.0	79.2	73.3	85.7	105.4	115.2	116.7	118.1	120.0	119.0	118.4
1892	121.4	126.2	122.7	117.4	114.9	112.0	109.1	104.7	103.8	106.7	109.1	109.0
1893	110.0	113.2	113.2	114.6	116.0	106.1	86.0	63.7	50.9	48.1	54.8	60.8
1894	63.3	68.5	75.5	75.6	55.4	47.1	65.6	89.3	99.6	100.0	102.2	103.1
1895	99.1	97.8	93.0	92.3	93.6	98.3	105.5	112.9	119.9	122.3	121.7	117.5
1896	112.6	108.0	102.8	101.6	100.0	98.1	91.1	77.5	64.4	60.5	67.5	74.8
1897	82.0	84.7	85.9	84.9	84.0	83.1	82.5	88.9	96.9	100.7	104.4	103.7
1898	105.0	105.6	105.9	103.2	101.0	98.1	94.3	94.0	96.0	96.6	98.2	97.9
1899	99.4	95.2	96.8	98.5	100.3	103.4	107.1	108.2	110.4	112.5	112.2	110.4
1900	111.1	109.4	107.5	104.5	106.6	105.7	96.9	87.1	82.1	78.5	77.1	82.8
1901	92.3	98.3	100.0	98.1	102.4	105.0	105.9	103.3	102.3	105.6	104.1	93.8
1902	104.3	99.3	102.7	105.3	108.0	105.5	104.8	105.9	103.9	104.9	101.5	105.9
1903	99.8	102.1	104.4	106.8	111.1	113.9	105.1	105.7	105.2	93.8	68.8	54.5
1904	58.5	80.1	88.1	96.3	92.9	82.8	71.0	73.5	85.5	89.7	92.5	98.0
1905	106.8	103.5	110.8	112.6	113.2	108.7	105.6	109.3	112.8	117.0	118.5	116.8
1906	117.6	116.5	117.0	116.0	114.9	114.3	115.5	108.5	110.6	116.1	122.4	120.0
1907	119.2	118.3	130.4	117.9	121.9	124.1	124.1	120.6	116.2	116.8	96.2	63.7
1908	54.3	57.6	60.0	58.5	59.4	58.1	64.2	68.1	72.0	74.7	77.9	85.9
1909	89.4	90.5	86.3	84.7	92.1	98.5	106.1	110.4	115.5	109.0	123.3	125.3
1910	125.6	122.6	118.8	116.6	111.8	110.2	103.3	98.9	95.5	91.9	89.3	81.6
1911	82.4	88.4	95.1	93.3	84.6	83.3	82.5	86.7	88.1	89.0	90.4	91.1
1912	93.1	96.1	101.7	103.5	107.5	109.4	106.9	109.0	105.9	109.9	114.5	120.4
1913	122.5	118.6	112.8	115.7	115.6	113.3	109.3	106.6	104.1	100.8	94.1	83.0
1914	79.9	83.7	92.6	92.4	82.7	79.7	80.5	81.0	75.9	68.7	61.9	61.5

[a] Computed from data published in the *Iron Age* and representing prior to October, 1901, estimates made from statistics of furnaces in blast, and subsequent thereto, direct data on production. For method of making adjustments for seasonal variation and trend, see Chapter III.

INDEX

c=chart; n=footnote; t=table.

251

DATE DUE

GAYLORD			PRINTED IN U.S.A.